ANGELA ASHWIN
JEFF ASTLEY
SARAH DYLAN BREUER
ANDREW DAVISON
MALCOLM GUITE
CHRISTOPHER HERBERT
PAUL KENNEDY
ANN LEWIN
JAN MCFARLANE
DAVID MOXON
HELEN ORCHARD
MARTYN PERCY
SUE PICKERING
BEN QUASH
TOM SMAIL

REFLECTIONS
FOR
DAILY PRAYER

ADVENT **2010** TO
CHRIST THE KING **2011**

Church House Publishing
Church House
Great Smith Street
London SW1P 3AZ

ISBN 978 0 7151 4229 5

Published 2010 by Church House Publishing
Copyright © The Archbishops' Council 2010

The opinions expressed in this book are those of the
authors and do not necessarily reflect the official policy of
the General Synod or The Archbishops' Council of the
Church of England.

Designed and typeset by Hugh Hillyard-Parker
Printed by CPI Bookmarque, Croydon, Surrey

Contents

About the authors

Angela Ashwin is a writer and speaker on spirituality. She has written several books about prayer and life with God, the latest of which is *Follow the Fool: Risk and Delight in the Christian Adventure*, about the wisdom of foolishness and our call to be 'fools for Christ'. She and her husband live in Southwell, Nottinghamshire.

Jeff Astley is Honorary Professorial Fellow in Practical Theology and Christian Education, University of Durham, and Director of the North of England Institute for Christian Education. He has worked in parish ministry, university chaplaincy and higher education and is the author of several books, including *Christ of the Everyday*.

Sarah Dylan Breuer is a public theologian – someone called to do theology and help others to claim their gifts as theologians in our varied contexts. She serves on the Executive Council of the Episcopal Church and as the executive director of its New England dioceses, and travels extensively as a teacher, preacher, retreat facilitator and worship leader.

Andrew Davison is Tutor in Doctrine at Westcott House, Cambridge. Before that, he was part-time Tutor in Doctrine at St Stephen's House in Oxford and junior chaplain of Merton College. He has written on prayer and on apologetics, and in praise of the parish and its significance for mission. He served his curacy in south-east London.

Malcolm Guite is Chaplain of Girton College, Cambridge. He is also a poet and singer-songwriter, and is author of various essays and articles and a book about contemporary Christianity. He lectures widely in England and the USA on poetry and theology.

Christopher Herbert was Bishop of St Albans from 1995 to 2009. He has an interest in, and love for, all forms of literature and is a prolific author in his own right. Much of his writing is based on the themes of prayer and spirituality, for both children and adults. Among his best-known books are *Ways into Prayer* and *Pocket Prayers*.

Paul Kennedy is Rector of East Winchester, a socially diverse multi-parish benefice which seeks to be 'Joining God in building faith and community on the eastern side of Winchester'. He is also a Benedictine oblate at the Anglican Alton Abbey and blogs at http://earofyour-heart.com/wp/

Ann Lewin was a secondary-school teacher for 27 years (RE and English) and ended her working life as a Welfare Adviser for International Students at Southampton University. She writes (e.g. *Watching for the Kingfisher*, published by Canterbury Press), and leads retreats and quiet days. Interests include reading, birdwatching, music, theatre and the company of friends.

Jan McFarlane is the Archdeacon of Norwich and Director of Communications in the Diocese of Norwich. She has served as Chaplain to the Bishop of Norwich, Chaplain of Ely Cathedral and Curate in the Stafford Team Ministry. A former speech therapist, she has a lifelong interest in communications and broadcasts regularly on local radio.

David Moxon is Bishop of Waikato, the Senior Bishop of the New Zealand Dioceses, and Archbishop and Primate of the Anglican Church in Aotearoa, New Zealand and Polynesia. He holds two Masters of Arts degrees: in Education with honours from Massey University, and in Theology from Oxford. He also has a Licenciate of Theology (Aotearoa) and a Diploma of Maori Studies from Waikato University.

Helen Orchard is Chaplain and Fellow of Exeter College, Oxford. She was previously a curate in the Guildford Diocese, and before ordination worked for the National Health Service. Her publications include works on John's Gospel and on spirituality and healthcare.

Martyn Percy is Principal of Ripon College Cuddesdon and the Oxford Ministry Course. He is also Professor of Theological Education at King's College London, Professorial Research Fellow at Heythrop College London and an Honorary Canon of Salisbury Cathedral.

Sue Pickering is an Anglican priest living in New Zealand. She holds an MA in Applied Theology from the University of Kent, and has been involved nationally in the formation of spiritual directors. Sue is currently a Canon of Taranaki Cathedral Church and chaplain to a retirement community. Her publications include retreat resources, an introduction to spiritual direction, and articles on spirituality in everyday life.

Ben Quash was Chaplain and Fellow of Fitzwilliam College, Cambridge, and a lecturer in the Cambridge Theological Federation from 1996 to 1999. He then returned to Peterhouse as Dean and Fellow until he came to King's College as Professor of Christianity and the Arts in 2007.

Tom Smail was Vice-Principal and Lecturer in Doctrine at St John's College, Nottingham from 1979 to 1984, and then led a church in Croydon until his retirement in 1994. He is an acclaimed speaker, and continues to lecture and preach in the UK and abroad.

About *Reflections for Daily Prayer*

Based on the *Common Worship Lectionary* readings for Morning Prayer, these daily reflections are designed to refresh and inspire times of personal prayer. The aim is to provide rich, contemporary and engaging insights into Scripture.

Each page lists the lectionary readings for the day, with the main psalms for that day highlighted in **bold**. The Collect of the day – either the *Common Worship* collect or the shorter additional collect – is also included.

For those using this book in conjunction with a service of Morning Prayer, the following conventions apply: a psalm printed in parentheses is omitted if it has been used as the opening canticle at that office; a psalm marked with an asterisk may be shortened if desired.

A short reflection is provided on either the Old or New Testament reading. Popular writers, experienced ministers, biblical scholars and theologians will be contributing to this series. They all bring their own emphases, enthusiasms and approaches to biblical interpretation to bear.

Regular users of Morning Prayer and *Time to Pray* (from *Common Worship: Daily Prayer*) and anyone who follows the lectionary for their regular Bible reading will benefit from the rich variety of traditions represented in these stimulating and accessible pieces.

Monday 29 November

Isaiah 42.18-end

'Who is blind like my dedicated one ...?' (v.19)

The servant or messenger figure described as 'dedicated one' (or 'covenanted one') in verse 19 of this passage may actually be being given his proper name: 'One-in-Covenant'. The word in Hebrew is analogous to the Arabic word 'Muslim', meaning one who submits to God.

But in this passage full of vexed utterances, of fury and love, we find that the messenger-servant shares the deafness and blindness of the people as a whole, whom he embodies. And what use is a messenger who is unable to receive or understand the message he is to carry?

The voice of God rails against the obduracy of his chosen ones – their failure to attend to him in the present, to think about the needs of the future, and to obey the law. But this anger cannot altogether disguise a compassion at the way these same children are trapped in holes and hidden in prisons. They are their own worst enemies (and this makes them also the prey of others), but they are so helpless.

One of the great messages of the Old Testament is that it is possible to fail and fail again in keeping specific injunctions in the law, but the covenant *behind* the law (which generated the law in the first place as a way of living with God – of being in loving relationship to him) still stands: God remains at the negotiating table.

Even the spent, useless, disobedient servant of God can still hear God tenaciously sustaining the bond, naming him still 'One-in-Covenant'.

COLLECT

Almighty God,
give us grace to cast away the works of darkness
and to put on the armour of light,
now in the time of this mortal life,
in which your Son Jesus Christ came to us in great humility;
that on the last day,
when he shall come again in his glorious majesty
    to judge the living and the dead,
we may rise to the life immortal;
through him who is alive and reigns with you,
in the unity of the Holy Spirit,
one God, now and for ever.

Psalms 47, 147.1-12
Ezekiel 47.1-12
John 12.20-32

Tuesday 30 November

Andrew the Apostle

Ezekiel 47.1-12

'... and it was a river that I could not cross' (v.5)

Carol Bialock, an American missionary sister working in Chile, wrote a poem that describes what it is to lose your footing when great waters rise. She talks about how 'when the sea comes calling, you stop being good neighbours', and instead 'you give your house for a coral castle' and 'you learn to breathe under water'.

There is so much in human nature – not least in the practices of worship – that can reinforce our sense of having everything under control, our footing fast. The God we serve is a river we can cross, or a sea contained within its boundaries – or so we think. Here, Ezekiel shows us a river that just keeps getting bigger and bigger. It flows from the temple out to the wider world – a reminder that the object of our worship (God) cannot be confined within any walls we make, and that our worshipping of this God is to change us, carrying us beyond ourselves.

The uncrossable river may initially seem terrifying. It may make us think of death and drowning; it may make us want to run away. But, like Bialock's ocean (which delivers wonderfully transformed life in which impossibilities become possible), Ezekiel's river gives life wherever it goes. Maybe as Christians, we find in the river gushing from the threshold of the temple a reminder of the water and blood from Christ's side, flowing for the healing of all peoples. We can never manage this stream; our task is to live from its blessings.

Almighty God,
who gave such grace to your apostle Saint Andrew
that he readily obeyed the call of your Son Jesus Christ
and brought his brother with him:
call us by your holy word,
and give us grace to follow you without delay
and to tell the good news of your kingdom;
through Jesus Christ your Son our Lord,
who is alive and reigns with you,
in the unity of the Holy Spirit,
one God, now and for ever.

COLLECT

3

Wednesday 1 December

Isaiah 43.14-end

'I will make a way in the wilderness' (v.19)

Unlike the carefully manicured lawns of Oxbridge colleges, which have alert porters to guard them from straying tourists and undergraduates, the lawns of university campuses in the US are regularly criss-crossed by students. And there is a name for the beaten paths that emerge most clearly and consistently as the grass is worn away: 'paths of convenience'. These paths tell you important things about the routes that those who live in the place most want and need to travel.

The university authorities have two options at the end of each academic year. They can re-seed them, in the hope that a new generation will find a different way to travel from A to B. Or they can acknowledge the value of the paths of convenience, give in, and pave them!

The route that God most wants and needs to travel takes him across surprising terrain that few would normally cross: not precious grass, but the terrifying waters of ocean chaos, and the deadly expanses of desert wilderness. He chooses this way in order to reach the prison where his children are being kept, so as to set them free. It is, you might say, a path of *in*convenience, but for God it is travelled in love. At the end of the reading, we are invited, by contrast, to think about how poorly the paths we take compare with God's: our love of *convenience* makes us poor travellers whose footsteps need re-seeding.

COLLECT

Almighty God,
give us grace to cast away the works of darkness
and to put on the armour of light,
now in the time of this mortal life,
in which your Son Jesus Christ came to us in great humility;
that on the last day,
when he shall come again in his glorious majesty
    to judge the living and the dead,
we may rise to the life immortal;
through him who is alive and reigns with you,
in the unity of the Holy Spirit,
one God, now and for ever.

Isaiah 44.1-8

'I am the Lord's ...' (v.5)

The naming of cats is a difficult matter, wrote T. S. Eliot. It's difficult partly because each cat has a unique character, which is hard to capture. But it's also difficult because naming brings demanding consequences. To know a cat's name is to be in *relationship* with it. And, from that point on, it's no merely anonymous cat; you can't overlook its needs in the same way as you might have done before. It can't ever again be invisible to you. If it's hungry, it will be harder for you not to feed it once it has a name. And yet its arrival in your life may not have been something you especially chose.

In this passage, we hear the words of God to a people who are rediscovering all over again the miracle of deliverance. And that, in turn, looks to them like a sort of recapitulation of creation itself, when God drew the world into being from what was just void. This section of the Book of Isaiah loves to draw those links. Above all, it shows a God infinitely attentive to particularity, who knows each person's name and identity, names and identities that have not been effaced by the anonymity of the ghetto and the powerlessness of exile. These lost cats who are to come back from Babylon find themselves named, and there is a promise that goes with that naming – a renewed promise to maintain relationship with them, to care for them, to love them whatever the consequences.

Almighty God,
as your kingdom dawns,
turn us from the darkness of sin to the
light of holiness,
that we may be ready to meet you
in our Lord and Saviour, Jesus Christ.

COLLECT

Friday 3 December

Psalms **25**, 26 or 17, **19**
Isaiah 44.9-23
Revelation 21.22 – 22.5

Isaiah 44.9-23

'For the Lord has redeemed Jacob, and will be glorified in Israel' (v.23)

Let's read this passage backwards. There are three verses at the end that a Christian reader may find it hard not to hear as a celebration of the triune God – the true God, who is the origin and end of all things, and no puppet.

This God formed us and remembers us everlastingly (v.21) – in other words, this God is the creator and origin of all things. This God also redeems his people's sins (v.22), which are as mere vapour before him – in other words, this God is a saviour. And, finally, this God invites praise and glorification, making the whole creation sing (v.23) – in other words, this God shapes creation for a life of delight and joy that is inexhaustible. Source of all, saviour of all, and nurturer of joy in all: Father, Son and Holy Spirit.

Now look back at the poor god the idolater makes from the leftovers of his tree (v.17), having first made sure he has looked after his bodily needs for warmth and food. This god of the leftovers is an optional extra to life, and the human being who fashions this object of devotion is *its* origin and end. Such a human being inhabits a great existential loneliness, wholly responsible for him- or herself, with no everlasting arms beneath, to hold, protect and uplift. What a transforming insight is vouchsafed to Israel by the knowledge – hard won but then hard held to – that its God is bigger than it is; that it does not need to save itself; that it has more to look forward to than a meal of ashes.

COLLECT

Almighty God,
give us grace to cast away the works of darkness
and to put on the armour of light,
now in the time of this mortal life,
in which your Son Jesus Christ came to us in great humility;
that on the last day,
when he shall come again in his glorious majesty
    to judge the living and the dead,
we may rise to the life immortal;
through him who is alive and reigns with you,
in the unity of the Holy Spirit,
one God, now and for ever.

Isaiah 44.24 – 45.13

'... who says of Cyrus, "He is my shepherd"' (44.28)

A peculiar and surprising way into understanding Cyrus, King of Persia, is through a comparison with someone superficially utterly different: Mary, the mother of Jesus. *He* ruled one of the greatest and most extensive empires the world has ever known. *She* was a teenage girl from an obscure, provincial town in the north of occupied Palestine. By any measure – including those of wealth, sex and political influence – they seem worlds apart.

But think a little further, and parallels begin to emerge. Both are individuals who say an astonishing 'yes' to the prompting of God: both say 'let it be' to a proposal that will utterly change history. Both become vehicles of a purpose they may only very indistinctly perceive. Cyrus lets the exiled people of Israel begin to return to their own land, and undertakes to rebuild the city and temple of Jerusalem. Mary accepts the invitation to build in her body the 'new temple', which (as Christ himself will put it) is his own body: the body that will be pulled down and rebuilt in just three days.

These two temple-builders are testimony to God's versatility, and to the fact that there is no one place – palace or hovel, Jewish community or Gentile – where servants of God are anointed for God's purposes; no one race, sex or class of person. The great movements of God in history often begin just where you aren't expecting them. He 'makes fools of diviners' (44.25).

Almighty God,
as your kingdom dawns,
turn us from the darkness of sin to the
light of holiness,
that we may be ready to meet you
in our Lord and Saviour, Jesus Christ.

COLLECT

Psalms **44** *or* 27, **30**
Isaiah 45.14-end
I Thessalonians I

Isaiah 45.14-end

'Assemble yourselves and come together' (v.20)

There are two powerful dynamics in this chapter. The first is a competitive one, in which it is assumed that the triumph of a particular people must entail the subservience of all others. This is a 'zero sum game' model of the world. There is only so much salvation to go round, and a favoured and redeemed people must necessarily have as their counterpart an audience of other nations who stand in chains.

But the second dynamic subverts and undercuts the first. It proclaims a God who is God of all – of 'every knee'. He is the one, true God, and the idea that he is so at the expense of other gods makes no sense – there *are* no others. This God created both heaven and earth, and all that is in them. He does not need to enter a wrestling ring with the gods of other peoples.

So this God *distinguishes* in order, finally, to *unite*. The apparently 'competitive' distinction between those who worship truly and those who worship idols (the raising up of one and disgracing of another) is only a step on the way towards something better – towards all people seeing what *true* worship is. There is no zero sum game here; God did not create the world 'to be a chaos' of eternal competition.

God's greatest answer to the chaos of competitive nations lies in his power to *assemble* (v.20). A partisan God's powers of assembly could only be very limited. This God calls all the ends of the earth to be saved.

COLLECT

O Lord, raise up, we pray, your power
and come among us,
and with great might succour us;
that whereas, through our sins and wickedness
we are grievously hindered
in running the race that is set before us,
your bountiful grace and mercy
may speedily help and deliver us;
through Jesus Christ your Son our Lord,
to whom with you and the Holy Spirit,
be honour and glory, now and for ever.

Psalms **56**, 57 *or* 32, **36**
Isaiah 46
1 Thessalonians 2.1-12

Isaiah 46

'I have made, and I will bear' (v.4)

Bel and Nebo are names for the gods of Babylon (we hear them echoed in the names of Babylonian kings like Belshazzar and Nebuchadnezzar). Just as in the chapters before and after it, this chapter of the Book of Isaiah is relentless in exposing these gods as without substance: the fictions of human minds. They are gods who have to be carried around in graven form; they are just one more category of possession. There is a nice play on the way that these heavy objects make the beasts who carry them bow down, and in doing so find *themselves* bowing down as no self-respecting god should.

By contrast with these gods who are a burden to *us*, the God of Israel is a god to whom we can allow ourselves to be burdensome. He can take it. This covenanting God does not make creatures in order to dump them when they get heavy; he abides with his handiwork – 'I have made, and I will bear' (v.4).

Given that we are transgressors, this is an uplifting and extraordinarily comforting message of hope. And it means that we do not have to accrue power (like the kings of Babylon) in order to compensate for a secret fear that our gods are too weak to save us. We can emerge from our defended spaces in the knowledge that we will still be held – that there are everlasting arms beneath us, freeing us to risk dispossession, the unknown, a life of faith.

Almighty God,
purify our hearts and minds,
that when your Son Jesus Christ comes again as
judge and saviour
we may be ready to receive him,
who is our Lord and our God.

COLLECT

Wednesday 8 December

Psalms **62**, 63 *or* **34**
Isaiah 47
1 Thessalonians 2.13-end

Isaiah 47

'... you said in your heart, "I am,
and there is no one besides me"' (v.10)

Perhaps this passage startles us; it seems misogynistic, derisive – even viciously so. It takes pleasure in imagining how the personification of Babylon's power (a 'daughter') will be exposed, humiliated and subjected to disgrace and the shameful scrutiny of gloating and hostile eyes. What do we do with this passage?

Here are two suggestions for how we might read it so as to grow in wisdom. First, we can read it in order to try to understand something more of what it must have been like to be an exiled slave. This was Israel's fate in Babylon. Its people were deprived of homes and homeland, of choice and freedom, and, above all, at times, of the right to worship the God they knew and loved. Instead, they watched profane values reign over them, and worked under a heavy yoke. Can we begin to understand their anger, as we hear it in this passage?

A second way to relate to this passage is to turn it upon ourselves, and ask ourselves critically: how might we in turn be in danger of becoming 'daughter Chaldea'? Jews and Christians ever since the Exodus have had to beware that they do not repeat the atrocities of Pharaoh, especially when handling political authority. And if we all have Pharaoh in us, then in like fashion – maybe – we have aspects of this Babylonian personification too. So, can we read this passage alert to the temptations of 'security in our wickedness', pleasure in our power?

COLLECT

O Lord, raise up, we pray, your power
and come among us,
and with great might succour us;
that whereas, through our sins and wickedness
we are grievously hindered
in running the race that is set before us,
your bountiful grace and mercy
may speedily help and deliver us;
through Jesus Christ your Son our Lord,
to whom with you and the Holy Spirit,
be honour and glory, now and for ever.

Thursday 9 December

Isaiah 48.1-11

'... who came forth from the loins of Judah' (v.1)

The critical spotlight is turned back on Israel in this passage; the people's faults are clearly described as rebellion, treachery and imperviousness to God's speech. These descriptions stand under the banner of an invocation of *Judah* at the beginning of the chapter: the fourth son of Jacob, so Genesis tells us, and older brother of Joseph (as well as an ancestor of Jesus). It is from his loins that the nation of Judah is descended.

And Judah is a complex forefather to have. Judah was complicit in the deed whereby Joseph was sold into slavery, and his father's heart was broken. Despite being a voice for clemency, and persuading his brothers to sell Joseph rather than to kill him, he shares responsibility for their treachery, obduracy and rebellion.

But maybe it is precisely because of this that he also offers hope to a later people who have also failed God. Later in the story, he undergoes trials and sufferings, and will plead to be allowed to sacrifice himself in his youngest brother Benjamin's place – out of love and concern for his father, and in evident sense of guilt for his past misdeeds.

So, his failings did not have to define him. He learned compassion; he learned to be self-sacrificial and to go beyond the borders of himself. The message of this chapter is that his descendants can do the same. God will not cut them off; he intends to refine them, and this is because his ultimate aim is to give them his glory.

Almighty God,
purify our hearts and minds,
that when your Son Jesus Christ comes again as
judge and saviour
we may be ready to receive him,
who is our Lord and our God.

COLLECT

Psalms 85, **86** *or* 31
Isaiah 48.12-end
I Thessalonians 4.1-12

Isaiah 48.12-end

'Then had thy peace been like a river' (AV, v.18)

'No rest for the wicked', we say.

When we use the phrase, we probably have in mind the endless deferral of rest. Peace is somewhere up ahead of us, but continually receding.

This passage tells us quite the opposite, however. For the great theme in this passage – as in so many others in this part of Isaiah – is not what lies ahead, in some indistinct future, but what lies at our origins: the Creation. We are asked to imagine the founding of the earth, and all the good things that were established right from the start – including its *peace*. God rested in Genesis; rest was part of the primal state of things. Our problem is not that peace will never be given, but that it *has* been given and we cannot accept the gift.

The prospect of return from exile in Babylon is also compared with the *Exodus*. It is a new Exodus *as well as* a new Creation. The God who liberates from slavery is in a sense creating his people all over again. Or, to put it another way, putting them back in touch with the blessings he always wanted them to have and from which they keep getting detached. Peace is one of these blessings; the mark of the wicked is not knowing that it's there for the taking. Our way to it is to honour the God who laid the earth's foundations and who asks us to follow him in the present.

COLLECT

O Lord, raise up, we pray, your power
and come among us,
and with great might succour us;
that whereas, through our sins and wickedness
we are grievously hindered
in running the race that is set before us,
your bountiful grace and mercy
may speedily help and deliver us;
through Jesus Christ your Son our Lord,
to whom with you and the Holy Spirit,
be honour and glory, now and for ever.

Psalms **145** *or* 41, **42**, 43
Isaiah 49.1-13
1 Thessalonians 4.13-end

Isaiah 49.1-13

'I will give you as a light' (v.6)

The servant in this passage is first of all described as like a weapon: a weapon of God. The servant is 'like a sharp sword', hidden dangerously in the shadow of God's hand, or again like 'a polished arrow' stored in God's quiver until its moment comes.

The servant has had this destiny – to be a weapon of God – right from the womb. The womb is another image of a place of secrecy and preparation, like the hand and the quiver. In all three cases, the servant lies dormant, waiting to be released upon an unsuspecting world.

The breathtaking turn the passage then takes is to transmute this weapon – the servant – into something wholly unexpected: *light*. Drawn from behind the hand, slid from the quiver, emerging from the womb, God's weapon is not going to draw blood. It is going to shine.

If it still makes sense to talk of his being a weapon at all, then the servant's target is the gloom and desolation in which so many people are imprisoned. When this weapon strikes home, what will its effect be? 'Kings shall *see*' (v.7); and those in darkness will be *made visible* (v.9). When this weapon strikes home, the 'wound' it gives is the wound of sight. How may we, as God's servants today, be instruments of light in God's hands, and what darknesses may we illuminate with the help of his grace?

Psalms **40** *or* **44**
Isaiah 49.14-25
I Thessalonians 5.1-11

Isaiah 49.14-25

'See, I have inscribed you on the palms of my hands' (v.16)

What a contrast comes with that little word 'but'! Just a verse before, we have had a declaration that the Lord has comforted his people, *but* Zion says: 'I still feel forsaken and forgotten'! To read Isaiah is to encounter a series of jagged juxtapositions of hope and despair, to be given glimpses of light that sometimes seem to make the surrounding darkness even deeper. But life is like that too. Zion is too deeply bereaved to hear, and hope deferred makes her heart sick. Sometimes for us too, in our daily readings, some gospel promise seems only to underscore God's absence.

How does God respond to Zion's heart-sickness, when she is too choked with grief to hear good news? How does he respond to ours? These verses show the way. To Zion, who has lost her children, he comes as a mother who can't stop loving the lost ones, and to all of us who are pierced with the wounds of this world, he comes as one who has made our scars his own, and has graven our names on the palms of his hand. As we move through these prophecies towards our Advent servant songs, we will know again how his palms were graven with nails that fastened his compassion to our wounds.

COLLECT

O Lord Jesus Christ,
who at your first coming sent your messenger
to prepare your way before you:
grant that the ministers and stewards of your mysteries
may likewise so prepare and make ready your way
by turning the hearts of the disobedient to the wisdom of the just,
that at your second coming to judge the world
we may be found an acceptable people in your sight;
for you are alive and reign with the Father
in the unity of the Holy Spirit,
one God, now and for ever.

Isaiah 50

'Where is your mother's bill of divorce?' (v.1)

Divorce and debt! The two most destructive, most personally undermining features of contemporary life, two of our most taboo topics – and God names them both in the very first verse of this chapter! This prophecy goes right to the heart of the wretchedness of both; to be rejected or betrayed within the bonds of love, to be always owing and have every effort undermined, every reward removed, because all we earn just sinks unseen into the pit of debt. If there is no good news for the divorced and indebted among us, then there is no gospel for any of us. But the Lord says: 'whoever has divorced you, there is no Decree Absolute between you and your maker; whatever you owe to the banks, I have never put you in hock to any creditor, and whatever you may owe me, I will more than redeem.'

Zion felt both divorced and indebted, doubly condemned, and many of us feel the same. 'Not so', says the Lord; 'let us stand up together', he says to Zion and to us, so that we too can say: 'behold the Lord God will help me – who is he that shall condemn me?'

God for whom we watch and wait,
you sent John the Baptist to prepare the way of your Son:
give us courage to speak the truth,
to hunger for justice,
and to suffer for the cause of right,
with Jesus Christ our Lord.

COLLECT

Psalms **75**, 96 *or* **119.57-80**
Isaiah 51.1-8
2 Thessalonians 1

Isaiah 51.1-8

'... he will comfort all her waste places' (v.3)

Do we make a desert of the earth because of the desert in our hearts? The state of the land, the feel of the earth herself, seem to embody Zion's inner state, each with their waste places, their wilderness and their desert. Both outwardly in the land and inwardly in her heart, Zion needs to hear a word of comfort. She needs to know that Eden is not lost forever, that the desert may yet become a garden. And so she needs to remember where she came from. The Lord reminds her that she herself was dug up from the earth she treads upon, not just in her descent from Abraham and Sarah but also in her derivation from the first person, the Adam who was himself God-breathed earth.

And so it is with us. Might our wastelands, both outer and inner, turn to Eden again if we could remember where we come from, whose image we bear and whose spirit we breathe? Even as we remember our kinship with the rocks from which we are hewn, we too might glimpse again that salvation that both sustains and outlasts the world to which we belong.

COLLECT

O Lord Jesus Christ,
who at your first coming sent your messenger
to prepare your way before you:
grant that the ministers and stewards of your mysteries
may likewise so prepare and make ready your way
by turning the hearts of the disobedient to the wisdom of the just,
that at your second coming to judge the world
we may be found an acceptable people in your sight;
for you are alive and reign with the Father
in the unity of the Holy Spirit,
one God, now and for ever.

Isaiah 51.9-16

'Was it not you ... who pierced the dragon?' (v.9)

Today is 'O *Sapientia*', the day the Advent antiphons begin with the acclamation, 'O Wisdom coming forth from the most high ... mightily ordering all things'. The same confidence in the reach and wisdom of the creator is also invoked in this primal image of victory over the dragons of the deep. The dragons embody those powers that oppress, the waters, those forces that overwhelm us.

In response to the terror of these primal fears, Isaiah gives us an image at once of creation *and* redemption. It was the creative power of love that separated the waters in Genesis and made the peaceful and ordered space in which humanity might flourish. It was the redemptive power of love that divided the waters of the Red Sea and made a way for the ransomed to cross.

Feeling lost and forgotten on the margins of Babylon, with its culture of oppressive power, Zion needs to remember, as we do, the powers of love; that the God who comes to comfort us is the one who made us, has made a way for us, and is coming to make and be that way for us in Christ.

God for whom we watch and wait,
you sent John the Baptist to prepare the way of your Son:
give us courage to speak the truth,
to hunger for justice,
and to suffer for the cause of right,
with Jesus Christ our Lord.

COLLECT

Isaiah 51.17-end

'See, I have taken from your hand the cup of staggering' (v.22)

There is a terrible scene in the Michael Caine gangster film *Get Carter* in which Caine's character takes vengeance on one of his enemies by forcing him to keep drinking whisky until he is killed by it. It's horrible to watch as the very sign of conviviality and friendship is turned inexorably into the means of torture and death.

Zion feels like that, as though one horrible dose after another is being forced down her throat as the Lord of history forces her to drain to the dregs the cup of suffering. Her children have been killed, and now she herself is dying. In *Get Carter,* Caine is out to revenge the suffering inflicted on his family, but when God comes to take the cup of trembling away from Zion, it is not, as Isaiah in his anger supposed, to force that cup on some other suffering victim. Instead he comes to drain it himself, to the dregs, on behalf of all humanity, there in the blood and sweat of Gethsemane, so that, thereafter, the only cup we need take from the Lord's hands is the cup of salvation, filled with his love: 'that liquor sweet and most divine, which my God feels as blood but I as wine' (George Herbert, *The Agonie*).

COLLECT

O Lord Jesus Christ,
who at your first coming sent your messenger
to prepare your way before you:
grant that the ministers and stewards of your mysteries
may likewise so prepare and make ready your way
by turning the hearts of the disobedient to the wisdom of the just,
that at your second coming to judge the world
we may be found an acceptable people in your sight;
for you are alive and reign with the Father
in the unity of the Holy Spirit,
one God, now and for ever.

Psalm **71** *or* **68**
Isaiah 52.1-12
Jude

Isaiah 52.1-12

'The Lord has bared his holy arm' (v.10)

For the third day running, Isaiah calls us to wake up! For grief is a kind of stupor, and oppression brings its own exhaustion. Sometimes, even when a way out of our sorrow has been made for us, we can be too weary to take it. Hence this triple wake-up call. The way has indeed been made, and, weary as we are, we need not try to find it ourselves; the herald has been sent, and his feet are already on those mountains behind which our sun will rise. Something is about to happen that will bring the whole world wide awake!

Isaiah tries to glimpse it and finds the phrase: 'The Lord has bared his holy arm ... and all the ends of the earth shall see the salvation of our God' (v.10). Perhaps he imagines a warrior stripping for battle, baring his arm to deal a mighty blow. But God says to him: 'my thoughts are not your thoughts, nor are your ways my ways' (Isaiah 55.8). And when this prophecy was fulfilled, and the Lord did indeed bare his holy arm for all the world to see, it was the outstretched arm of a suffering servant, receiving, and not striking the blows, but laying bare, nevertheless, the love that makes and redeems us all.

God for whom we watch and wait,
you sent John the Baptist to prepare the way of your Son:
give us courage to speak the truth,
to hunger for justice,
and to suffer for the cause of right,
with Jesus Christ our Lord.

COLLECT

Monday 20 December

Isaiah 52.13 – 53.end

'... as one from whom others hide their faces' (v.53)

At the 1975 gathering of the World Council of Churches, a sculpture called 'The Tortured Christ', by Brazilian artist Guido Rocha, himself the victim of torture, was displayed in the lobby where delegates met for their plenary, but it proved to be so horrific and disturbing that they asked for it to be removed. And so it was put down into a basement room, where only those who were looking would find it.* The conference was meant to highlight torture but, ironically, even the image of such suffering was hidden away in just such a dark basement as forms the scene of so much modern torture.

Isaiah knows that some pain is so gross, some visages so marred, that we turn our own faces away. But God does not turn his face away; rather, he enters into our suffering with such compassionate attention that his own face becomes the face of the tortured. It is unbearable to think how those who are marred and maimed in our conflicts were once babes whom some mother loved. But, as we look to the Advent of Christ, Isaiah reminds us that he was born to bear the grief we cannot bear, and carry the sorrows of those from whom we have averted our eyes.

*Story recounted by Maggie Dawn in *The Writing on the Wall* (Hodder & Stoughton, 2010)

COLLECT

God our redeemer,
who prepared the Blessed Virgin Mary
to be the mother of your Son:
grant that, as she looked for his coming as our saviour,
so we may be ready to greet him
when he comes again as our judge;
who is alive and reigns with you,
in the unity of the Holy Spirit,
one God, now and for ever.

Psalms **121**, 122, 123
Isaiah 54
2 Peter 1.16-2.3

Isaiah 54

'For a brief moment I abandoned you, but with great compassion I will gather you' (v.7)

Sometimes it is a recent memory that maims us and an older memory that has the power to heal. The immediate past may be devastating, but buried somewhere deep within us is a memory of goodness or love that carries the seeds of hope. So it is with Zion: her recent history leaves her feeling bereaved and barren, and Isaiah starts there, with the way she feels now. He calls her 'O barren one who did not bear' (v.1), but he also digs deep and reminds her again of the buried memory of Sarah, the matriarch, the one who was called barren, but who bore a child against all expectation and called him 'Laughter'.

Zion knows that her very existence is owed to that miracle, for she is descended from Isaac, the boy who nearly died, the fragile seed of promise, and it gives her hope. The deep past and the promised future make a great arc beneath which her present distress is seen in a new perspective – a small moment between great mercies.

As we follow the last stages of Mary's pregnancy, we also remember Sarah and Isaac. Sarah's son came to the brink of self-sacrifice for obedience's sake; for Love's sake, Mary's Son went all the way.

Eternal God,
as Mary waited for the birth of your Son,
so we wait for his coming in glory;
bring us through the birth pangs of this present age
to see, with her, our great salvation
in Jesus Christ our Lord.

COLLECT

Isaiah 55

'Why do you spend your money for that which is not bread?' (v.2)

Nightly on the news, you see the faces of the drained and laden, trudging home from shopping centres somehow disappointed by their retail therapy, the sad and cynical faces of the wealthy West, puzzled at how happiness has passed them by. But sometimes, on the same news, in a clip from some poor part of the earth, you see gaggles of giggling and radiantly smiling children, happy with nothing but the torn shirts on their backs and a home-made football.

How bitterly we have learned what it is to spend our money 'for that which is not bread' and our labour 'for that which does not satisfy' (v.2). Could it be that the secret of happiness for many of the world's poorest people is that they have come already to drink from the waters of this prophecy? That the generous and generative Word Isaiah speaks of here is already unfolding and feeding them? Perhaps only when we put down the shopping, let go of the burden, and receive instead the gift of this Word as a seed in our hearts, will we, who have come in with such sadness, at last go out with joy (v.12).

COLLECT

God our redeemer,
who prepared the Blessed Virgin Mary
to be the mother of your Son:
grant that, as she looked for his coming as our saviour,
so we may be ready to greet him
when he comes again as our judge;
who is alive and reigns with you,
in the unity of the Holy Spirit,
one God, now and for ever.

Psalms 128, 129, **130**, 131
Isaiah 56.1-8
2 Peter 3

Isaiah 56.1-8

'...for my house shall be called a house of prayer for all peoples' (v.7)

So far, Isaiah has been helping forsaken Zion to call on her deep memory, to remember those special stories embedded in her faith and culture, the tales of Sarah, the badges of her racial and religious identity. But now, just as she recovers her joy, he tells her this: this joyful news, patterned as it is in your memory, is not just for you, but for all the nations, all the races. You, who were outcast, must welcome other outcasts too, especially the ones you yourself cast out – the foreigners and the eunuchs, the once whose race, whose bodies, whose genders or identities could never fit your rules.

Israel, the outcast, had made her outcasts too, but here is the astonishing paradox, the liberality of God's love: the God of Israel nevertheless 'gathers the outcasts of Israel'. The one to be born on Christmas Day, the one who fulfils, page by page, all these prophecies of Isaiah, came to break down just those barriers of race and religion that pride had set across the temple gates. For the promised one came to the temple, as he comes to our churches now, with a scourge in his hand and these words on his lips: 'my house shall be called a house of prayer for all peoples' (v.7).

Eternal God,
as Mary waited for the birth of your Son,
so we wait for his coming in glory;
bring us through the birth pangs of this present age
to see, with her, our great salvation
in Jesus Christ our Lord.

Friday 24 December

Christmas Eve

Psalms **45**, 113
Isaiah 63.1-6
2 John

2 John

*'Be on your guard, so that you do not lose
what we have worked for' (v.8)*

So, on the eve of Christmas, we leap from the Old Testament to the New, from Isaiah to John. But something remains the same; Isaiah writes to Zion as the beloved but forsaken mother who is to be comforted, and John the elder writes to the Church as the 'elect lady', a beloved mother of children. He too speaks grace and peace, but he also warns of danger. The whole Gospel, foreshadowed in Isaiah, and celebrated in John, turns on incarnation, on the Word made flesh. Might the day come when the Church forgot that? Might we turn away from the God who meets us in compassionate flesh, and turn back instead to an abstract and bloodless religion?

'The word made flesh is here made words again', lamented Scottish poet Edwin Muir, and God is made 'three angry letters in a book'! This holy night, John asks us to be on our guard, so that we 'do not lose what we have worked for' (v.8) but learn again on Christmas morning to find him, in his holy flesh, which is also our own and our neighbours'.

COLLECT

Almighty God,
you make us glad with the yearly remembrance
of the birth of your Son Jesus Christ:
grant that, as we joyfully receive him as our redeemer,
so we may with sure confidence behold him
when he shall come to be our judge;
who is alive and reigns with you,
in the unity of the Holy Spirit,
one God, now and for ever.

Psalms **110**, 117
Isaiah 62.1-5
Matthew 1.18-end

Matthew 1.18-end

'... they shall name him Emmanuel...' (v.23)

And so we come to the day that 'fulfils' what was spoken by the prophet; all those promises of comfort, our daily reflection with Isaiah, those images of redemption and return, of mighty salvation. The watchmen are up on the tower looking out for a strong-armed man on the mountains, a warrior to tread the winepress of righteous wrath. But, while they look up to the strongholds, Matthew looks down among the weak and weary and finds our saviour with the poor, a child pursued by Herod, almost a victim at birth, carried from the scenes of slaughter as a refugee, an asylum-seeker in a strange land before he has even learned a word of his own language. And that is why he is 'Emmanuel' – God with us. He is with us on the inside of life, not looking in from outside, or down from above, but feeling from within the hurts and helplessness, absorbing and transforming the pain. And he remains Emmanuel past Christmastide, past Passiontide and Eastertide, past the last page of the Scripture.

For today, God steps free from the pages of his own book and walks with us, and in us, into every human encounter. We find him now not just in daily reflections on Scripture, but reflected to us daily in the faces of everyone, even the least of those whom we may meet or feed or clothe or love today.

Almighty God,
you have given us your only-begotten Son
to take our nature upon him
and as at this time to be born of a pure virgin:
grant that we, who have been born again
and made your children by adoption and grace,
may daily be renewed by your Holy Spirit;
through Jesus Christ your Son our Lord,
who is alive and reigns with you,
in the unity of the Holy Spirit,
one God, now and for ever.

COLLECT

25

Monday 27 December

John, Apostle and Evangelist

Psalms **21**, 147.13-end
Exodus 33.12-end
1 John 2.1-11

1 John 2.1-11

'Whoever says, "I am in the light", while hating a brother or sister, is still in the darkness' (v.9)

Fine words need to be matched by appropriate deeds, and the author of 1 John is challenging members of his church community who seem quite happy to quote Jesus' sayings without taking on board the implications for their own lives. For example, his readers claim to 'abide in' Jesus (recalling passages about Jesus as the 'bread of life' and the 'true vine' in John 6.35,56 and 15.1-11). But this is inadequate if they do not also live as Jesus did (v.6).

Similarly, they know Jesus as the 'light of the world', who calls on his followers to walk in that light (John 8.12, 12.35), but they still need to be reminded that Christians cannot hate each other and walk in the light at the same time. Integrity and mutual love are absolute requirements for believers.

For us today, it is not particularly demanding to read and quote sublime sayings of Jesus about light, love and transparency. The difficulty is practising what we preach. But there is mercy when we fail: 'if anyone does sin, we have an advocate with the Father, Jesus Christ the righteous ...' (v.1). Perhaps, in our current Church disputes, we need to expose our lack of love and mutual respect to the purifying light of Christ, so that we too may find forgiveness.

COLLECT

Merciful Lord,
cast your bright beams of light upon the Church:
that, being enlightened by the teaching
of your blessed apostle and evangelist Saint John,
we may so walk in the light of your truth
that we may at last attain to the light of everlasting life;
through Jesus Christ your incarnate Son our Lord,
who is alive and reigns with you,
in the unity of the Holy Spirit,
one God, now and for ever.

Psalms **36**, 146
Baruch 4.21-27
or Genesis 37.13-20
Matthew 18.1-10

Tuesday 28 December
The Holy Innocents

Matthew 18.1-10

'Take care that you do not despise one of these little ones' (v.10)

The smallest, the youngest and the least powerful among us are as important to God as the strong, experienced and famous. This message underlies much of today's passage, which is chosen because it refers to children, a theme pertinent to Holy Innocents' Day. On this day, we recall Herod's massacre of the baby boys of Bethlehem (Matthew 2.16-18), and are also reminded of our fearsome responsibility never to damage innocent or vulnerable people (vv.6,10).

Jesus often focuses his attention on the little people, those at the bottom of the pile because of poverty, stigma or misfortune. He also has a good rapport with children, delighting in their company when the disciples are busy disapproving (Matthew 19.13-15). So, it is not surprising that he says we need to become like small children in order to enter the kingdom. Perhaps he is thinking of children's natural openness and willingness to trust and explore without cynicism. But he goes further: 'Whoever becomes humble like this child is the greatest in the kingdom of heaven' (v.4). This is a radical overturning of the social norms of first-century Palestine, and speaks to us, too, if we are tempted to look down on those who are not clever, respectable or important in worldly terms.

COLLECT

Heavenly Father,
whose children suffered at the hands of Herod,
though they had done no wrong:
by the suffering of your Son
and by the innocence of our lives
frustrate all evil designs
and establish your reign of justice and peace;
through Jesus Christ your Son our Lord,
who is alive and reigns with you,
in the unity of the Holy Spirit,
one God, now and for ever.

Wednesday 29 December

Stephen, Deacon, First Martyr

Psalms 13, 31.1-8, 150
Jeremiah 26.12-15
Acts 6

Acts 6

'... they saw that his face was like the face of an angel' (v.15)

The story of Stephen, like the Christmas narratives themselves, contains vivid contrasts between light and hope on the one hand, and jealousy and suffering on the other. St Stephen's Day, which normally falls on Boxing Day, reminds us that birth and death are never far apart in the gospel. Over these Christmas days, we have encountered a bright star, glory and angels, but also the acute danger to Jesus resulting from Herod's vicious paranoia. Now, in the early Church, Stephen's grace-filled ministry is becoming such a threat to members of a Jerusalem synagogue that he will soon be killed.

We see human nature at its best and its worst here. A squabble about food distribution to widows is met with a positive, generous response, as the apostles appoint deacons to organize the provisions for the needy. Stephen's outstanding gifts of wisdom and healing soon attract attention, and, when his enemies realize that they cannot defeat him through argument, they hire false witnesses to condemn him, just as others had done with Jesus (Mark 14.56-9). Stephen will also be like Jesus when he prays that his murderers may be forgiven (Acts 7.60; Luke 23.34).

No matter how strong evil appears, God's light and love remain unquenchable.

COLLECT

Gracious Father,
who gave the first martyr Stephen
grace to pray for those who took up stones against him:
grant that in all our sufferings for the truth
we may learn to love even our enemies
and to seek forgiveness for those who desire our hurt,
looking up to heaven to him who was crucified for us,
Jesus Christ, our mediator and advocate,
who is alive and reigns with you,
in the unity of the Holy Spirit,
one God, now and for ever.

Psalms 111, 112, 113
Isaiah 59.1–15a
John 1.19-28

John 1.19-28

*'I am the voice of one crying out in the wilderness,
"Make straight the way of the Lord"' (v.23)*

John faces a barrage of questions from suspicious members of the religious establishment in Jerusalem, who are probably threatened by his bold preaching and by the size of the crowds who flock to him for baptism. His response is striking. First, he refuses to be categorized by popular expectations. He is not the Messiah, nor is he, at least in this Gospel, adopting the mantle of Elijah or another prophet as a messianic forerunner. Instead he is a witness to somebody of unimaginable significance whom they do not yet know (vv.26-27). Secondly, he sees himself as simply a messenger or 'voice' (v.23), pointing away from himself towards the one whose sandal he is unworthy to untie. Finally, John's quotation from Isaiah emphasizes his vocation to be in the wilderness, the tough landscape where humans are exposed and stripped to the bare essentials.

The Baptist is an inspiring example of faithful discipleship, with his freedom of spirit, his humility and his willingness to stay in a place where there is no easy escape from harsh challenges. For John, as for us, Christ is the centre and purpose of our faith. And Christ is here with us now, just as he was with John that day, standing quietly among the crowds by the Jordan.

Almighty God,
who wonderfully created us in your own image
and yet more wonderfully restored us
through your Son Jesus Christ:
grant that, as he came to share in our humanity,
so we may share the life of his divinity;
who is alive and reigns with you,
in the unity of the Holy Spirit,
one God, now and for ever.

COLLECT

Friday 31 December

John 1.29-34

'Here is the Lamb of God who takes away the sin of the world!'
(v.29)

The young man Jesus, with a unique role and ministry to fulfil, is only just beginning to appear in public. Yet, already, there is a hint of his suffering and death when John heralds him as 'the Lamb of God'. Lambs are associated with daily sacrifices in the Jerusalem temple, and this phrase also carries overtones of the Suffering Servant of Isaiah 53, who bears our sins and afflictions and is led like a lamb to the slaughter (Isaiah 53.4-5,7). The Passover lamb without blemish, killed on the eve of Israel's deliverance from Egypt, is another Old Testament link (Exodus 12.21-27) – and, in this Gospel, Jesus dies at the moment when the Passover lambs are killed (cf. John 19.14,31). Yet the deliverance Jesus brings is greater than anything seen before, because he himself is the Lamb.

Jesus' death is not the appeasement of a vengeful deity, or the substitution of a sinless victim, enduring a barbaric execution in our place to satisfy a distorted concept of justice. Jesus the Lamb is the innocent one, taking into himself all our sin and evil, and releasing into the world an energy of reconciling love through the power of the Holy Spirit. It is that same Spirit that descends on him at his baptism, and enables John to understand and proclaim Jesus' true identity (v.33).

COLLECT

Almighty God,
who wonderfully created us in your own image
and yet more wonderfully restored us
through your Son Jesus Christ:
grant that, as he came to share in our humanity,
so we may share the life of his divinity;
who is alive and reigns with you,
in the unity of the Holy Spirit,
one God, now and for ever.

Psalms **103**, 150
Genesis 17.1-13
Romans 2.17-end

The Naming and Circumcision of Jesus

Romans 2.17-end

'… real circumcision is a matter of the heart – it is spiritual and not literal' (v.29)

As Paul addresses controversies in the Roman Church about circumcision and the keeping of the Jewish law, he touches on one of the main issues that led to Jesus' death. Jesus himself was a faithful son of Israel, circumcised on the eighth day and always passionate about the spirit rather than the letter of the law. Yet his enemies plotted to kill him because of his revolutionary attitude to practices such as Sabbath observance, ritual purity and temple offerings. Jesus was sweeping away all that was based on externals and opening up the possibility of repentance, salvation and faithfulness of heart for every person. And that would become the very core of Paul's teaching.

Now, to Paul's horror, certain Christians in Rome are complacent about their spiritual status simply on the basis of being circumcised. Paul insists that this physical state is meaningless without obedience to the essential principles of the Jewish law (vv.17-24). On this day in the Church, we are celebrating Jesus' own circumcision, which was an outward sign of what would become his total dedication to the Father. A spiritual exercise for this New Year might be to ask ourselves whether our own external religious practices, whatever they are, express the true desires of our hearts and the integrity of our lives.

Almighty God,
whose blessed Son was circumcised
in obedience to the law for our sake
and given the Name that is above every name:
give us grace faithfully to bear his Name,
to worship him in the freedom of the Spirit,
and to proclaim him as the Saviour of the world;
who is alive and reigns with you,
in the unity of the Holy Spirit,
one God, now and for ever.

COLLECT

31

John 1.43-end

'Jesus answered, "I saw you under the fig tree before Philip called you"' (v.48)

Nathanael's first encounter with Jesus is fascinating. This future disciple (cf. John 21.2) is peacefully sitting under his fig tree when Philip suddenly appears, announcing that he has found the Messiah in Jesus of Nazareth. Nathanael is amazed: 'Can anything good come out of Nazareth?' Philip then takes him to Jesus, who is aware of Nathanael's scepticism yet does not chide him. Instead he commends him as someone totally without guile (vv.46-47).

Jesus knows our inmost thoughts and our limitations, as he knows Nathanael. Yet he accepts and affirms us as we are, without condemning us when we question or misunderstand our faith. As Nathanael begins to acknowledge Jesus' unique status, he uses traditional Jewish terminology: 'King of Israel' and 'Son of God' – which could refer to an angel, a king, a just man, or Israel itself (v.49). He still has only a partial grasp of Jesus' significance, which is not surprising considering how little time he has had to learn. But Jesus assures him that he will see greater things than he could ever have imagined. We too are invited to open our hearts and minds to the life-changing impact of Jesus, who can expand our vision so that we recognize heaven on earth, both in Jesus himself and in the ways he is at work in the world (cf. vv.50-51).

COLLECT

Almighty God,
in the birth of your Son
you have poured on us the new light of your incarnate Word,
and shown us the fullness of your love:
help us to walk in his light and dwell in his love
that we may know the fullness of his joy;
who is alive and reigns with you,
in the unity of the Holy Spirit,
one God, now and for ever.

Psalm **89**.1-37
Isaiah 61
John 2.1-12

John 2.1-12

*'Jesus did this, the first of his signs, in Cana of Galilee,
and revealed his glory' (v.11)*

This story has certain similarities with another incident where Jesus
banters with a woman who asks for a miracle, and then appears to
change his mind. In Mark 7.24-30, a Syro-Phoenician woman inter-
rupts Jesus' time off and begs him to heal her sick daughter. Here,
Mary asks him to rescue an embarrassing situation at a wedding.

In both cases, Jesus is initially cautious, because his actions could cause
problems. In the Gentile territories, Jesus could be swamped by people
needing healing. As a single human being, he can only work among
the Jews, and it will be his followers who minister more widely. But he
makes an exception out of compassion for this woman. Again at Cana,
if Jesus fulfils Mary's request, this could be misconstrued as the act of
a popular wonder-worker, whereas he will steadfastly refuse to
perform signs on demand (Luke 11.29, 23.8-9). In addition, the time
for his inevitable clash with the establishment (often exacerbated by his
miracles) has not yet come (v.4). But he does risk an act of kindness in
the end.

To the Evangelist, this miracle at Cana reveals Jesus' divine glory. The
old, rule-bound order of the Jewish institution is being replaced by the
generous wine of the gospel, and all our mundane lives can be
transformed into something joyous, loving and grace-filled.

God our Father,
in love you sent your Son
that the world may have life:
lead us to seek him among the outcast
and to find him in those in need,
for Jesus Christ's sake.

COLLECT

33

Wednesday 5 January

John 2.13-end

*'Jesus answered them, "Destroy this temple, and in three days
I will raise it up"' (v.19)*

Why this startling behaviour of Jesus? Traders are making a handsome
and often unscrupulous profit out of people's religious observances.
Temple commerce has become an end in itself rather than part of the
service of God, and the noise and bustle of barter and exchange
detract from the necessary atmosphere of reverence in this holy place.
But the reasons for Jesus' action go deeper. A total cleansing and
renewal of vision is needed at the heart of the Jewish faith, which is,
itself, in danger of becoming like a marketplace with God. Sacrifices
and other external practices are widely seen as bargaining chips for
earning God's acceptance without necessarily touching people's inner
lives. So, you could destroy the temple building without losing what
actually matters. Furthermore, the purpose of the temple is now
fulfilled in Jesus himself, since we have God's indwelling in the world
in Jesus' own person. Such ideas probably form the background to
Jesus' shocking words in verse 19, which Christians would later apply
especially to his death and resurrection.

Unlike the other Gospel-writers, John places this incident at the
beginning of Jesus' ministry, pointing to the radical transformation
about to be offered to Judaism and the world. Jesus knows what is in
all our hearts (vv.24-25). The question is whether we are willing to
open ourselves up to his purifying energy.

COLLECT

Almighty God,
in the birth of your Son
you have poured on us the new light of your incarnate Word,
and shown us the fullness of your love:
help us to walk in his light and dwell in his love
that we may know the fullness of his joy;
who is alive and reigns with you,
in the unity of the Holy Spirit,
one God, now and for ever.

Psalms **132**, **113**
Jeremiah 31.7-14
John 1.29-34

Jeremiah 31.7-14

*'They shall come and sing aloud on the height of Zion,
and they shall be radiant over the goodness of the Lord' (v.12)*

At Epiphany, we celebrate the revealing of Christ's glory in the world, especially in the visit of the Magi to Bethlehem, in Jesus' own baptism and in the miracle at the wedding in Cana of Galilee. Today's reading gives us a glimpse of glory from an Old Testament perspective, as Jeremiah promises hope and restoration to the Israelites exiled in Babylon (in the sixth century BC). This poetic passage presents a utopian picture of a vulnerable community (including the blind, the disabled and the pregnant, v.6) returning to their own land and finding prosperity and peace after great suffering. The Hebrew verb 'to be radiant' in verse 12 means both 'to flow along' and 'to become bright', suggesting a joyful procession of people who reflect something of the divine light themselves as they recognize God's goodness at work.

Jesus manifests God's radiance, although not in the triumphant or spectacular ways that many expected. His birth, baptism, miracles and even his suffering reveal the divine glory for those with eyes to see (cf. John 2.11, 13.31), and the purpose of his entire ministry is to free us from our own 'exile' experiences of guilt, legalism or despair. As we ponder the inner healing and new life that Jesus offers, our best response is to seek to be transparent to his light ourselves.

COLLECT

O God,
who by the leading of a star
manifested your only Son to the peoples of the earth:
mercifully grant that we,
who know you now by faith,
may at last behold your glory face to face;
through Jesus Christ your Son our Lord,
who is alive and reigns with you,
in the unity of the Holy Spirit,
one God, now and for ever.

1 John 3

*'See what love the Father has given us, that we should be called
children of God; and that is what we are' (v.1)*

Thanks to Jesus' coming into the world, it is possible for us to become
'children of God', taken up into the profound love-relationship that
we see between Jesus and God his Father. In this season of Epiphany,
the Church recalls Jesus' baptism, when his unique status is
dramatically confirmed by the voice from heaven: 'You are my Son,
the Beloved' (Mark 1.11). Today's reading reiterates the incredible truth
that we, in all our weakness, are called to share in that intimate
communion of Christ with the Father. Paul puts it another way when
he encourages us to pray 'Abba! Father!' as Christ himself had prayed
(Romans 8.15).

This insight can enrich our prayer, as we reach out with childlike
surrender and trust to the Father, and ask to be filled with the same
Spirit that infused Jesus. Life as sons and daughters of God also gives
us a foretaste of eternity. Ultimately, we shall reflect Jesus' very nature,
in a way that we cannot now fully grasp: 'when he is revealed, we will
be like him, for we will see him as he is' (v.2). We have already been
created in the divine image, but Jesus will enable us to realize this
potential fully. Our response can only be wonder and gratitude,
because this is pure gift, pure grace.

COLLECT

O God,
who by the leading of a star
manifested your only Son to the peoples of the earth:
mercifully grant that we,
who know you now by faith,
may at last behold your glory face to face;
through Jesus Christ your Son our Lord,
who is alive and reigns with you,
in the unity of the Holy Spirit,
one God, now and for ever.

Psalms **46**, 147.13-end *or* **76**, 79
Isaiah 64
1 John 4.7-end

1 John 4.7-end

'God is love, and those who abide in love abide in God,
and God abides in them' (v.16)

This passage needs to be read aloud if we are to do full justice to its power and poetry. The repeated words 'God', 'love' and 'abide' lead us ever more deeply into the movement of divine love in which we are invited to participate. This is the language of prayer, appealing to our hearts, minds and wills as we grow in our vocation to love because God first loved us. The writer echoes Jesus' commandment at the Last Supper, that we should love one another as God has loved us (John 13.34), but gives it a startling new twist: if we fail to love, we do not know God, because God's essential nature *is* love. So, to be unloving while still claiming to be a Christian is to make oneself a 'liar' (v.20). These are strong words, because this is crucial.

Christians sometimes disagree about what lies at the heart of our faith, and a recent church discussion group ended up as a tug-of-war between love and judgement. It is easy to emphasize either of these at the expense of the other. But, in the end, we are judged by love. And it is the astonishing love of God, seen in Jesus' sacrificial death for us, that exposes our betrayals and makes us want to be more loving ourselves, more like him.

Creator of the heavens,
who led the Magi by a star
to worship the Christ-child:
guide and sustain us,
that we may find our journey's end
in Jesus Christ our Lord.

COLLECT

Monday 10 January

1 Corinthians 1.1-17

'... *called to be saints, together with all those who in every place call on the name of our Lord Jesus Christ, both their Lord and ours*' (v.2)

Church factions are nothing new, and Paul starts this letter by tackling the divisions and misunderstandings that have arisen among Christians in Corinth. He begins with a passionate reminder that all believers, 'in every place', share the calling to be 'saints' or 'the sanctified' – a general term used at this time for all church members (cf. Philippians 4.22; Ephesians 1.1). We can take heart from the fact that those early conflicts did not quench the spread of the gospel, nor have denominational boundaries stopped people living and dying for Christ ever since. God's grace is greater than all our schisms and limitations.

What do we have in common? This is Paul's central question as he first encourages and then chides the Corinthians. The answer is Christ, who cannot be divided, and whose presence in the hearts of each other we ignore at our peril. A key concept here is 'fellowship' or *koinonia* (v.9), a word that has nothing to do with cosy, inward-looking faith, but rather challenges us to share in the very life of God's Son, and to remember that even the Christians whom we find most difficult are fellow disciples, loved by Jesus as we are.

COLLECT

Eternal Father,
who at the baptism of Jesus
revealed him to be your Son,
anointing him with the Holy Spirit:
grant to us, who are born again by water and the Spirit,
that we may be faithful to our calling as your adopted children;
through Jesus Christ your Son our Lord,
who is alive and reigns with you,
in the unity of the Holy Spirit,
one God, now and for ever.

Psalms 8, **9** *or* 87, **89.1-18**
Amos 2
1 Corinthians 1.18-end

1 Corinthians 1.18-end

'For God's foolishness is wiser than human wisdom, and God's weakness is stronger than human strength' (v.25)

These words of Paul are so potentially shocking that one modern translation of the Bible paraphrases the verse to read, 'What seems to be God's foolishness' and 'what seems to be God's weakness' (*Good News Bible*, HarperCollins 2009). But we cannot dodge the scandalous heart of our faith: that the power of divine love is revealed in and through the humiliating barbarity of a crucifixion. To follow Jesus on the way of the cross is a tough assignment, and we may be reluctant to accept any threat to our comfort, security or reputation. Yet it is our calling to be taken up into a gospel where the first are last, the persecuted are blessed, and our enemies are to be loved rather than crushed (cf. Mark 9.35; Matthew 5.10,44).

Paul's primary concern here is the arrogance of warring factions among Corinthian believers, some of whom pride themselves on their intellectual and social status. But they, like us, need to remember that everything we do well is God's gift: 'He is the source of your life in Christ Jesus' (v.30). Jesus was neither successful nor powerful in worldly terms, and true wisdom is found in the foolishness of the love that gives itself away, not in the boasting that thinks it knows more about God than everybody else.

Heavenly Father,
at the Jordan you revealed Jesus as your Son:
may we recognize him as our Lord
and know ourselves to be your beloved children;
through Jesus Christ our Saviour.

COLLECT

Wednesday 12 January

Psalms 19, **20** *or* **119.105-128**
Amos 3
I Corinthians 2

1 Corinthians 2

'... we speak of these things in words not taught by human wisdom but taught by the Spirit' (v.13)

Paul continues his challenge to those who claim superiority in the Corinthian church by raising the question of how we can know about God at all. This issue is still alive today, as prominent atheists use rational argument to attack their versions of our faith. But Paul is adamant that 'God's wisdom, secret and hidden', cannot be fully grasped by intellect or the 'wisdom of this age' alone (vv.6-7). He recalls how nervous and hesitant he felt when he first proclaimed the gospel to them (although this is hard to believe in view of the courage and intellectual stature that we see in him elsewhere). Yet Paul's listeners had still responded to him, not because of his eloquence, but because God's power was at work through the message of the cross.

For Christians, the gift of reason is a necessary tool in seeking to understand life and faith. But God's ways are ultimately beyond human comprehension. We can speak confidently about mercy, healing and the call to serve, because we know these things in the depth of our hearts. Faith and trust do not come from thinking alone, but from loving, listening and surrender – elements that remain a mystery to worldly wisdom.

COLLECT

Eternal Father,
who at the baptism of Jesus
revealed him to be your Son,
anointing him with the Holy Spirit:
grant to us, who are born again by water and the Spirit,
that we may be faithful to our calling as your adopted children;
through Jesus Christ your Son our Lord,
who is alive and reigns with you,
in the unity of the Holy Spirit,
one God, now and for ever.

Psalms **21**, 24 *or* 90, **92**
Amos 4
1 Corinthians 3

1 Corinthians 3

'… you should become fools so that you may become wise' (v.18)

Paul returns to his key theme that God works through powerlessness and vulnerability rather than worldly might and human cleverness. Outraged by the party strife among Corinthian Christians, he asks, 'What then is Apollos? What is Paul?', insisting that he and the other apostles whose names are used by warring factions are simply fellow-labourers in God's field, while God alone gives the growth (vv.5-9). Our current divisions in the Church show how badly we still need this spirit of humility, recognizing God's grace at work in others and heeding Paul's challenge to become fools if we want to be wise.

Countless individuals down the centuries have sensed the calling to be 'holy fools', from early desert hermits and Russian eccentrics to counter-cultural Christians in our own time. They have often defied worldly ambition in dramatic ways, but there is a 'fool for Christ' to be found in us all (cf. 1 Corinthians 4.10). Divine foolishness turns upside-down worldly standards of success, value and achievement, helping us to be childlike, not to take ourselves too seriously and to accept our total dependence on God. Paul concludes with the marvellous phrase: 'For all things are yours' (v.21), reminding us that everything good is God's generous gift, not our own. To be humble is to be thankful.

Heavenly Father,
at the Jordan you revealed Jesus as your Son:
may we recognize him as our Lord
and know ourselves to be your beloved children;
through Jesus Christ our Saviour.

COLLECT

41

Friday 14 January

Psalms **67**, 72 *or* **88** (95)
Amos 5.1-17
1 Corinthians 4

1 Corinthians 4

*'... do not pronounce judgement before the time,
before the Lord comes' (v.5)*

The way in which we perceive and judge each other is a key issue here. Paul is concerned about people in Corinth who are 'puffed up' with pride as they criticize others and divide the congregation (v.6). God alone is our judge, he insists, since only God knows our inmost hearts. What is more, our own apparent failure or humiliation may be the very place where God works most effectively. The apostles frequently endured hardship and abuse when they preached the gospel, yet their weakness and 'rubbish' status had been used by God to make strong believers out of others (vv.9-13). We cannot judge by appearances, nor do we have the right to condemn the faith of fellow-Christians, as if we knew all about their personal spiritual life.

Arrogance is always a danger for the Church, especially when outreach and mission result in transformed lives and growing congregations. The heady experiences of success and power need to be tempered by humility. It is when we acknowledge our total dependence on God that grace floods in: 'What do you have that you did not receive?' (v.7). The world may be attracted by popular orators and claims of absolute certainty, but fools for Christ often discover that the Spirit works through vulnerability, littleness and the willingness to listen before we judge.

COLLECT

Eternal Father,
who at the baptism of Jesus
revealed him to be your Son,
anointing him with the Holy Spirit:
grant to us, who are born again by water and the Spirit,
that we may be faithful to our calling as your adopted children;
through Jesus Christ your Son our Lord,
who is alive and reigns with you,
in the unity of the Holy Spirit,
one God, now and for ever.

1 Corinthians 5

'And you are arrogant! Should you not rather have mourned?' (v.2)

This is a difficult chapter. Paul seems willing to condemn a member of the congregation, even though he has just been berating them for judging each other. One reason for his hard-line approach here is the seriousness of the situation, exacerbated by the Corinthians' nonchalant arrogance as regards his authority. Paul is tackling a case of incest according to the Torah (Leviticus 18.8) and adopts a ruthless tone: 'hand this man over to Satan for the destruction of the flesh, so that his spirit may be saved …' (v.5). But why so harsh? Other chapters indicate that the self-styled 'wise' in Corinth may be interpreting the man's relationship with his father's wife as an expression of his Christian freedom (cf. 1 Corinthians 6.12ff.). Paul realizes that this combination of boastfulness and immorality ('malice and evil'), could affect the whole church, like stale yeast in a lump of dough (v.8), so he pronounces a classic excommunication: send the man back to a world already in Satan's grip. If painful or destructive things happen to him there, it will at least be good for his soul (cf. v.5).

We may baulk at the lack of mercy here. Yet there can be situations when Christians are right to denounce the abuse or oppression of others, especially when such things are done by those who claim to serve and worship God.

Heavenly Father,
at the Jordan you revealed Jesus as your Son:
may we recognize him as our Lord
and know ourselves to be your beloved children;
through Jesus Christ our Saviour.

COLLECT

Monday 17 January

Psalms 145, **146** or **98**, 99, 101
Amos 6
1 Corinthians 6.1-11

1 Corinthians 6.1-11

'... to have lawsuits at all with one another is already a defeat for you' (v.7)

The very idea that Christians should take each other to court is anathema to Paul. He sees the world as essentially under the judgement of God and belonging to 'the unrighteous', making it totally inappropriate for believers to try to settle their quarrels in the civil courts. Only the Church, he argues, is competent to judge grievances between its own members. Paul may also have in mind instances of corruption when he says, 'the saints will judge the world' (v.2), and he maintains that it is better to accept injustice within a local congregation than to seek redress in a secular trial (v.7).

Two thousand years later, those of us who live under an independent judiciary probably see the processes of law in a different light. In spite of our tendency to be an over-litigious society, countless people of integrity, including Christians, work within our legal system. However, some years ago I saw the damage done both to individuals and to the gospel when someone took his own diocese to court over a procedural dispute. Legalism and the desire to defeat one's opponents by whatever means, no matter how harmful, are as unhealthy in Christian circles now as they were in Paul's day.

COLLECT

Almighty God,
in Christ you make all things new:
transform the poverty of our nature by the riches of your grace,
and in the renewal of our lives
make known your heavenly glory;
through Jesus Christ your Son our Lord,
who is alive and reigns with you,
in the unity of the Holy Spirit,
one God, now and for ever.

Psalms **132**, 147.1-12
or **106*** (*or* 103)
Amos 7
1 Corinthians 6.12-end

1 Corinthians 6.12-end

'... do you not know that your body is a temple of the Holy Spirit within you?' (v.19)

Christian freedom is being misinterpreted as licence by certain believers in Corinth, who claim that their bodily behaviour is irrelevant because they are now spiritual people and therefore above the law (v.12). Paul counters this by insisting that our spiritual and physical lives are inextricably linked. The body and its functions are not basically bad, as many have mistakenly taught down the ages, but are 'meant ... for the Lord' (v.13). Furthermore, our bodies are 'temples' or sanctuaries of the Holy Spirit within us (v.19). This is a refreshingly positive view of the body, quite different from the dualism that wants to shun the material world and crush all bodily needs and desires in order to achieve holiness.

If, as Paul teaches, our bodies are a gift from God and belong to God, we should treat food, sex and all other corporeal aspects of life with reverence and integrity. Promiscuity and greed constitute sacrilege against ourselves and others, and also against Christ whose 'members' or limbs we are (v.15). Everything we do, whether in work, relaxation, creative activity or the service of others, is part of our single 'Yes' to God, involving our whole selves, body, mind and spirit.

Eternal Lord,
our beginning and our end:
bring us with the whole creation
to your glory, hidden through past ages
and made known
in Jesus Christ our Lord.

COLLECT

Wednesday 19 January

Psalms **81**, 147.13-end
or 110, **111**, 112
Amos 8
1 Corinthians 7.1-24

1 Corinthians 7.1-24

*'… let each of you lead the life that the Lord has assigned,
to which God called you' (v.17)*

Corinth is a place of extremes. Having dealt with the libertarian element in the Church, Paul now comes up against some severe ascetics who are advocating total sexual abstinence for everyone. He is sufficiently experienced as a pastor to know that this is unrealistic. To remain unmarried is still the ideal, he suggests, but if you cannot control your passions it is better to allow yourselves the normal intimacy of married life (vv.1-7). This betrays an inescapably negative attitude to human sexuality. However, Paul's overriding concern is that his flock will remain faithful and stable in their relationships, and his limited view of sex is part of his wider message that they should all live according to their God-given nature.

Countless individuals down the centuries have sensed a genuine calling to the celibate life, while others have tried to force themselves into a mould that is not right for them. Paul's words encourage us to discern our own giftedness and vocation rather than try to emulate others: 'each has a particular gift from God, one having one kind and another a different kind' (v.7). Our task is to start where we are, seeking to live out our Christian discipleship within our present situation, rather than assuming that God can only be found somewhere else.

COLLECT

Almighty God,
in Christ you make all things new:
transform the poverty of our nature by the riches of your grace,
and in the renewal of our lives
make known your heavenly glory;
through Jesus Christ your Son our Lord,
who is alive and reigns with you,
in the unity of the Holy Spirit,
one God, now and for ever.

Psalms **76**, 148 *or* 113, **115**
Amos 9
1 Corinthians 7.25-end

1 Corinthians 7.25-end

'I say this for your own benefit ... to promote good order and unhindered devotion to the Lord' (v.35)

There is an additional factor behind Paul's teaching in this chapter. Like others of his time, Paul thinks that Jesus will soon return to establish God's kingdom on earth once and for all. Assuming that the end of the present world order and the 'impending crisis' are imminent, many Christians are therefore wondering if they should separate themselves from all worldly concerns, including marriage and possessions (cf. vv.26,31). Paul agrees that the single state is preferable in these circumstances, because it frees believers to focus all their energy and attention on 'the affairs of the Lord' (v.32). But he also reiterates his more positive view of marriage for those who need it, giving the go-ahead for those keen to marry a 'virgin' or young girl just out of puberty (vv.25ff.).

We see many things differently today. We know that Jesus' second coming did not happen as expected, and we probably do not regard family ties and paid work as inevitable hindrances to life with God (even though we may wish we had more time for prayer). Yet the challenge is still there, to consider how far our lifestyle reflects our true priorities. 'The affairs of the world' (v.33) are not necessarily bad. But are we allowing everyday concerns to squeeze out our prayer, worship and service of others?

Eternal Lord,
our beginning and our end:
bring us with the whole creation
to your glory, hidden through past ages
and made known
in Jesus Christ our Lord.

COLLECT

Friday 21 January

1 Corinthians 8

*'Anyone who claims to know something does not yet have the
necessary knowledge; but anyone who loves God is known by him'*
(vv.2-3)

What sort of knowledge matters most in the Christian life? This
question underlies Paul's arguments here, and is as important today as
it was in the first century. Knowing something intellectually does not
guarantee the deeper knowledge that is true wisdom. Certain
believers in Corinth are inflated with pride about their grasp of the
thorny issue of food offered to idols, and Paul mocks their resultant
claim to 'possess knowledge' (v.1). To those sophisticated people, it
seems perfectly obvious that consuming food from pagan temples
carries no significance, because idols are not real. Yet, for all their
cleverness, they lack sensitivity to the needs of other Christians who
are either offended by their actions or are being misled into thinking
that standards can be compromised: 'take care that this liberty of yours
does not somehow become a stumbling-block to the weak' (v.9).

We need reason and common sense, and it is good to be well
informed about our faith in order to engage intelligently in debate
about issues of doctrine and discipleship. But a deep and prayerful
knowledge of God is about love, not facts, and can never be
possessed. Arrogance makes brainpower into an idol, but truly to
know God is simply to understand in our deepest being that we are
loved (v.3).

Almighty God,
in Christ you make all things new:
transform the poverty of our nature by the riches of your grace,
and in the renewal of our lives
make known your heavenly glory;
through Jesus Christ your Son our Lord,
who is alive and reigns with you,
in the unity of the Holy Spirit,
one God, now and for ever.

Psalms **122**, 128, 150
or 120, **121**, 122
Hosea 2.2-17
1 Corinthians 9.1-14

1 Corinthians 9.1-14

*'Am I not free? Am I not an apostle? Have I not seen Jesus
our Lord?' (v.1)*

Here we see Paul as a cross and exhausted human being. He has given himself unstintingly to the work of preaching the gospel, but now finds himself criticized for assuming that the church in Corinth will feed and support him. Two things are striking here. The first is the sheer vehemence of his outburst, with its stream of indignant questions and arguments. We may be able to relate to his exasperation, especially in the way that aggrieved and self-justifying thoughts pour through his mind – an experience common to many of us when we feel we have been unjustly treated.

Secondly, it is, sadly, not unusual for church members to find fault with their leaders for the slightest reason. This is not to say that congregations should be mutely subservient to the clergy, or that clergy should not be answerable for their actions. But it is easy to jump to unfair and hurtful conclusions, for example, about the way our ministers manage their time and resources. Corinthian Christians failed to give Paul the benefit of the doubt, even though he was willing to earn his keep as a tent-maker if necessary (cf. Acts 18.3). If we ourselves are about to blame someone behind their back, the wisest course may be to pause and reflect before we speak.

COLLECT

Eternal Lord,
our beginning and our end:
bring us with the whole creation
to your glory, hidden through past ages
and made known
in Jesus Christ our Lord.

Monday 24 January

Psalms 40, **108**
or 123, 124, 125, **126**
Hosea 2.18 – 3.end
1 Corinthians 9.15-end

1 Corinthians 9.15-end

*'... though I am free with respect to all,
I have made myself a slave to all' (v.19)*

This reading reveals the passion, complexity and even the psychology of the apostle Paul. Psychologically, it clearly mattered to Paul that he was a *real* apostle, although not one of the original Twelve. He foregoes his 'rights' as an apostle, but he lets us know that he has those rights all the same.

Paul's treatment of reward shows how complex he can be: no one can rob him of his right to boast as a preacher, but then, he has no right to boast in the first place, since he is obliged to preach. Even so, he merits a reward, yet he lays this reward aside.

Paul's zeal is seen in his purposefulness. He does not 'run aimlessly' but runs so as to win the prize. This prize is not something for himself alone; it is that many should share with him in eternal life.

Paul's method is to 'become all things to all people'. This expression can spell blandness. For Paul, it means quite the opposite. Among Jews, he threw himself into living and arguing as a Jew. Among Gentiles, he argues with a Gentile frame of reference. We see this in his preaching at Athens, where he made full use of the religious, literary and philosophical culture of his Greek audience. There is nothing bland about Paul.

COLLECT

Almighty God,
whose Son revealed in signs and miracles
the wonder of your saving presence:
renew your people with your heavenly grace,
and in all our weakness
sustain us by your mighty power;
through Jesus Christ your Son our Lord,
who is alive and reigns with you,
in the unity of the Holy Spirit,
one God, now and for ever.

Psalms 66, 147.13-end
Ezekiel 3.22-end
Philippians 3.1-14

Tuesday 25 January

The Conversion of Paul

Philippians 3.1-14

'... whatever gains I had, these I have come to regard as loss because of Christ' (v.7)

Today is the main feast day of Paul the apostle. In our reading, we encounter the same passion and purposefulness we did as yesterday. It presents Paul from more angles than any other half-chapter in his epistles. We see his fiery and protective love for his spiritual children; he is like a she-bear defending her cubs. Then comes a potted early life story and a theological thumbnail sketch of his conversion: I regard my prior advantages, he writes, 'as rubbish', or, to give the Greek its full force, as 'mire', as 'sewage in the streets'.

The passage ends with Paul at his best, seamlessly weaving doctrine and devotion. He wants us to be serious about both. His theology is precise: salvation is 'in Christ', by faith, through his death and resurrection. Yet there is nothing dry or abstract about this. It is also the warp and weft of his life of labour and prayer. Paul wants to know Christ, to share with him, to become like him.

He closes with one of his most characteristic of paradoxical combinations: all is grace ('Christ Jesus has made me his own'), but this inspires us to action rather than absolving us from it ('I press on to make it my own').

Almighty God,
who caused the light of the gospel
to shine throughout the world
through the preaching of your servant Saint Paul:
grant that we who celebrate his wonderful conversion
may follow him in bearing witness to your truth;
through Jesus Christ your Son our Lord,
who is alive and reigns with you,
in the unity of the Holy Spirit,
one God, now and for ever.

COLLECT

Wednesday 26 January

Psalms 45, **46** *or* 119.153-end
Hosea 5.1-7
1 Corinthians 10.14 – 11.1

1 Corinthians 10.14 – 11.1

'… flee from the worship of idols' (v.14)

We are faced with idolatry just as much today as Paul was. Then, it was a matter of polytheism; for us, it is more likely a matter of consumerism. Idols are a problem because we treat them seriously, but they are also a problem because they are worthless. Most of all, idolatry is a problem because both things are true.

Worship is always an act of dedication and a search for union. For the people of Israel, sacrifices formed a bond between them and God. Paul goes on to stress that, for Christians, this sharing is even more profound. He calls our Eucharist 'a sharing' in the body and blood of Christ.

Like the Israelite sacrifices, Paul says, or the Eucharist, idolatry unites us with what we worship. It also joins person to person, creating a community. Worship does this whether it is the worship of the true God or its idolatrous parody – think of the common feeling between present-day devotees of a celebrity or craze in fiction.

'Is an idol anything?' Paul asks. 'No' is the answer. Idols have power, but they are also nothing. That is precisely the point. When we worship an idol, we join ourselves to a nothing, an emptiness, a void. But worship God and we are joined to the 'most real': the source of all reality.

COLLECT

Almighty God,
whose Son revealed in signs and miracles
the wonder of your saving presence:
renew your people with your heavenly grace,
and in all our weakness
sustain us by your mighty power;
through Jesus Christ your Son our Lord,
who is alive and reigns with you,
in the unity of the Holy Spirit,
one God, now and for ever.

Psalms **47**, 48 *or* 143, 146
Hosea 5.8 – 6.6
1 Corinthians 11.2-16

1 Corinthians 11.2-16

*'... in the Lord woman is not independent of man or man
independent of woman' (v.11)*

Faced with a reading such as today's, our problem is not living 2,000
years ago. What we take for granted after two millennia of Christian
culture was revolutionary to Paul's audience. Conversely, what we find
difficult or extraordinary about this passage would hardly have
attracted the notice of Paul's first audience.

A text like this one poses all sorts of interpretative questions. We
cannot simply brush under the carpet things that we do not like. All
the same, we get closer to Paul's message if we ask what would have
struck his first readers as a bombshell and not simply have confirmed
their cultural status quo.

Paul's writings about men and women are unremarkable for their time
when they address female subordination or concerns over hair,
clothing and jewellery. They are revolutionary when they tell Christian
men to love their wives as Christ loves the Church or, in this passage,
that there is genuine equality: 'just as woman came from man, so man
comes through woman' and 'in the Lord, woman is not independent
of man or man independent of woman'.

Yes, Paul also wrote things that were unremarkable for his time. He
also wrote revolutionary things. Our emphasis should be on the latter.

God of all mercy,
your Son proclaimed good news to the poor,
release to the captives,
and freedom to the oppressed:
anoint us with your Holy Spirit
and set all your people free
to praise you in Christ our Lord.

COLLECT

53

Psalms 61, **65** *or* 142, **144**
Hosea 6.7 – 7.2
1 Corinthians 11.17-end

1 Corinthians 11.17-end

'... wait for one another' (v.33)

In the New Testament, we find the words with which Christ instituted the Eucharist four separate times: three times in the Gospels and here in this epistle. When St Paul comes to pass them on, it is in the middle of a rebuke about divisions in the Christian community and a lack of interest in the poor. It is sobering that we should encounter them here.

Paul has a profound reverence for the Lord's Supper. It is a participation – a 'sharing' – in the body and blood of Christ (1 Corinthians 10.16). He has an equally profound reverence for the Church. It too is the body of Christ.

The Corinthians had been sharing communion with enmity against one another in their hearts. For some, it had become an opportunity for indulgence, with contemptuous disregard for the poor and hungry.

Paul calls this a failure to 'discern the body'. It is a failure of discernment twice over: they do not discern in the sacrament the seriousness it deserves as the body of Christ, nor do they discern the presence of Christ in his people, and especially in the needy.

If our emphasis is usually on the bread as Christ's body, this passage directs us also to the Church. If our emphasis is on Jesus in his people, Paul reminds us that the bread and the cup are a unique participation in Christ.

COLLECT

Almighty God,
whose Son revealed in signs and miracles
the wonder of your saving presence:
renew your people with your heavenly grace,
and in all our weakness
sustain us by your mighty power;
through Jesus Christ your Son our Lord,
who is alive and reigns with you,
in the unity of the Holy Spirit,
one God, now and for ever.

Psalms **68** *or* **147**
Hosea 8
1 Corinthians 12.1-11

1 Corinthians 12.1-11

*'... concerning spiritual gifts, brothers and sisters,
I do not want you to be uninformed' (v. 1)*

The gifts of the Holy Spirit, such as healing or prophecy, can be a source of tension and disunity in the Church. They have certainly been so in the past. When we read St Paul today, we see that this is a particular tragedy. The gifts are 'services' – they are given to someone not for his or her own sake but for the sake and service of the community as a whole. The gifts are also 'activities' – something done for a purpose. The purpose, Paul writes, is building up 'the common good'.

Every Christian should be open to the gifts that the Spirit might give. These include the gifts listed here, but also any number of others. The keynote of the Spirit's distribution of gifts, as we read today, is 'variety'.

Paul urges Christians unfamiliar with this territory to 'strive for the spiritual gifts' (1 Corinthians 14.1) – the gifts are for service, and he wants us to be fully equipped for that task. On the other hand, if the charismatic gifts are more central to the life of your local church, Paul's reminder is that service, and seeking the good of others, are to be their distinguishing marks.

God of all mercy,
your Son proclaimed good news to the poor,
release to the captives,
and freedom to the oppressed:
anoint us with your Holy Spirit
and set all your people free
to praise you in Christ our Lord.

COLLECT

Monday 31 January

1 Corinthians 12.12-end

'... you are the body of Christ and individually members of it' (v.27)

In last Thursday's reading, we tried to discern the central feature of Paul's teaching about men and women, husbands and wives, by putting ourselves in the shoes of his first readers. The same approach will be helpful today.

It is a commonplace to describe a group of people as a 'body' and to talk of 'members' (which means something like 'arms and legs') and 'corporate identity'. What is familiar to us was new to Paul's readers. When he described the Church as a body, he was not using a well-worn image; he was inventing a new one. Paul's images are thoroughly theological, and never more so than when he is talking of the Church, for instance as the bride of Christ, or as his Body.

If we understand the Church as the Body of Christ, there are immediate consequences. This image makes it clear that we need one another, that diversity is a good thing and that we should open ourselves up to the happiness and sadness of others.

This sort of interrelation is a noble goal to seek for wider society, but Paul is clear that it begins with the Church. This corporate belonging together is not a general hope but a theological one. Paul calls for a revolution in the way we live. If it does not begin in the Church, it will not begin anywhere.

COLLECT

God our creator,
who in the beginning
commanded the light to shine out of darkness:
we pray that the light of the glorious gospel of Christ
may dispel the darkness of ignorance and unbelief,
shine into the hearts of all your people,
and reveal the knowledge of your glory
    in the face of Jesus Christ your Son our Lord,
who is alive and reigns with you,
in the unity of the Holy Spirit,
one God, now and for ever.

Psalms **93**, 97 *or* **5**, 6 (8)
Hosea 10
1 Corinthians 13

1 Corinthians 13

'... the greatest of these is love' (v.13)

Paul's discussions of church order, sexual ethics, the Eucharist and charismatic gifts are crowned by his hymn on the theme of love. Here we find the summation of all that he has been saying in this letter.

'Faith, hope, and love abide, these three; and the greatest of these is love.' Why, we might ask, should *love* be the greatest? For an answer, we can turn to St Thomas Aquinas (1225–64), one of the greatest of all Christian writers on the theology of love.

Love, he writes, is greater even than faith or hope because they always imply a certain distance from God, whereas love concerns union with God. By definition, 'faith is directed to what is not seen, and hope is directed to what is not possessed' (*Summa Theologiae* I-I, 66.6). On the other hand, we already possess what we love: 'the beloved is, in a way, in the one who loves'.

God has given himself to us and also promises an ever-fuller friendship: 'the one who loves is drawn by desire to be one with the beloved'. Aquinas points us to 1 John 4.16: 'those who abide in love abide in God, and God abides in them'. Faith and hope will 'abide', but one day their work will be done. When we see God face to face, love will grow only stronger.

God of heaven,
you send the gospel to the ends of the earth
and your messengers to every nation:
send your Holy Spirit to transform us
by the good news of everlasting life
in Jesus Christ our Lord.

COLLECT

Wednesday 2 February

The Presentation of Christ in the Temple

Romans 12.1-5

*'... we, who are many, are one body in Christ,
and individually we are members one of another' (v.5)*

If we did not know where our reading came from, we might think that today's reading continues where we left off yesterday. We read today that the Church is a body and Christians are members; there are diverse and inter-related functions within the whole; we are to show forbearance and seek the good of others.

However, the reading is from Romans, not 1 Corinthians. We have it because today is the feast of the Presentation of Christ in the Temple. The message of this feast underlines Paul's arguments in 1 Corinthians: we live for others because God came among us and lived for others; we show forbearance because God showed forbearance, not coming as judge until he had first come as redeemer; Christ is united to his Church in order to extend the most wonderful union of all: the bodily union of God and humanity in Christ's own person.

Throughout 1 Corinthians, we encounter the body frequently: the ecclesial body, the Eucharistic body, the body honoured or dishonoured in marriage. The body matters to Paul because it mattered to God. As the Prayer Book's collect has it, today God was 'presented in the temple in substance of our flesh'. As the second-century theologian Tertullian put it, for Christian theology 'the flesh is the hinge of salvation'.

COLLECT

Almighty and ever-living God,
clothed in majesty,
whose beloved Son was this day presented in the Temple,
in substance of our flesh:
grant that we may be presented to you
with pure and clean hearts,
by your Son Jesus Christ our Lord,
who is alive and reigns with you,
in the unity of the Holy Spirit,
one God, now and for ever.

1 Corinthians 14.20-end

'… be infants in evil, but in thinking be adults' (v.20)

Growing up as a bird involves learning to fly. Growing up as a human being involves learning to speak. It is no coincidence that Paul begins this passage on speaking in tongues with an invocation of infancy and maturity: 'be infants in evil, but in thinking be adults'.

Throughout his letters, Paul desires two things: that those who have not encountered Christ should become new Christians, and that new Christians should grow into their faith. We can see these as two related aspects of conversion. In one sense, conversion is stepping over a line; in another sense, it is beginning to walk along the line of Christian discipleship.

Whether the scene Paul paints today is familiar or strange, some general points stand out. They relate to Christian maturity. When we meet together, Christians should think about the outsider – a healthy Church community should bowl the newcomer over. The basic organizing principle for Christian gathering should be mutual up-building: 'Let all things be done for building up'. We should seek the Holy Spirit's inspiration, but not suppose that this removes our will – even the prophet retains control. God is given most space to speak when things are done in an orderly fashion, since he is 'a God not of disorder but of peace'.

Almighty God,
by whose grace alone we are accepted
and called to your service:
strengthen us by your Holy Spirit
and make us worthy of our calling;
through Jesus Christ your Son our Lord,
who is alive and reigns with you,
in the unity of the Holy Spirit,
one God, now and for ever.

COLLECT

Friday 4 February

Psalms 17, **19**
Hosea 13.1-14
I Corinthians 16.1-9

1 Corinthians 16.1-9

'On the first day of every week ...' (v.2)

Millennia before the invention of the Friendly Society or the savings coupon, St Paul saw the value of regular saving. 'Put something aside every week', he tells the Corinthians, 'so that you will have a collection for the poor ready when I arrive.'

As Christians, the principle remains that we should give away some of what we earn for the work of the Church and the relief of the poor. The Church of England advises five per cent to the Church and five per cent to other charities.

What we do with our money gets close to the heart of where our commitments really lie. Just as indicative is what we do with our time. Several passages in the New Testament document a revolution in the way the early Christians organized their week. Today's passage is one of them.

From the earliest days, Christians made Sunday their principal day for gathering and giving praise to God, moving from the Jewish sabbath. They met on Sunday in honour of the resurrection. Sunday worship was not necessarily at all convenient, but the resurrection had reordered their lives. Today's reading highlights some of the really very few obligations that the Church lays on her children: to give of their time and to give of their money, to support the Church and the poor, and to gather for worship on Sunday.

COLLECT

Almighty God,
by whose grace alone we are accepted
      and called to your service:
strengthen us by your Holy Spirit
and make us worthy of our calling;
through Jesus Christ your Son our Lord,
who is alive and reigns with you,
in the unity of the Holy Spirit,
one God, now and for ever.

Saturday 5 February

1 Corinthians 16.10-end

'Let all that you do be done in love' (v.14)

At the end of a letter from St Paul, we step into a different world. The tone becomes practical and the setting almost domestic. It seems that he wrote these endings himself and not through a secretary. This intriguing detail also suggests that he had poor eyesight: 'See what large letters I make when I am writing in my own hand!' (Galatians 6.11).

Paul's endings resemble a cross between a report from a human-resources department and a quartermaster's memo: people are sent here and there; mundane objects are requisitioned – in one case a cloak – as the winter sets in.

In his more polished theological prose, Paul teaches Christian solidarity: 'We do not live to ourselves, and we do not die to ourselves' (Romans 14.7). In the far more ragged writing of his letters' conclusions, the same message is underlined in the biographical detail. He has taught that: 'The one who plants and the one who waters have a common purpose, and each will receive wages according to the labour of each' (1 Corinthians 3.8). Here, that is made clear: just as no Christian lives or dies alone, neither does any Christian work alone. Paul – the apostle with the ego – is at pains to stress inter-relation. He lives by what he has taught us: we are members together of the body of Christ.

God of our salvation,
help us to turn away from those habits
which harm our bodies
and poison our minds
and to choose again your gift of life,
revealed to us in Jesus Christ our Lord.

COLLECT

Monday 7 February

John 13.1-11

'Lord, not my feet only but also my hands and my head!' (v.9)

John doesn't give an account of the institution of the Holy Communion as the other Gospel-writers do. Instead he describes how Jesus gave himself to his followers at the last meal he and his disciples had together before the crucifixion.

It was a natural expression of hospitality in their culture and climate for people to have their feet washed. When Jesus began to perform this servant's work for the disciples, Peter found it difficult. Surely it should have been the other way round, with Peter kneeling before Jesus to wash his feet? Peter's instinct was to refuse to let Jesus do it. But Jesus told him that if he wouldn't let him minister to him, Peter wouldn't really belong to him. Peter, with his endearing impetuosity, immediately went to the other extreme – 'Not just my feet, Lord, but my hands and my head too – I want to belong to you completely'. We can almost hear the laughter in Jesus' voice as he told Peter that he didn't have to go over the top: 'Just let me minister to you, you don't need to do anything more, you belong.'

There is a sombre subtext in this passage, though. Judas had his feet washed too. But there was no acceptance of the love that Jesus was offering. Judas submitted to the act but made no loving commitment in response.

The question we are left with is: how wholehearted is our response?

COLLECT

Almighty God,
by whose grace alone we are accepted
    and called to your service:
strengthen us by your Holy Spirit
and make us worthy of our calling;
through Jesus Christ your Son our Lord,
who is alive and reigns with you,
in the unity of the Holy Spirit,
one God, now and for ever.

Psalms 32, **36**
1 Chronicles 13
John 13.12-20

John 13.12-20

'... wash one another's feet' (v.14)

We sometimes re-enact the foot-washing on Maundy Thursday. And we often miss the point in two ways. Most people who have their feet washed will probably have washed them before they come, partly out of consideration for those who will do the washing, but also because we find it difficult to let people handle our feet as they really are – blistered, calloused, perhaps painful. We want to tidy them up a bit, make them presentable. Our feet are a metaphor for our inner selves – we don't find it easy to let ourselves be seen as vulnerable. We like to present a good image. We're not good at letting people minister to us.

The second way in which we can miss the point is by not letting the action be two-way. We don't all wash each other's feet. If we are always the ones who minister, we diminish others by implying that they have nothing to give us. There has to be a mutuality of service if we are to obey Jesus' command. For he didn't say, 'wash everyone else's feet'; he said, 'wash one another's feet'.

How ready are we to let other people see our vulnerability? Can we let others minister to us at our real point of need? If, on the other hand, we are always on the receiving end of ministry, are we missing out on an opportunity to use our gifts in the service of others?

God of our salvation,
help us to turn away from those habits
which harm our bodies
and poison our minds
and to choose again your gift of life,
revealed to us in Jesus Christ our Lord.

COLLECT

63

Wednesday 9 February

John 13.21-30

'And it was night' (v.30)

There was a shadow hanging over the disciples as they gathered for the last meal they were to have with Jesus before his death, and it intensifies as the narrative continues. All through John's Gospel, there is a contrast between light and darkness. Jesus came to be light shining in darkness that would not be able to quench it. Nicodemus came to Jesus out of the darkness (John 3.2), spoke up in his defence when the Pharisees were denouncing Jesus, and at the end was openly on Jesus' side when he helped Joseph of Arimathea bury Jesus' body.

Judas, who had been in the light, one of the chosen Twelve, decided to go back into the darkness as he left the supper table to continue his arranged betrayal. John says starkly as Judas went out: 'And it was night'. This is more than an indication of the time of day. It points to the choice that Judas had made to give up on Jesus' way of being light to the world. There has been much speculation about Judas' motives for acting as he did. What is clear is that he removed himself from the light into which he had been called.

We have been called out of darkness to live in light, too (1 Peter 2.9-10). We need to keep very close to Jesus if we are not to slip back into darkness again.

COLLECT

Almighty God,
by whose grace alone we are accepted
    and called to your service:
strengthen us by your Holy Spirit
and make us worthy of our calling;
through Jesus Christ your Son our Lord,
who is alive and reigns with you,
in the unity of the Holy Spirit,
one God, now and for ever.

Psalm **37***
1 Chronicles 17
John 13.31-end

John 13.31-end

'... love one another' (v.34)

This is the moment of glory. It seems an extraordinary thing to say immediately after Judas has gone out into the night. Chapter 13 began with Jesus saying that he knew his hour had come, in contrast to earlier occasions when he had held back from declaring himself. At the wedding in Cana (John 2.4), he told his mother: 'My hour has not yet come.' Later he chose not to go openly to Jerusalem for the Feast of Tabernacles (John 7.8) because his hour 'had not yet fully come'. But, after the triumphal entry into Jerusalem (John 12.20), his tone changed. When some Greeks came asking to see him, he said to the disciples: 'The hour has come for the Son of Man to be glorified', and he went on to speak of his death.

Now Jesus tells his disciples that he must leave them, and they will not be able to follow immediately, though later they will. Understandably, they are bemused. Peter rushes in, as he had done before with a declaration of loyalty, expressing his willingness to die for Jesus. But Jesus isn't asking for anything so dramatic. He tells the disciples to do something very practical about their lifestyle, and love one another.

How faithful are we in witnessing to Jesus in the humdrum business of life? Or do we long to do something dramatic?

God of our salvation,
help us to turn away from those habits
which harm our bodies
and poison our minds
and to choose again your gift of life,
revealed to us in Jesus Christ our Lord.

COLLECT

65

Friday 11 February

Psalm 31
I Chronicles 21.1 – 22.1
John 14.1-14

John 14.1-14

'I am the way, and the truth, and the life' (v.6)

The first words of this passage are often used at funerals to reassure people that there is ample provision for them to enjoy God's continuing love after death. In this context, though, the disciples are not sure what Jesus is talking about. He has said that he is going on a journey they cannot share (John 13.33-36); now he says that he will return and take them to be with him, in a place they already know.

Thomas articulates their bewilderment, and in response Jesus says: 'I am the way, and the truth, and the life. No one comes to the Father except through me' (v.6). 'Father' was the word Jesus used when he addressed God, and he commended it to his followers too. This is the unique contribution Jesus made to our understanding of God. When he says: 'Whoever has seen me has seen the Father' (v.9), he is saying that if they want to understand the nature of God, they only have to look at him, the one who has shown that love means service and self-giving – that is what the Father, God, is like.

As Archbishop Michael Ramsey said: 'God is Christlike, and in him there is no un-Christlikeness at all.'

COLLECT

Almighty God,
by whose grace alone we are accepted
    and called to your service:
strengthen us by your Holy Spirit
and make us worthy of our calling;
through Jesus Christ your Son our Lord,
who is alive and reigns with you,
in the unity of the Holy Spirit,
one God, now and for ever.

Psalms 41, **42**, 43
1 Chronicles 22.2-end
John 14.15-end

John 14.15-end

'I will not leave you orphaned' (v.18)

The disciples are anxious because of all that Jesus has said about leaving them. How will they cope without him? Now Jesus promises that he will still be around for them, but in a new way, through the Spirit the Father will send.

Jesus has already said that, because he is leaving them to go to the Father, if they trust him they will be able to do what he has done – even greater things in fact, as they live in his life. It is through the Spirit that this will be possible, for the Spirit will strengthen and encourage, remind them of all that Jesus had taught them and enlighten them with God's truth. This new relationship with Jesus will not be like having him alongside physically; it will be much more intimate than that, a real indwelling. And this relationship will bring them peace and strength to go on in spite of their feelings of inadequacy.

We all long for peace, but we have to learn that it is not simply the end of tension and aggression. That is what the world means by peace. God's peace comes from the inner certainty that God is ultimately in control – and it is God's gift in the middle of times of stress and upheaval.

God of our salvation,
help us to turn away from those habits
which harm our bodies
and poison our minds
and to choose again your gift of life,
revealed to us in Jesus Christ our Lord.

COLLECT

Monday 14 February

Psalm **44**
I Chronicles 28.1-10
John 15.1-11

John 15.1-11

'... apart from me you can do nothing' (v.5)

The imagery of the vine is very rich, and describes the demands discipleship makes on us as well as its rewards. As branches of the vine, Jesus' followers are expected to bear fruit. If they don't, they will be cut out and thrown onto the bonfire. When they do bear fruit, they still need to be pruned in order to be more fruitful. There is no option of being left alone to grow in our own way. The important fact about branches is that they are an integral part of the plant, not add-on extras. Branches share the vine's life and bear its fruit. They can produce nothing without the main stem.

As Christ's followers, we don't just tag along, we share his life, live in his love, witness to his transforming power. We have to keep close contact with Jesus in order to do that. But the joy of knowing that we are sharing in all that Jesus wants to give us is to know fullness of life.

Pruning is never going to be a comfortable process. But we all need de-cluttering from time to time. Where should the cuts come for us?

COLLECT

O God,
you know us to be set
in the midst of so many and great dangers,
that by reason of the frailty of our nature
we cannot always stand upright:
grant to us such strength and protection
as may support us in all dangers
and carry us through all temptations;
through Jesus Christ your Son our Lord,
who is alive and reigns with you,
in the unity of the Holy Spirit,
one God, now and for ever.

Psalms **48**, 52
1 Chronicles 28.11-end
John 15.12-17

John 15.12-17

'You did not choose me but I chose you' (v.16)

This great commandment, to love one another as Jesus loves us, has no limits set to its scope. It has been given a narrow focus through verse 13 often being inscribed on war memorials, as though being killed in battle is the ultimate expression of love. Perhaps using the verse in that way has helped people to cope with the senseless losses of war. But being killed in the course of doing one's duty does not necessarily have anything to do with love, and Jesus did not have that kind of warfare in mind when he gave the commandment.

Jesus was talking about love and obedience in relationship to him, defined as being his friends. We often talk about choosing to follow Jesus; the reality is that he has chosen us. We may find it hard to believe that we are worth choosing – that hasn't always been our experience in life. Think back to the experience of teams being picked in the playground, or more long-lasting rejections in the course of growing to adulthood. The truth is that Jesus has chosen us to be his friends, to show by the way we live in a spirit of service what loving one another means.

Lord of the hosts of heaven,
our salvation and our strength,
without you we are lost:
guard us from all that harms or hurts
and raise us when we fall;
through Jesus Christ our Lord.

COLLECT

Wednesday 16 February

John 15.18-end

'You also are to testify' (v.27)

Being one of Jesus' friends doesn't necessarily lead to instant popularity. Jesus warns us that living in his way may result in being treated in the same way as he was. Sometimes the goodness of people who try to do what they understand to be God's will proves to be an uncomfortable challenge to those who live by a different agenda, and ridicule or sidelining or more physical attacks may be the result. But Jesus never offered his friends an easy life. His friends are the signs of God's truth at work in the world, truth to which the Spirit of God will witness in due time.

Holding on to the belief that we have been chosen and are precious to God through our friendship with Jesus will give us the confidence to be faithful in our co-operation with the Spirit of truth. Our witness springs from the spilling over of that indwelling that Jesus spoke of earlier.

When being a Christian gets tough, we need to cling on even more tenaciously to our membership of the vine, and draw on the life-giving strength of Jesus' love.

COLLECT

O God,
you know us to be set
in the midst of so many and great dangers,
that by reason of the frailty of our nature
we cannot always stand upright:
grant to us such strength and protection
as may support us in all dangers
and carry us through all temptations;
through Jesus Christ your Son our Lord,
who is alive and reigns with you,
in the unity of the Holy Spirit,
one God, now and for ever.

Psalms 56, **57** (63*)
I Chronicles 29.10-20
John 16.1-15

John 16.1-15

'When the Spirit of truth comes,
he will guide you into all the truth' (v.13)

What is truth? Pilate asked that question, but he didn't wait for an answer.

People view truth in different ways. For some, it means finding a place of safety, where certainties protect from the discomfort of having to answer awkward questions. Keeping company with like-minded people can give the illusion of invincible strength. For others, discovering truth is more like being on a journey, in the company of people who push boundaries and discover riches and nourishment in the process. Perhaps that is how the Spirit of truth operates. For Jesus didn't say that the truth would keep us safe, he said that the truth would set us free (John 8.32).

That is quite a frightening thought, for if we are free, we have to take responsibility for our decisions and actions. It is tempting to want to retreat to the castle where nothing needs to be questioned. But the Spirit won't let us rest with less than the truth, and continually leads us on to explore the riches of God's nature.

The only certainty we need is to know that God won't let us down, and to that the Spirit bears witness.

COLLECT

Lord of the hosts of heaven,
our salvation and our strength,
without you we are lost:
guard us from all that harms or hurts
and raise us when we fall;
through Jesus Christ our Lord.

71

John 16.16-22

'... you will have pain, but your pain will turn into joy' (v.20)

There were times when nothing seemed to make sense to the disciples – and those last days before the crucifixion were no exception. Jesus seemed to be talking in riddles – what on earth did he mean: 'A little while and you will no longer see me, and again a little while and you will see me' (v.17)? And what did 'going to the Father' mean? Jesus' response to their unspoken questions didn't help much either: 'You are going to be sad when the world (those against me) is rejoicing, but your sorrow will be turned to joy, just as the pain of childbirth gives way to joy when a child is born.' It was all very confusing.

There are times when what we experience makes no sense, when we can't see any purpose to what we are going through, or any prospect of it ending. But Jesus encourages us to see our suffering, whatever it is, as the birthpangs of new life emerging from our struggle. That's not easy. Jesus didn't find it easy either, as he faced death. Perhaps it's only in retrospect that we can recognize that God has been at work. We won't be able to give thanks for everything that happens to us, but we can practise giving thanks in everything because God is faithful and will never let us go.

COLLECT

O God,
you know us to be set
in the midst of so many and great dangers,
that by reason of the frailty of our nature
we cannot always stand upright:
grant to us such strength and protection
as may support us in all dangers
and carry us through all temptations;
through Jesus Christ your Son our Lord,
who is alive and reigns with you,
in the unity of the Holy Spirit,
one God, now and for ever.

Psalm **68**
2 Chronicles 1.1-13
John 16.23-end

John 16.23-end

'But take courage; I have conquered the world!' (v.33)

This passage contains great promises. The time will come when everything will be made plain. In that day, the promise that in the power of the Spirit the disciples will be able to do the kind of things that Jesus did will be fulfilled, and anything they ask in Jesus' name will be granted. It sounds wonderfully simple, but asking in Jesus' name doesn't just mean tacking 'through Jesus Christ our Lord' onto the end of a request. It means being so aligned with his will that what we desire is what he desires. It's the fruit of abiding in him and being indwelt by him.

It sounds wonderful – but human frailty gets in the way. The disciples think they have understood, but Jesus knows that a testing time is coming when they will lose their confidence and desert him. Then the presence of his Father will be his only source of strength. That will be our source of strength too, because we are loved by the Father, whatever happens to us. So, we can indeed take courage. We won't escape trials and tribulations, but Jesus has defeated their power, and in that truth lies our peace.

Lord of the hosts of heaven,
our salvation and our strength,
without you we are lost:
guard us from all that harms or hurts
and raise us when we fall;
through Jesus Christ our Lord.

COLLECT

73

John 17.1-5

'Father ... glorify your Son so that the Son may glorify you' (v.1)

The drama of the Last Supper continues to unfold as we reach the high priestly prayer – Jesus prays to the Father. It is a prayer from the heart and in the shadow of the cross. Unlike at the Cana wedding, Jesus' hour has now come. His divine glory is to be openly revealed, but only in and through the shame of the cross.

We are invited into this glory. Paradoxically, the cross and death of Jesus are our invitation into eternity, and we get there by knowledge. This is no dry academic exercise but means entering into an intimate relationship of love. Bernard, the twelfth-century abbot of Clairvaux, equates knowledge with 'understanding and love' which are the 'two arms of the soul'. This is the knowledge that resides within the Trinity, a knowledge only achieved in intimate relationship.

Eternal life breaks into the everyday as the love we share within God deepens. Jesus refers to his pre-incarnate glory in the presence of the Father – a perfect mutual relationship. In trying to understand the intimacy of this love, the Holy Spirit is sometimes referred to as the bond of love that exists between them. Jesus' earthly passion reveals the passion that exists within God and invites us to be beguiled.

COLLECT

Almighty God,
who alone can bring order
to the unruly wills and passions of sinful humanity:
give your people grace
so to love what you command
and to desire what you promise,
that, among the many changes of this world,
our hearts may surely there be fixed
where true joys are to be found;
through Jesus Christ your Son our Lord,
who is alive and reigns with you,
in the unity of the Holy Spirit,
one God, now and for ever.

Tuesday 22 February

John 17.6-19

'I ask you to protect them from the evil one' (v.15)

Earlier, during the Last Supper, Jesus referred to the ruler of this world, or Satan. He is not saying that the world itself is evil. He is recognizing that the world is ordered in an alluring way that can lead to harm. Jesus is now asking for the grace of God in our hour of temptation. Traditionally John's writing ends, with the book of Revelation, in a cosmic battle between good and evil. Now, John recalls Jesus' prediction of a personal battle between each of his followers and the evil one. It is a personal and interior battleground.

Should we think of evil as an abstract force or a person? Some of the Bible verses are ambiguous: this one could also be translated as 'evil' instead of 'evil one', while the Lord's Prayer can be translated as 'deliver us from the evil one'. At other times, evil is clearly personified as Satan.

Personally, I find the personification of evil to be helpful. We personify good in God and grace in Jesus; evil in the devil follows this pattern. However the pattern of evil, from Nazi death camps to abusive crimes, demonstrates how evil relies on human participation. In recognizing the prince of this world, we must also deny his power.

Eternal God,
whose Son went among the crowds
and brought healing with his touch:
help us to show his love,
in your Church as we gather together,
and by our lives as they are transformed
into the image of Christ our Lord.

COLLECT

75

John 17.20-end

'... that they may be one, as we are one' (v.22)

Jesus' prayer concludes, and now he intercedes for the unity of the Church. This unity mirrors the unity of the Trinity. It is a mystical passage where Christians are encouraged to share in the nature of God.

We can struggle to understand this divine nature in which we share. Often, the Trinity is seen in a hierarchical way – the Father as the head, with the Son doing what he is told, and the Holy Spirit obeying them both. If that is our Trinitarian model, it may also be our model of the Church: one that requires a strong unifying authority. On one level, this model has attractions, offering certainty about our faith and membership, with strong adherence to inherited understandings of Scripture and tradition. However, is it 'one as we (the Father and Son) are one'?

Another way of viewing the Trinity is as a relationship where Father, Son and Holy Spirit break down possible barriers with an intimacy and equality that is sometimes likened to a dance. There is no one head, no one way of being, as the *persons* of the Trinity remain distinctive. Such a model of Church will celebrate difference. If we disagree over Scripture, lively and loving debate can be the fruit of diversity.

COLLECT

Almighty God,
who alone can bring order
to the unruly wills and passions of sinful humanity:
give your people grace
so to love what you command
and to desire what you promise,
that, among the many changes of this world,
our hearts may surely there be fixed
where true joys are to be found;
through Jesus Christ your Son our Lord,
who is alive and reigns with you,
in the unity of the Holy Spirit,
one God, now and for ever.

Psalm **78.1-39***
2 Chronicles 6.1-21
John 18.1-11

John 18.1-11

'Judas, who betrayed him' (vv.2,5)

Isn't it the greatest of all betrayals? Startlingly, in his book *The Fidelity of Betrayal,* Peter Rollins asks whether 'the betrayal of Judas' is really Judas betraying Jesus, or Judas being betrayed *by* Jesus.

If Judas was betrayed, it was because he had a false understanding of what Jesus was to accomplish. Thinking that Jesus, the saviour, was going to redeem Israel from Roman occupation and temple corruption, Judas could have reasoned that, by instigating violent conflict, he was provoking Jesus into liberating action.

There are several ironies in the arrest of Jesus. One is that the betrayal of Judas, however understood, was necessary. To fulfil what Jesus was to accomplish, he has to be delivered up, and Jesus was fully aware of this. Judas plays a vital role. The second irony is that Judas fails to recognize God's action in Jesus, but the police and soldiers, who came to arrest him, recognize God. When Jesus says 'I am he', which recalls the Jewish name for God, the members of the arresting party step back and fall to the ground.

Today's reading may warn us not to be like Judas, putting our agenda upon God, and not to be like the soldiers and police, who briefly recognize God's presence but fail to accept it.

Eternal God,
whose Son went among the crowds
and brought healing with his touch:
help us to show his love,
in your Church as we gather together,
and by our lives as they are transformed
into the image of Christ our Lord.

COLLECT

Friday 25 February

Psalm **55**
2 Chronicles 6.22-end
John 18.12-27

John 18.12-27

'Again Peter denied it' (v.27)

Jesus is arrested and brought before Annas. Peter follows, but, despite his previous protestations, he three times denies knowing Jesus. Betrayed by one friend and denied by another, Jesus is to suffer alone. The pain that Jesus is to bear is not just physical and the shame of public humiliation; it is also the grief of loneliness. Why such a depth of pain?

An answer is offered by the second-century bishop Irenaeus. He said that Jesus, in the incarnation, had to *recapitulate* or sum up every aspect of human life. He had to go through infancy, growth and adulthood. As Jesus remains God, while being human, he makes every aspect of human life divine. By implication, Jesus had to go through the reality of suffering and death so that even this may be touched by divinity. The death he suffered was one of physical pain, public humiliation and personal abandonment. Many people suffer these in their own death. However, the Christian can take comfort in God alongside them in such an hour. Because God in Jesus recapitulated such a horrific experience of death, God remains alongside every person – including those in the depths of pain, shame or despair. This is an implication of the line 'He descended into hell' in the Apostles' Creed.

COLLECT

Almighty God,
who alone can bring order
to the unruly wills and passions of sinful humanity:
give your people grace
so to love what you command
and to desire what you promise,
that, among the many changes of this world,
our hearts may surely there be fixed
where true joys are to be found;
through Jesus Christ your Son our Lord,
who is alive and reigns with you,
in the unity of the Holy Spirit,
one God, now and for ever.

Psalms **76**, 79
2 Chronicles 7
John 18.28-end

Saturday 26 February

John 18.28-end

'… to testify to the truth' (v.37)

Jesus is delivered to Pilate, but his captors remain outside Pilate's residence, thus avoiding ritual defilement. Jesus is subjected to an illegal, sham trial, with no clear accusation, while certain legal regulations are minutely followed. In this, the authorities fail to act truthfully. When confronted with Jesus, Pilate asks, 'What is truth?', but he is dismissive and fails to await an answer or engage with Jesus.

Earlier (chapters 14 to 16), Jesus has promised another advocate, who is the Spirit of truth. We receive this Spirit by keeping the commandments of Jesus. Belonging to the truth is equated with listening and responding to the voice of Jesus.

The clamour of our lives may prevent us from hearing the truth of God expressed in Jesus. Jesus' captors failed to hear as his voice was crowded out by ritual tradition. Pilate failed to hear in the compromise of political expediency. Later on, the crowd will fail to hear as the mob sets the agenda.

In the sixth century, Benedict wrote a rule for monks. This opens with a command to listen with the 'ear of your heart'. This implies an attentive, intuitive listening – where we are fully present to the other. The ultimate other is God, and we can listen to him in his Word, Jesus Christ.

Eternal God,
whose Son went among the crowds
and brought healing with his touch:
help us to show his love,
in your Church as we gather together,
and by our lives as they are transformed
into the image of Christ our Lord.

COLLECT

Monday 28 February

John 19.1-16

'Hail, King of the Jews!' (v.3)

True words spoken in cruel mockery, but what do they mean? Jesus has proclaimed that his kingdom was not of this world. He is a new kind of king who lays power aside, even at the risk that it is turned against him. He has the trappings of a king, but these have been subverted – his stately crown has become the crown of thorns, his robes of state replaced by a purple robe of mockery, his prestigious throne replaced by the shameful cross.

The other striking redefinition of the kingly role is silence. A king will usually make royal pronouncements from his throne. This king – who is the Word of God – has become silent. 'Like a lamb that is led to the slaughter' (Isaiah 53.7), he makes no further defence to Pilate.

Paul says that Jesus is 'in the form of God', but he 'emptied himself, taking the form of a slave' (Philippians 2.7). Before Pilate and the crowd, that process of emptying means that Jesus lays aside all claims to worldly kingship, respect or even life. Privilege is laid down and we, in turn, are invited to pick it up. The fourth-century bishop of Alexandria, Athanasius, who championed the incarnation, strikingly concludes that 'the Son of God became human so that we might become God'.

COLLECT

Almighty God,
you have created the heavens and the earth
and made us in your own image:
teach us to discern your hand in all your works
and your likeness in all your children;
through Jesus Christ your Son our Lord,
who with you and the Holy Spirit reigns supreme over all things,
now and for ever.

Psalms 87, **89.1-18**
2 Chronicles 10.1 – 11.4
John 19.17-30

John 19.17-30

'It is finished' (v.30)

John's account of the crucifixion records Jesus in control and purposefully completing his mission. Not only is Jesus planning the care of his mother after his death, but also Psalm 22 is fulfilled, unconsciously, by Roman soldiers as they gamble over his tunic. Jesus then intentionally fulfils Scripture in his need for a drink. However, the clear completion of his mission is shown in his final words, 'It is finished', before he gives up, or hands over, his spirit.

But what is finished? Archbishop Desmond Tutu summarizes this crucifixion completion well: 'Christ when he was lifted up did not say "I draw some people to myself", He said "I draw all, all, ALL"' (www.inclusivechurch2.net). His Church lived through the oppressive violence of South African apartheid. The key insight gained from this is the radical inclusive nature of Christ reigning from the cross. The completion of Christ's mission is the breaking down of all barriers, including the ultimate barrier between humanity and God.

The message of the cross is that Jesus chose to die for all, including those who are socially, ethnically, religiously or sexually different from us. The Chief Rabbi Jonathan Sacks comes to a similar conclusion from the creation story: 'The religious challenge is to find God's image in someone who is not in our image' (*The Dignity of Difference*, Continuum International Publishing, 2002).

Almighty God,
give us reverence for all creation
and respect for every person,
that we may mirror your likeness
in Jesus Christ our Lord.

COLLECT

John 19.31-end

'... at once blood and water came out' (v.34)

Reading the Bible is like peeling an onion; there are so many layers. Passages, like this reference to the blood and water, may be considered both historical and symbolic. The historical level is to emphasize the reality of Jesus' physical death, with the flow of blood and water mingled together.

The symbolic level has been unpacked from the Church's earliest days. Augustine saw a clear reference to the sacraments of baptism and Eucharist, and their significance in the plan of salvation. John Chrysostom, archbishop of Constantinople, supported this but also saw the formation of the Church. Just as Eve, the bride of Adam, was formed from Adam's side, so the Church, the bride of Christ, is formed from Christ's side. There is also a Passover reference. Previously, in Egypt, blood was sprinkled on doorposts, so that the angel of death passed over the Israelite houses. Now blood is shed from Christ's side. When Christians receive this blood in the Eucharist, then, like those Israelite dwellings, we are protected from evil.

Medieval altar pieces often tie in the Eucharist with the death of Jesus by depicting his blood being collected by angels using chalices. Today, in our literary culture, we may struggle with symbolism, but does that restrict our Bible reading?

COLLECT

Almighty God,
you have created the heavens and the earth
and made us in your own image:
teach us to discern your hand in all your works
and your likeness in all your children;
through Jesus Christ your Son our Lord,
who with you and the Holy Spirit reigns supreme over all things,
now and for ever.

Psalms 90, **92**
2 Chronicles 13.1 – 14.1
John 20.1-10

John 20.1-10

'... he saw and believed' (v.8)

The enigmatic disciple, whom Jesus loved, believed on encountering the empty tomb. However, he does not understand and returns to where he is staying. Later, all the apostles will fail to understand as they retreat, in fear, to their room.

There is a difference between believing and understanding. For faith, the difference is between believing that something is true and then faithfully acting on that belief. As a baby, I was baptized, but it was not until my early twenties that I became a *practising* Christian. A belief, experienced in primary-school nativity plays, became a faith in which I believed. I was gradually coming to understand the profound implications of the Word becoming flesh, and living and dying among us.

What did the beloved disciple believe? He knew that the tomb was empty, and he believed that this was not due to grave-robbers. This he would have concluded from the neatly folded and valuable grave clothes. However, his understanding is not yet engaged, and the fulfilment of the promises to Israel remains unclear.

Faith is a lifetime's journey. Faith we can never *fully* understand as, from our mortal perspective, we are gazing upon a dim mirror. However, understanding grows and develops through practice. Do we really practise the resurrection life by bringing life to others?

Almighty God,
give us reverence for all creation
and respect for every person,
that we may mirror your likeness
in Jesus Christ our Lord.

COLLECT

83

John 20.11-18

'Do not hold on to me' (v.17)

John's Gospel highlights the angels in Jesus' empty tomb, 'one at the head and the other at the feet'. Archbishop Rowan Williams shows the connections that may be made: 'Iconographically, it recalls ... the mercy-seat of the ark, flanked by the cherubim' (*On Christian Theology,* Blackwell, 2000). Israelite tradition held that God dwelt between the cherubim that were mounted on the ark and leant towards each other across the throne or mercy-seat. However, the ark's throne contains no image of God – God is both there and absent, seen and not seen. Archbishop Rowan calls this a 'paradoxical manifestation'.

This paradoxical manifestation is carried forward into the resurrection. We have Mary Magdalene and those on the road to Emmaus failing to recognize the risen Christ. The Jesus whom they previously knew is both there and absent. A fundamental change has taken place. The change is not to deny the reality of the resurrection but to affirm that Jesus has risen into something new, and his rising continues in the looking forward to the ascension.

'Do not hold on to me,' Jesus said to Mary Magdalene. This may be better translated as 'do not keep clinging'. Mary has to let go of her personal relationship with the physical Jesus and embrace the mystical presence/absence that now inspires the Church.

COLLECT

Almighty God,
you have created the heavens and the earth
and made us in your own image:
teach us to discern your hand in all your works
and your likeness in all your children;
through Jesus Christ your Son our Lord,
who with you and the Holy Spirit reigns supreme over all things,
now and for ever.

Psalms 96, **97**, 100
2 Chronicles 15.1-15
John 20.19-end

John 20.19-end

'As the Father has sent me, so I send you' (v.21)

Possibly, this verse should be called *the* great commission. Following the resurrection, we are sent, as the Father sent his Son. We are to participate intimately in God's activity, in the Trinity's very nature. But what does this imply?

In today's passage, Jesus says 'Peace be with you' three times. Peace, *shalom*, is the nature of the triune God. This is not peace in a political or economic sense; the disciples will go on to face persecution. The peace of the Father and Son is the peace of forgiveness and wholeness. It is also a peace that we offer to others by being their servant, as Christ was the servant of many. We are sent, as was Christ, metaphorically and literally to empty ourselves and wash feet. The peace we proclaim is likely to become increasingly vital in our society, which is facing economic and structural transition.

Re-creation is also present in today's passage. The Holy Spirit is given to the disciples by Jesus breathing over them. This recalls the wind, breath or Spirit of God moving over the face of the waters at the beginning of creation. Life came forth then, just as new life is now experienced in the risen Christ.

Go and do likewise.

Almighty God,
give us reverence for all creation
and respect for every person,
that we may mirror your likeness
in Jesus Christ our Lord.

COLLECT

Jeremiah 1

'I am with you to deliver you' (v.8)

Traditionally, Jeremiah is regarded as a prophet preaching from 627 BC until the fall of Jerusalem to the Babylonians in 587 BC. He spoke to the people of ancient Israel, and to many others since.

As with all the prophets, his words are not simply the 'words of Jeremiah' (v.1). What is important is the 'word of the Lord' sounding through them (vv.4,11). In verses 4 to 10, Jeremiah is called and commissioned to this ministry. God has taken the initiative, even before Jeremiah's conception. But God's initiative does not preclude our free response, and – along with others – Jeremiah baulks at the call. His reluctance is based on a proper sense of inadequacy, and, in turn, God responds with reassurance, and divine enabling and strengthening.

These things are necessary for the prophet – and for anyone who feels called to speak uncomfortable truths that others would rather not hear. Such behaviour was as unlikely to lead to popularity, power or promotion in ancient Israel as it is in our society today. So, the prophet is always vulnerable, always at risk. He needs, therefore, to be strengthened – fortified against his audience (v.18). And it is only faith in God's promises that can build this fortification: 'I am with you to deliver you' (vv.8,19).

COLLECT

Almighty Father,
whose Son was revealed in majesty
before he suffered death upon the cross:
give us grace to perceive his glory,
that we may be strengthened to suffer with him
and be changed into his likeness, from glory to glory;
who is alive and reigns with you,
in the unity of the Holy Spirit,
one God, now and for ever.

Psalm 106* (*or* 103)
Jeremiah 2.1-13
John 3.22-end

Jeremiah 2.1-13

'... my people have changed their glory' (v.11)

God's word to Israel begins gently and positively enough, as did their early relationship after the escape from Egypt. This was their honeymoon period: a time of 'devotion', 'love' and 'following', when Yahweh (the Hebrew name of Israel's God, usually translated 'the Lord') and his bride Israel belonged to one another, exclusively and faithfully.

It did not last. The prophets indict their nation for breaking the faithful, loyal relationship with Yahweh. While God was true to his word, the people and their leaders forgot him, no longer rehearsing the story of their deliverance and the gift of the Promised Land. The priests did not seek him; the judges did not embrace his justice; the prophets sought the words of other gods (v.8).

So, Jeremiah proclaims what the Old Testament scholar Walter Brueggemann calls the 'prophetic "therefore"': 'Therefore ... I accuse you, says the Lord' (v.9). First the indictment, then the declaration of judgement. It is for this, God declares, that disaster is coming upon you. There is no parallel to their crime. Even the heathen did not change gods, but Israel has abandoned Yahweh (its 'glory', v.11) for a pretend, nothing-deity. It has walked away from the source of all life, 'the fountain of living water', for a leaky, DIY-job of cowboy plumbing. The prophet and his God stand appalled.

Holy God,
you know the disorder of our sinful lives:
set straight our crooked hearts,
and bend our wills to love your goodness
and your glory
in Jesus Christ our Lord.

COLLECT

Lent

Wednesday 9 March

Ash Wednesday

Psalm **38**
Daniel 9.3-6,17-19
1 Timothy 6.6-19

1 Timothy 6.6-19

'Fight the good fight of the faith' (v.12)

At the beginning of Lent, we read of temptation (v.9) and 'the good fight of the faith' (v.12 – the fight being an image from competitive athletics rather than warfare). Scholars have suggested that verses 11 to 16 come from a baptismal liturgy, or perhaps an ordination address.

Lent is a time for spiritual realism. The author follows Job in recognizing our intrinsic poverty (v.7, cf. Job 1.21). Lacking possessions, we come to crave them. Self-interest, famously presented here as the love of money, is one of those root sins that spiritually distract us from focusing on God, the only source of true riches (vv.10, 17). We then drown in spiritual self-destruction. There are references to the future (v.19). But, as in John's Gospel, 'eternal life' is presented as something that can be Timothy's *present* possession (v.12). This is true life, real life, life directed towards God. It is no transient thing; it must be fulfilled. But fighting the good fight is a matter of grasping hold of it *now*.

Part of this, key to the Lenten life, is a deeper sort of 'grasping': a matter of understanding – of seeing the point of – life. Spiritual realism knows that life is really about giving, not getting-and-holding (v.18) – as is the God of Jesus (v.13).

COLLECT

Almighty and everlasting God,
you hate nothing that you have made
and forgive the sins of all those who are penitent:
create and make in us new and contrite hearts
that we, worthily lamenting our sins
and acknowledging our wretchedness,
may receive from you, the God of all mercy,
perfect remission and forgiveness;
through Jesus Christ your Son our Lord,
who is alive and reigns with you,
in the unity of the Holy Spirit,
one God, now and for ever.

Psalms **77** *or* 113, 115
Jeremiah 2.14-32
John 4.1-26

Jeremiah 2.14-32

'... my people have forgotten me' (v.32)

God seems puzzled. Israel's northern kingdom fell to Assyria in 722 BC.
The southern kingdom of Judah, where Jeremiah prophesies, is now
threatened by enemies. Why? Is it because of its lowly status (v.14)?

Yahweh, God alone, knows the real reason for their suffering: in
breaking her marriage vows and abandoning her faithful partner
(v.17), Israel has found only the freedom of the prey at the mercy of
lions (v.15).

Freedom is often a two-edged sword. We yearn for it when restrained
by parents, employers, spouses, life. But, although the freedom to
choose is always good, it is the same freedom that allows us to
embrace and create what is bad – for ourselves sometimes, often for
others. It is not enough just to be free. It depends on what we are
freeing ourselves from and freeing ourselves for, and how we use that
freedom. Jeremiah paints a poignant picture of an unrestrained,
degenerate freedom that becomes an indiscriminate, unfulfilling and
'hopeless' love of strangers (vv.20-25).

Yahweh laments his lost love, who turned her back on his faithfulness
and refuses to give up her freedom and return home (v.31). Here is a
God who *feels*, who can be *hurt*: a God who is vulnerable, and truly
cares whether we still love him or not.

Holy God,
our lives are laid open before you:
rescue us from the chaos of sin
and through the death of your Son
bring us healing and make us whole
in Jesus Christ our Lord.

COLLECT

Jeremiah 3.6-22

'I thought you would call me, My Father' (v.19)

When spurned lovers or hurt parents confide in a trusted friend, talking of their betrayal, they will speak of pain and recrimination. But, if love is still alive in the damaged relationship, deeper feelings of affection and forgiveness will eventually tumble into expression.

Is God very different? We might expect that a just God, who can alone occupy the moral high ground without fear of slipping, would maintain his righteous indignation longer than we could. But not so. God is infinite in all things, but limitless love always trumps untrammelled justice. Ultimately, God's forgiveness can know no bounds. He *yearns* for us.

The northern kingdom, Israel, sinned first – and fell to the Assyrians. Southern Judah is going the same way – indeed, she is already further along it (vv.6-11). But Yahweh's faithfulness and love, as husband and father, will not allow him to 'be angry for ever'. He will bring whoever will come – from both Israel and Judah – back to Jerusalem (vv.14,18), despite their fickleness.

Few texts are as poignantly expressive of the character of God, and the hope implicit in the human response, than verses 19 to 22: I thought you would call me 'father', but you have turned, left and forgotten me. Come back ... Be healed ...

COLLECT

Almighty and everlasting God,
you hate nothing that you have made
and forgive the sins of all those who are penitent:
create and make in us new and contrite hearts
that we, worthily lamenting our sins
and acknowledging our wretchedness,
may receive from you, the God of all mercy,
perfect remission and forgiveness;
through Jesus Christ your Son our Lord,
who is alive and reigns with you,
in the unity of the Holy Spirit,
one God, now and for ever.

Psalms **71** *or* 120, **121**, 122
Jeremiah 4.1-18
John 4.43-end

Jeremiah 4.1-18

'... a destroyer of nations has set out' (v.7)

The German Protestant theologian, Rudolf Otto, wrote of the experience of holiness as two-sided. The holy is entrancing, attractive. We speak of it – of him/her – as good. But there is dread and terror as well. Moses before the burning bush and the disciples witnessing the transfiguration were captivated and enthralled, but fearful too. Talk of judgement articulates this stormy side of God's love.

This is how it is: turning away from the light and warmth of grace, we stumble into the cold, dark side of holy fear. 'Do not be deceived ... you reap whatever you sow' (Galatians 6.7).

A stroppy, defiant adolescent might respond to a parent's demand by shouting 'Or else what ...?' Israel and Judah, by betraying God's love, now face the answer to that question.

So, the mood changes and the sky darkens. Turn your back on God, and you face what is not-God, and must face it alone. God's love is personal. His 'wrath', however, sounds like an impersonal, unavoidable force: the virulent consequence of human evil (v.4). The images pile up – the lion, the destroyer, the scorching from the desert, the whirlwind. In plain language: 'besiegers ... from a distant land' (v.16).

The enemies of Israel are come, because of her rebellion. 'This is your *doom*.'

COLLECT

Holy God,
our lives are laid open before you:
rescue us from the chaos of sin
and through the death of your Son
bring us healing and make us whole
in Jesus Christ our Lord.

Jeremiah 4.19-end

'The whole land shall be a desolation; yet ...' (v.27)

The prophet spells out in vivid, personal images what this disaster will mean to the 'stupid children' of Israel. It means the destruction of tents (v.20), the noise of armies and the chaos of flight (v.29), and the terrified cry of 'daughter Zion' (v.31). In verses 23 to 27, the national and personal tragedies appear as a cosmic catastrophe. God's dark side is the undoing of creation, its return to the chaos, darkness and emptiness that preceded the love of God's creative Spirit (Genesis 1.1-2).

Imagine the prophet spitting out these words. He is addressing not only the people, prophets and priests, but also the officials and the king himself (look back to 4.9-10). These destructive events have not yet happened, so Jeremiah's audience is not yet 'appalled' or 'astounded'. So, Jeremiah must escalate his language, in the desperate hope that they will *listen*. But, from their perspective, all seems well. 'No problem', as people say. Alas, they are self-deceived – and deceive one another. The prophet alone will face and name the terrible reality of God's inevitable judgement in response to his children's rejection.

And yet, is there no hope? A glimmer, at least? Perhaps an ambiguous whisper may be heard in verse 27: 'yet I will not make a full end'.

COLLECT

Almighty God,
whose Son Jesus Christ fasted forty days in the wilderness,
and was tempted as we are, yet without sin:
give us grace to discipline ourselves in obedience to your Spirit;
and, as you know our weakness,
so may we know your power to save;
through Jesus Christ your Son our Lord,
who is alive and reigns with you,
in the unity of the Holy Spirit,
one God, now and for ever.

Psalms **44** *or* **132**, 133
Jeremiah 5.1-19
John 5.19-29

Jeremiah 5.1-19

'... see if you can find one person who acts justly' (v.1)

Verses 1 to 13 read like a lawsuit, with judgement following the formal accusation.

Yahweh suggests a search to try to find a single just person in Jerusalem. No one can be found. This is not unexpected among the poor and unlearned (v.4). But the prophet expects better of the powerful, who are schooled in the faith. But again, no one. So, 'How can I pardon you?', asks the Lord (v.7). 'Shall I not bring retribution on a nation such as this?' (v.9).

The metaphorical wild animals – lion, wolf, leopard – are to be unleashed (v.6); the symbolic devouring fire of God's words will consume the people (v.14). Literally, a foreign nation, 'an enduring ... ancient nation' of warriors will destroy them (vv.15-17).

Is there still a 'yet'? Searching for straws to grasp, we come across two verses that again suggest that the destruction will not be total: that God will not 'make a full end' of the people of Israel (vv.10,18). But their only hope is the hope of exile, far away from the land of God's promises. Once again, as in Egypt before the Exodus, before they knew the grace of God; once again, 'you shall serve strangers in a land that is not yours'.

Heavenly Father,
your Son battled with the powers of darkness,
and grew closer to you in the desert:
help us to use these days to grow in wisdom and prayer
that we may witness to your saving love
in Jesus Christ our Lord.

COLLECT

Wednesday 16 March

Jeremiah 5.20-end

'Shall I not punish them for these things?' (v.29)

In both the Old Testament and the New, the theological logic goes: God is like this, God has done and does this; *therefore* you must be and do that. God has brought you out of slavery to this land, *therefore* ... God in Christ has healed and redeemed our lives, *therefore* ...

In verses 22 to 24, it is God's creative power and providential care, expressed in creation, that is presented as the indicative (the statement) that implies the imperative (the exhortation or command) that Israel should acknowledge her creator. But this logic is lost on her. She doesn't fear or tremble. She sees nothing, understands nothing. Stubborn and rebellious to the last, she turns aside. The people's hearts are alienated from their God.

This is not just about a spiritual or religious failing. Verses 25 to 29 present a thoroughgoing *moral* indictment of what has been called the 'practical atheism' of the fat, sleek scoundrels who neglect the claims of the poor and fatherless.

Again, then, the prophet voices God's rhetorical question – 'shall I not bring retribution on a nation such as this?' (v.29). The opportunity for repentance is now past. So, the dreadful question must be posed to Judah: 'what will you do when the end comes?'

COLLECT

Almighty God,
whose Son Jesus Christ fasted forty days in the wilderness,
and was tempted as we are, yet without sin:
give us grace to discipline ourselves in obedience to your Spirit;
and, as you know our weakness,
so may we know your power to save;
through Jesus Christ your Son our Lord,
who is alive and reigns with you,
in the unity of the Holy Spirit,
one God, now and for ever.

Psalms **42**, 43 *or* **143**, 146
Jeremiah 6.9-21
John 6.1-15

Jeremiah 6.9-21

'... because they have not given heed' (v.19)

Jeremiah was called to a ministry of grape-harvesting. It is a 'gleaning' (v.9) that involves searching and picking up the last of the grapes (cf. Jeremiah 49.9). A – literally – fruitless task. There is nothing left, for the vines have been stripped by the nation's faithlessness and her Lord's judgement (Jeremiah 5.10-11).

Yahweh sounds resigned and wounded – but also weary at holding back the anger of his love, the consequence of his people breaking their covenant (v.11). All will suffer its inevitable effects, for all have sinned 'from the least to the greatest' – but the leaders most, by speaking of *shalom* (peace, well-being) instead of warning Israel about its perilous state. Did they feel no shame? (vv.13-15).

We must again imagine the scene in which the prophet speaks out against the status quo and its values, taking on the powerful. We rarely hear such bold critiques, even in safe societies under the rule of impartial law. This is the hard task of prophecy – standing up for something, speaking out for something, preaching before kings the radical word of the Lord.

It is not as though they were ignorant of 'where the good way lies' (v.16) and what the words of God imply. But they have taken no 'heed' (vv.17,19). And so ...

Heavenly Father,
your Son battled with the powers of darkness,
and grew closer to you in the desert:
help us to use these days to grow in wisdom and prayer
that we may witness to your saving love
in Jesus Christ our Lord.

COLLECT

Jeremiah 6.22-end

'I have made you a tester and a refiner' (v.27)

This prophecy of destruction is unremitting ('terror is on every side', v.25). But the note of sadness is also unquenched ('O my poor people', v.26). Amid the ever-increasing clamour of the invading army, we hear the lamentation of Israel – and that of her prophet, and of her Lord.

And then a personal word to Jeremiah (vv.27-30). Why is the flow of prophecy so often interrupted by such commentaries on the prophet's vocation? Doesn't it smack of self-concerned indulgence? We should recognize that the prophets always felt themselves to be on shaky ground. When you are a prophet, you are often in a minority of one. Everyone else takes a very different view. How could the prophets be sure that they were true, not false prophets? Were they speaking God's word, or just their own thoughts?

The prophet bears a unique, terrible responsibility. He is not just a gleaner of vines. He is also the metallurgist who must assay Israel, to test its character. He is the one authorized to remove its base impurities, so as to separate out the precious metals in the furnace of his speech and acts. And he knows that, should he fail in this vocation to refine Israel, then the Lord will reject his nation as so much dross.

COLLECT

Almighty God,
whose Son Jesus Christ fasted forty days in the wilderness,
and was tempted as we are, yet without sin:
give us grace to discipline ourselves in obedience to your Spirit;
and, as you know our weakness,
so may we know your power to save;
through Jesus Christ your Son our Lord,
who is alive and reigns with you,
in the unity of the Holy Spirit,
one God, now and for ever.

Psalms 25, 147.1-12
Isaiah 11.1-10
Matthew 13.54-end

Isaiah 11.1-10

'... and a little child shall lead them' (v.6)

The excuse – should we need one – for breaking our Lenten fast of Jeremiah with this magnificent passage is the reference in v.10 to Jesse, King David's father and the ancestor of the Joseph of the nativity story (see Matthew 1.6,16; Luke 3.23,32). But the shoot from this stump (Isaiah 11.1), which is described so beautifully and powerfully here, is essentially a prophetic expression of future hope for Israel.

In Isaiah's time, Assyria threatened Jerusalem; much later, Babylon would destroy it – and the Davidic monarchy. Nevertheless, Isaiah proclaims God's promise that a new David will arise. And he will be the bearer of God's Spirit, and of God's *vision* (not judging by superficialities, v.3) and *justice* (even for the poor and insignificant, v.4). Especially, he will bear, proclaim and enact God's *peace* (vv.6-9).

This universal peace is imagined as something beyond any peace to which human beings could aspire. It extends even to the natural enmity of predator and prey. This is a most powerful image of Israel's deepest yearning: for a life where none shall 'hurt or destroy'.

Did these words cross Joseph's mind as he looked on Mary's baby, born into an Israel that was still desperately in need of the clear-sighted justice and peace of God?

COLLECT

God our Father,
who from the family of your servant David
raised up Joseph the carpenter
to be the guardian of your incarnate Son
and husband of the Blessed Virgin Mary:
give us grace to follow him
in faithful obedience to your commands;
through Jesus Christ your Son our Lord,
who is alive and reigns with you,
in the unity of the Holy Spirit,
one God, now and for ever.

Monday 21 March

Jeremiah 7.21-end

'This is the nation that did not obey' (v.28)

This prose passage begins with harsh words against the sacrificial cultus of Israel (see also Jeremiah 6.20, 7.4). God doesn't care any longer about the niceties of ritual, says Jeremiah. This isn't because the prophet is a Protestant-before-his-time, overturning the ancient patterns of worship. He is rejecting not sacrifice as sacrifice, but any form of worship that is offered with *morally* unclean hands (cf. Micah 6.6-8) and without obedient listening and living (Jeremiah 7.23-24,26,28).

The correct order of things was shown at Sinai. The covenant with Yahweh and its moral stipulations are ratified first before the details of the cultic laws are handed down. What came first must come first. 'Obey my voice, and I will be your God, and you shall be my people; and walk only in the way ...' (v.23).

Hinnom is described in this passage as a place of alien, pagan worship (a 'high place', v.31) and even of human sacrifice, apparently of children. The prophet declares that it will become an open grave for those slaughtered by the invaders. In the New Testament, this valley, where the city's rubbish constantly burned close to the city walls of Jerusalem, is called 'Gehenna' and is used to speak of hell (Mark 9.43-48). Jeremiah is expecting a hell-on-earth.

COLLECT

Almighty God,
you show to those who are in error the light of your truth,
that they may return to the way of righteousness:
grant to all those who are admitted
    into the fellowship of Christ's religion,
that they may reject those things
    that are contrary to their profession,
and follow all such things as are agreeable to the same;
through our Lord Jesus Christ,
who is alive and reigns with you,
in the unity of the Holy Spirit,
one God, now and for ever.

Jeremiah 8.1-15

'Even the stork in the heavens knows its times' (v.7)

The criticism of Israel's rebellious worship continues, with harsh words for those who worshipped the gods of the heavens. In a final indignity – which surely reveals that 'nothing is sacred' (beyond what is truly sacred) – the bones of the honoured dead will be disinterred and scattered 'like dung' (v.2).

The inexplicable and unique nature of the sin of Israel is now underscored. Her continuing disloyalty is represented as an irrational, almost unnatural act. Other peoples would return (v.4), but not they. The rest of creation responds instinctively to the movements of nature, but Israel is unresponsive to God's law. Even the birds migrate when the right season comes round, yet the people of Israel resist to the end the promptings of their lawgiver.

Verse 8 is doubtless the kind of reply that Jeremiah regularly provoked as he preached his message. Their response doesn't matter. 'The wise shall be put to shame' (v.9). God is now pictured as the gleaner of last resort – seeking to harvest any grapes or figs from the withered plants of Israel. But, again, it is a fruitless search (v.13).

The only possibility left is to retreat in the face of the invader. The judgement of God marks their doom. There will be no more harvests.

Almighty God,
by the prayer and discipline of Lent
may we enter into the mystery of Christ's sufferings,
and by following in his Way
come to share in his glory;
through Jesus Christ our Lord.

COLLECT

Wednesday 23 March

Psalm **35** *or* **119.1-32**
Jeremiah 8.18 – 9.11
John 6.60-end

Jeremiah 8.18 – 9.11

'For the hurt of my poor people I am hurt' *(8.21)*

The roller-coaster experience continues with this heart-rending lament from Jeremiah and the inhabitants of Jerusalem, and perhaps from God. It is an expression of overwhelming grief. 'For the hurt of my poor people I am hurt.' 'Is there no balm in Gilead?' (8.21-22).

But Jeremiah (and Yahweh?) suffer a deep, internal conflict. Their grief for, and love towards, Israel is not in doubt (9.1). But human beings can only stand so much rejection before a desire wells up in their hearts *to leave* (9.2). Does God also feel the pull of these contradictory emotions?

With God it is worse. For all things are in the hands of the Creator God. Why, then, does God not stop these horrors? Jeremiah's answer would be 'because he causes them'. Recoiling at the bluntness of this claim, we might say that, in the providence of the justice of God, they are the inevitable consequence of the rejection of God: 'deceit upon deceit! They refuse to know me … *Therefore* …' (9.6-7).

So, verses 9.10 and 11 sit side by side, though uneasily: the cry of compassion, and the harsh reality of the history of the 'chosen people'. And between them lies the hinge on which everything hangs, the mystery of the just *and* loving God.

COLLECT

Almighty God,
you show to those who are in error the light of your truth,
that they may return to the way of righteousness:
grant to all those who are admitted
    into the fellowship of Christ's religion,
that they may reject those things
    that are contrary to their profession,
and follow all such things as are agreeable to the same;
through our Lord Jesus Christ,
who is alive and reigns with you,
in the unity of the Holy Spirit,
one God, now and for ever.

Psalms **34** *or* 14, **15, 16**
Jeremiah 9.12-24
John 7.1-13

Jeremiah 9.12-24

'Do not let the wise boast' (v.23)

At the heart of this passage is another powerful, poetic lament over the ruin of Jerusalem, and the indiscriminate slaughter that causes it. On either side of the dirge sits a prose reflection on wisdom. These passages do not plumb the depths of the wisdom literature of Job and Ecclesiastes, which wrestle with the most intractable issues of life. But they do clearly distinguish a worldly-wise understanding from the insight required to grasp 'the ways of the Lord'. Verses 13 to 15 are blunt. God is now an enemy to his people because they have disobeyed him, which is the logic we have seen elsewhere (see 9.5-9).

Verses 23 to 24 offer us a more profound insight. There is no ground for 'boasting' except in God, and therefore in the knowledge of God and in commitment to the values of God (steadfast love, justice, righteousness). Not in *me*, then, only in God. Paul takes up this theme in 1 Corinthians 1.20-31, where he contrasts the wisdom of the world with the apparent foolishness of choosing the 'low and despised', which is the wisdom of the cross.

Self-satisfaction is anathema to true religion. It has led Israel away from its destiny, and its Lord. The only way forward is through its crucifixion.

Almighty God,
by the prayer and discipline of Lent
may we enter into the mystery of Christ's sufferings,
and by following in his Way
come to share in his glory;
through Jesus Christ our Lord.

COLLECT

Friday 25 March
Annunciation of Our Lord
to the Blessed Virgin Mary

Romans 5.12-end

'... by the one man's obedience' (v.19)

To mark the announcement to Mary of her pregnancy and the status of her baby (Luke 1.26-38), we have this profound theological meditation.

Looking back at – rather than forward to – the mission of Christ, Paul sees Jesus as the saviour who cancelled, even reversed, the power of sin that has sucked human beings into enmity with God and the defeat of death. Paul's insight is that the historical Jesus is more than an individual. He is of universal significance: a sort of Adam (Hebrew for 'man'), who was another representative figure. Just as one man changed everything for the worse, so one man has changed everything for the better (vv.18-19).

Both Adam (the 'type of the one who was to come', v.14) and Christ define the character of an age. From the beginning until the coming of Christ, life is distinguished by rebellion, sin and death. But the gracious act ('free gift') of God in Jesus has put things right ('justification', instead of 'condemnation'), leading to the reign of 'righteousness' for others – as grace is made available to 'the many' of humankind.

The young, frightened girl we remember today did not imagine her baby's life in these terms. But she knew something about grace; and she called him 'Jesus', which is shorthand for God's salvation.

COLLECT

We beseech you, O Lord,
pour your grace into our hearts,
that as we have known the incarnation of your Son Jesus Christ
    by the message of an angel,
so by his cross and passion
we may be brought to the glory of his resurrection;
through Jesus Christ your Son our Lord,
who is alive and reigns with you,
in the unity of the Holy Spirit,
one God, now and for ever.

Jeremiah 10.17-24

'... not in your anger, or you will bring me to nothing' (v.24)

It is time for Judah to pack its bags and prepare for exile.

The prophet again anticipates the end and speaks of his personal anguish, which must for now stand in for the response of the nation and her own lament. Of course, they will eventually grieve themselves. But will they also recognize their distress as a punishment, as Jeremiah does? And will they, too, acknowledge that they 'must bear it' (v.19)? Will they judge their leaders ('the shepherds', particularly their kings) for stupidly ignoring the will of God?

Most significantly, perhaps, will they join with the prophet in his great prayer of repentance and his plea for a punishment from which they can learn? Israel can only bear a *corrective* punishment that mercifully takes account of human weakness – not the utter destruction of a *punitive* judgement, marked by a strict and just retribution. 'Not in your anger, or you will bring me [us] *to nothing*' (v.24).

Verse 23 might be read in different ways. It may speak of an intrinsic moral weakness in human beings (cf. Jeremiah 17.9), or of their ultimate inability to control their destiny (cf. Jeremiah 18.5-8). On either reading, it is a request for mercy. And the question remains: is God – after all and despite everything – a God of mercy? Will Yahweh stay his hand?

Almighty God,
you show to those who are in error the light of your truth,
that they may return to the way of righteousness:
grant to all those who are admitted
into the fellowship of Christ's religion,
that they may reject those things
that are contrary to their profession,
and follow all such things as are agreeable to the same;
through our Lord Jesus Christ,
who is alive and reigns with you,
in the unity of the Holy Spirit,
one God, now and for ever.

COLLECT

Psalms **5**, 7 or 27, **30**
Jeremiah 11.1-17
John 7.37-52

Jeremiah 11.1-17

'... he will set fire to it, and its branches will be consumed' (v.16)

When Jeremiah was called to be a prophet by God, he replied: 'Ah! Lord God I am not skilled in speaking ...' Perhaps Jeremiah's response was meant to be an accurate description of how he saw himself, but the fact is he was a remarkable wordsmith, a poet, a man who spoke with a burning energy.

Look carefully at today's passage and you will see some of those poetic skills being put to work. There is a metaphor which runs like a thread through the text: the metaphor of fire.

Jeremiah refers to the children of Israel having been created in a kind of furnace (v.4); then he refers (v.16) to the sound made by an olive tree when it is engulfed in a forest fire; and in verse 17, he rages against the sacrifices made by fire to Baal. In fact, fire is a theme that runs all the way through Jeremiah's work; for example, in chapter 5, verse 14, we read that God said to Jeremiah: 'I am now making my words in your mouth a fire, and this people wood, and the fire shall devour them.'

It's all terrifying stuff. But then, any attempt to speak the truth requires a kind of moral energy that can seem almost overwhelming. How can we be certain that the energy we feel within is really the voice of God? During Lent, we need to take stock of our capacity to deceive ourselves, and pray that we may live with integrity.

COLLECT

Almighty God,
whose most dear Son went not up to joy but first he
    suffered pain,
and entered not into glory before he was crucified:
mercifully grant that we, walking in the way of the cross,
may find it none other than the way of life and peace;
through Jesus Christ your Son our Lord,
who is alive and reigns with you,
in the unity of the Holy Spirit,
one God, now and for ever.

Jeremiah 11.18 – 12.6

'Why does the way of the guilty prosper?' (12.1)

It's a bit disingenuous of Jeremiah, isn't it, to describe himself as a pet lamb being led innocently to the slaughter by his own kith and kin? His fellow villagers in Anathoth cannot have been overjoyed to have this hot-headed prophet in their midst, foretelling chaos and invasion because of their apostasy.

Jeremiah rounds on them and calls on God to wreak vengeance. And God apparently promises that disaster will surely fall on the village. But that isn't enough for Jeremiah; he wants them to be dragged to the slaughter yards.

He sets up a kind of dualism: *I* am an innocent lamb; *they* are sheep who deserve to be killed. It's not very edifying stuff; his sense of betrayal by his own people fuels, perhaps understandably, his anger.

But he then recognizes some of the causes of that anger: 'Why does the way of the guilty prosper? Why do all who are treacherous thrive?' (v.1). His sense of what natural justice demands is in conflict with the evidence of his own eyes. He believes that righteous behaviour should be rewarded, but what seems to happen is the very opposite. He claims that there is a great gulf between what his people outwardly practise and what they inwardly believe. He is looking for an inward conversion, a purifying of the soul so that humankind can become truly integrated. It's a cry that echoes down the corridors of time. And the psychological confusion of his reactions, if we are honest, may have some resonance with how we occasionally feel.

Eternal God,
give us insight
to discern your will for us,
to give up what harms us,
and to seek the perfection we are promised
in Jesus Christ our Lord.

COLLECT

Jeremiah 13.1-11

'... the loincloth was ruined; it was good for nothing' (v.7)

Sometime Jeremiah lambasts his people with much sound and fury, and then we come across an episode like this in which the parable is quiet, understated and puzzling. This is not a parable for the outsider to ponder, but is one for Jeremiah himself to consider. He is told to buy a loincloth and to bury it in a crevice in some rocks. (There is some dispute about the word '*Perath*'. Some have argued that it suggests a visit to the river Euphrates, known in Hebrew as 'Perath'; others say that it refers to somewhere much closer to Anathoth. The latter seems inherently more likely, because the Euphrates was hundreds of miles away.)

Later, Jeremiah is told by God to go and find the hidden loincloth. He does so and discovers it in tatters. It's a sign that Jeremiah interprets as meaning that God will shred and tear and ruin the people of Judah and Jerusalem. Once they were bound as close to God as a loincloth is bound to a body, but soon they will be torn to shreds.

This passage seems to have two functions. First, it illustrates Jeremiah's growth in understanding. Secondly, it may represent a story remembered about Jeremiah which was seen later to have prophetic immediacy.

Whatever the origin of this strange episode, one thing is clear: Jeremiah believed that the relationship of God with his chosen people was at the point of destruction. He must have felt desperate and intensely alone, for no one seemed to accept what he was saying.

Pray this Lent that any loneliness you feel may be transformed by God into truth-filled courage.

COLLECT

Almighty God,
whose most dear Son went not up to joy but first he
    suffered pain,
and entered not into glory before he was crucified:
mercifully grant that we, walking in the way of the cross,
may find it none other than the way of life and peace;
through Jesus Christ your Son our Lord,
who is alive and reigns with you,
in the unity of the Holy Spirit,
one God, now and for ever.

Jeremiah 14

'... we are called by your name; do not forsake us!' (v.9)

There are moments in Jeremiah's life where his desire to speak what he believes to be the truth becomes internalized into prayer. This is one such moment. His love for his people is absolute. Is not the hot anger of truth-telling sometimes born of desire to see improvement because what you love is under threat?

Now he addresses not his people but the Almighty. It is a prayer of heartfelt intensity. Jeremiah yearns for the right relationship between God and his people to be re-established. He sees around him the effects of a drought (is not the description haunting?), and interprets it as a sign of God's absence. He feels as desolate as the parched earth, so he calls to God: 'Yet you, O Lord, are in the midst of us, and we are called by your name; do not forsake us!' (It is the kind of cry that should fill our hearts in Lent.)

The words spiral up into the air. A dialogue ensues, in which God answers that the people have been constantly disobedient, but Jeremiah courageously replies: 'Is it not you, O Lord our God? We set our hope on you ...' (v.22). He begs God to remember the closer-than-covenant relationship which he has with his people. And Jeremiah waits. He can do no more ...

Prayer of this kind is based on the belief that, in spite of all things, God remains faithful, true to himself, utterly holy, utterly compassionate.

We meet it in the cry of the man who encountered Jesus and said: 'Lord, I believe, help my unbelief ...' (Mark 9.24).

Eternal God,
give us insight
to discern your will for us,
to give up what harms us,
and to seek the perfection we are promised
in Jesus Christ our Lord.

COLLECT

Jeremiah 15.10-end

'Woe is me, my mother, that you ever bore me' (v.10)

It is worth remembering that someone, somewhere, once took a papyrus and a stylus and wrote these words that we now read. Perhaps it was Jeremiah himself who did so, which means that we ought to read this text a bit like we might read any other piece of literature. We need to listen to each 'voice', conscious that the 'voice' of God is like that of a character in a play. The words come from the lips of the character, but they began as words in the mind of the playwright.

Jeremiah expresses his sense of personal desolation: 'Woe is me, my mother, that you ever bore me ...' (v.10). And he expresses his despair over God: 'Truly, you are to me like a deceitful brook, like waters that fail' (v.18). It is a powerful and courageous lament.

God replies that he will rescue Jeremiah from the clutches of the wicked, from the hands of the ruthless.

Perhaps what we are being given here is a privileged insight into the workings of Jeremiah's soul; the kind of heartfelt conversation that is more often expressed in the solitude of prayer than in public discourse. Whatever its origins may be, and whatever the political situation in which this was written, we should take heart that people before us have felt able to speak to God in prayer with honesty. The more difficult part is then listening for the response, and trying to decide what may be from God and what may be from the deceits of our own nature.

COLLECT

Almighty God,
whose most dear Son went not up to joy but first he
    suffered pain,
and entered not into glory before he was crucified:
mercifully grant that we, walking in the way of the cross,
may find it none other than the way of life and peace;
through Jesus Christ your Son our Lord,
who is alive and reigns with you,
in the unity of the Holy Spirit,
one God, now and for ever.

Psalms **31** *or* 41, **42**, 43
Jeremiah 16.10 – 17.4
John 9.1-17

Jeremiah 16.10 – 17.4

'By your own act you shall lose the heritage that I gave you' (17.4)

There is no comfort for anyone in these verses. God has made his decision, declares Jeremiah. The people who were once his chosen ones have forsaken him. They have run after other gods. They have failed to keep his laws.

The consequences will be unbearable; they will be flung headlong out of the land and be taken to a strange and alien country. Ripped from God and ripped from their homes, they will experience loss of a terrible kind. And, of course, seen in the light of the Exile of 597 BC, this is what happened. The people were taken captive, and by the waters of Babylon sat down and wept.

How far these words of Jeremiah were purely religious prophecies and how far they were an astute reading of the turbulent politics of the Middle East at the time is not for us to know. In any case, for Jeremiah the distinction between politics and religion was not a part of his mental map. All that we can do, centuries later, is to acknowledge that there are times when our understanding of the relationship between God and the facts of history is unclear. The famous hymn, 'God is working His purpose out as year succeeds to year', written by an Old Etonian scholar and teacher, Arthur Campbell Ainger, might have caught the confident mood of late-nineteenth-century expansionist Britain, but in a post-Holocaust Europe, it might raise more questions than it answers.

The relationship between God and the events of our world require the thoughtful and humble attention of us all.

Eternal God,
give us insight
to discern your will for us,
to give up what harms us,
and to seek the perfection we are promised
in Jesus Christ our Lord.

COLLECT

Monday 4 April

Psalms **70**, 77 *or* **44**
Jeremiah 17.5-18
John 9.18-end

Jeremiah 17.5-18

'Let my persecutors be shamed ... destroy them with double destruction!' (v.18)

Proverbs are a good source of wisdom, for they encapsulate the experience of generations of our forebears. In ancient Israel, there was a long tradition of valuing sayings of this kind; you only have to look at the Book of Proverbs to realize that.

In today's passage from Jeremiah, there seem to be a number of sayings that have a proverbial character. For example, 'Blessed are those who trust in the Lord ... They shall be like a tree planted by water, sending out its roots by the stream' (vv.7-8), or 'Like the partridge hatching what it did not lay, so are all who amass wealth unjustly ...' (v.11).

Yet, interspersed with these Wisdom sayings are passages that are clearly meant to reflect the situation in which Jeremiah found himself. He had been warning his people for a long time, and they only responded by saying: 'Where is the word of the Lord? Let it come!' (v.15). In brief, they felt that Jeremiah had been calling 'wolf' for too long.

He was furious at their patronizing response to his message, and he yelled at God: 'Bring on them the day of disaster; destroy them with double destruction!' (v.18).

Is that kind of response to rejection ever justified?

COLLECT

Merciful Lord,
absolve your people from their offences,
that through your bountiful goodness
we may all be delivered from the chains of those sins
which by our frailty we have committed;
grant this, heavenly Father,
for Jesus Christ's sake, our blessed Lord and Saviour,
who is alive and reigns with you,
in the unity of the Holy Spirit,
one God, now and for ever.

Tuesday 5 April

Jeremiah 18.1-12

'... like the clay in the potter's hand, so are you in my hand' (v.6)

Almond trees, cauldrons, linen cloths – these were some of the everyday things through which Jeremiah somehow 'saw' God disclosing himself. In today's reading, it is a visit to a potter that enables him to see and hear what God might be saying to him. Watching a potter moulding pots on the wheel, Jeremiah 'sees', as it were, a theological meaning in the action. It is about God's ability to make and remake his people as he wishes. We are clay in his hands.

It is a metaphor that a number of biblical writers had used. Isaiah, for example (Isaiah 29.16), had spoken of the relationship of the clay to the potter, and, centuries later, St Paul used a similar image (Romans 9.20-21). It is unsurprising that everyday trades and crafts should have been the source of metaphors; the same is equally true today. We might say of someone, 'He's a robot', or 'She was programmed to do that'. What it raises is an interesting theological issue. When we use metaphors to talk about God, at what point do we acknowledge that ancient metaphors are no longer adequate? In the twenty-first century in Western Europe, does the metaphor of God as a potter have the power that it must once have had when the craft of pottery was visible on every street corner? When metaphors run out of steam, are we free to abandon them?

Another question: in a period of history when our mental map includes concepts about 'chaos theory' as well as concepts about 'certainty', are we able to talk of God being as free as a potter to make or unmake things at will? The questions are easier to ask than to answer. Perhaps all we can do, especially during Lent, is to try to have the same kind of creativity and integrity that Jeremiah had in how we attempt to speak about God.

Merciful Lord,
you know our struggle to serve you:
when sin spoils our lives
and overshadows our hearts,
come to our aid
and turn us back to you again;
through Jesus Christ our Lord.

COLLECT

Wednesday 6 April

Jeremiah 18.13-end

'May a cry be heard from their houses ...' (v.22)

Jeremiah was convinced that the Day of Reckoning was coming for his people. He longed for them to change their ways. He spoke passionately about their need to restore their relationship with God, but they refused to listen to him. No matter how powerful his words, no matter how arresting his poetry, they would not respond. They were set in their ways and refused to budge. At least, that is Jeremiah's version of events. It would be interesting to hear the viewpoint of some of those who disagreed with his analysis, but we do not have that available. What we do have is Jeremiah's anxious and fiery message straight, it would seem, from God: 'Like the wind from the east, I will scatter them before the enemy. I will show them my back, not my face, on the day of their calamity' (v.17).

It should have been no surprise to Jeremiah that his message made people so angry that they plotted to get rid of him. He responded with a full-throttle blast of invective: 'Bring raiders on them without warning, and let screaming be heard from their houses ...' (v.22).

It may be understandable as the response of a man who could not get his message across, but it all feels a very long way from the saying of Jesus, 'Blessed are the peacemakers'. But we should not forget that it was out of the long history of God's dealings with his people that Jesus' message arose. Salvation is not achieved overnight.

You might want to consider, this Lent, how strong your relationship is with God, and, if the relationship is fragile, how it can be restored.

COLLECT

Merciful Lord,
absolve your people from their offences,
that through your bountiful goodness
we may all be delivered from the chains of those sins
which by our frailty we have committed;
grant this, heavenly Father,
for Jesus Christ's sake, our blessed Lord and Saviour,
who is alive and reigns with you,
in the unity of the Holy Spirit,
one God, now and for ever.

Thursday 7 April

Jeremiah 19.1-13

*'So will I break this people and this city, as one breaks
a potter's vessel' (v.11)*

There are occasions in the Bible when the actual text seems a bit confused, as though an editor has sewn two sections together and has placed them in the wrong position. This may be the case in today's reading. If you read verses 1-2 and then jump straight to verse 10, the story makes sense. In the first verses, the people addressed are the elders and the priests. The second section, beginning at verse 3, is addressed not to the elders and priests but to the princes and the people of Jerusalem. It could be that the editor has put the two stories together because they both refer to a potter and his earthenware jars.

Whatever the cause of the textual confusion might be, the message is clear. Jeremiah proclaims in word and symbolic action that terrible trouble lies very close at hand. God is about to judge his people. And why? Because the people have been worshipping other gods and have been involved in the sacrificial killing of innocent children. So, Jeremiah smashes the earthenware pot and says that, just as the jar lies scattered and cannot be remade, so will their dead bodies be.

It is a chilling and awful proclamation, which was even more terrifying for those who believed that symbolic actions actually brought about the things that they foretold.

Merciful Lord,
you know our struggle to serve you:
when sin spoils our lives
and overshadows our hearts,
come to our aid
and turn us back to you again;
through Jesus Christ our Lord.

COLLECT

Psalms **102** or **51**, **54**
Jeremiah 19.14 – 20.6
John 11.1-16

Jeremiah 19.14 – 20.6

'... a terror to yourself and to all your friends' (20.4)

The tension created by Jeremiah's tough prophecies was bound to break sooner or later. In today's passage, we come to that moment.

Jeremiah's smashing of the earthenware pot had taken place at or very near Topheth, the place in the valley of Hinnom, where people had been sacrificing their children by burning them alive in honour of the god Moloch. Having berated the people for such an appalling practice, Jeremiah now re-enters Jerusalem. He goes to the centre of power, the temple, and there he continues his tirade, saying that God will bring destruction on all.

He was arrested by a priest called Passhur and was placed overnight in the stocks. The ordeal did nothing to cool Jeremiah's religious convictions. In the morning, he railed against Passhur, giving him a new name that meant 'fear/terror on every side', or 'terror let loose', and said that Passhur would be carried into captivity by the approaching enemy.

There is an underlying irony in this story. Jeremiah's name means 'Yahweh exalts'. And here he is, a man from an outlying village, whose very name should have been a warning to those who refused to listen, clashing with one of the most powerful priests in Jerusalem, one whose main function should have been to give glory to God through the sacrificial system at the temple. It's the outsider who would seem to be closer to God than the insider, and the outsider who says that everything in the centre will be demolished by God. It is radical in the extreme.

COLLECT

Merciful Lord,
absolve your people from their offences,
that through your bountiful goodness
we may all be delivered from the chains of those sins
which by our frailty we have committed;
grant this, heavenly Father,
for Jesus Christ's sake, our blessed Lord and Saviour,
who is alive and reigns with you,
in the unity of the Holy Spirit,
one God, now and for ever.

Psalms **32** *or* **68**
Jeremiah 20.7-end
John 11.17-27

Jeremiah 20.7-end

'Why did I come forth from the womb to ... spend my days in shame?' (v.18)

And then, having challenged one of the most powerful men of his city, and having withstood the loneliness and humiliation of the stocks, Jeremiah's confidence suddenly deserts him.

It is a moment of intense poignancy. Nothing we have read of Jeremiah's courage and resilient determination up to now can quite prepare us for the shock of this haunting passage. This is a soul in the very depths of despair: 'You have duped me, Lord, and I have been your dupe ...' God is nowhere to be found. He is appallingly absent. It is a cry of dereliction from the depths of Jeremiah's being. For a moment, we are left to wonder what will become of this audacious but now broken man.

His courage wells up. He recalls that trying not to speak of the things of God was impossible; it was like a fire burning in his heart. And, as soon as he remembers this inner reality, he calls out, 'But the Lord is with me like a dread warrior' (v.11), and soon he is singing out the praises of God, only to succumb almost immediately to spiritual anguish: 'Cursed be the day on which I was born!' (v.14).

There are some biblical passages where the very core of our humanity is exposed, our noblest and our most fragile self has nowhere left to hide. We are alone.

Words stop. All we can do is to wait in that place where certainty and uncertainty are one, and in our desolation call upon God for mercy.

Lent provides us with an opportunity to wait upon the merciful kindness of the Lord.

Merciful Lord,
you know our struggle to serve you:
when sin spoils our lives
and overshadows our hearts,
come to our aid
and turn us back to you again;
through Jesus Christ our Lord.

COLLECT

Jeremiah 21.1-10

'I am setting before you the way of life and the way of death' (v.8)

The historical context of this passage is clear. It is the year 588 BC. Jerusalem is being blockaded by the Babylonians. In terms of Middle Eastern politics, the rulers of Judah, prior to this, had tried to arrange an alliance with the Egyptians against the rising might of Babylon, but it was all to no avail. The Babylonian forces were now massing at the approaches to Jerusalem. The King of Judah, Zedekiah, sends a message to Jeremiah asking him to intercede with God for a miracle. Jeremiah's reaction is swift, brutal and uncompromising: 'Thus says the Lord, the God of Israel ... I myself will fight against you ... in anger, in fury, and in great wrath' (vv.3,5).

Jeremiah had spoken. But he did offer a piece of realpolitik advice: surrender to the besieging armies and you might survive; stay in the city and you will all be slaughtered.

It is not difficult to imagine the flurry of anxious consultations that must have gone on among the political leaders in Jerusalem once Jeremiah's advice was received: should they heed his warnings or not? It was hawks versus doves.

And what was Jeremiah thinking? For one who loved his country and his people passionately, he must have been heartbroken. His conscience would not allow him to compromise what he said, but where was God's plan in all of this?

COLLECT

Most merciful God,
who by the death and resurrection of your Son Jesus Christ
delivered and saved the world:
grant that by faith in him who suffered on the cross
we may triumph in the power of his victory;
through Jesus Christ your Son our Lord,
who is alive and reigns with you,
in the unity of the Holy Spirit,
one God, now and for ever.

Psalms **35**, 123 *or* **73**
Jeremiah 22.1-5,13-19
John 11.45-end

Jeremiah 22.1-5,13-19

'... obey this word' (v.4)

One of the difficulties in reading the Book of Jeremiah is that it is does not always follow a strict historical sequence. In yesterday's reading, we were looking at events in the year 588 BC; in today's reading, we seem to be many years earlier in the reign of Jehoiakim. He was the vassal king of Judah who had been put in place by Pharaoh Neko II in 608 BC. He played a devious political hand and switched allegiance to the Babylonians for three years, but then switched back to the Egyptians. It was not a clever move.

Meanwhile, he was assailed in Jerusalem by the uncompromising voice of Jeremiah, who forcefully reminded him of his religious and moral obligations, and of the consequences of failure to obey God: 'I shall consecrate an armed host to fight against you, a destructive horde ...'

In 599 BC, Nebuchadnezzar II of Babylon laid siege to Jerusalem. In 598 BC, Jehoiakim died, and within three months Jerusalem fell. Many of the leading citizens were exiled to Babylon, and the Babylonians installed a new vassal king in Jerusalem, Zedekiah. (We met him in yesterday's reading.)

No matter whether the king of Judah was a vassal of Egypt or of Babylon, Jeremiah did not waver. His message was that it was God who had to be obeyed, not man, and obeyed completely. Nothing less would do. That was Israel's solemn religious and moral duty.

Consider this Lent whether you feel you serve God obediently.

COLLECT

Gracious Father,
you gave up your Son
out of love for the world:
lead us to ponder the mysteries of his passion,
that we may know eternal peace
through the shedding of our Saviour's blood,
Jesus Christ our Lord.

Jeremiah 22.20 – 23.8

'I will raise up for David a righteous Branch' (23.5)

If only the editors of the Book of Jeremiah had had a stronger sense of chronology …

In today's readings (22.20-27), we have a prophecy about a future catastrophe when the people and their rulers will be taken captive; but this is immediately followed by a saying which implies that the exile has already begun. It does not make for easy reading.

The passage that follows, however, brings a rapid change of mood. We are introduced to a powerful lament ('O land, land, land …', 22.29), which takes us into Jeremiah's heart. He can see that the shepherds of Israel have not watched over God's own flock. They have failed to fulfil their God-given duty. And the result is a tragedy.

Nevertheless, even in such harrowing times, Jeremiah proclaims that God will one day make a righteous branch spring from David's line, a king who will 'deal wisely, and shall execute justice and righteousness in the land' (23.5). He foretells that the exile will end and that the people will be able to return to their own soil. In the midst of despair, he sees God-born hope.

The longing for a righteous king eventually fed into Jewish messianic expectations, and therefore into the life of Christ. Bring to mind Mary's song: 'He has come to the help of Israel his servant, as he promised to our forefathers; he has not forgotten to show mercy to Abraham and his children's children for ever.'

COLLECT

Most merciful God,
who by the death and resurrection of your Son Jesus Christ
delivered and saved the world:
grant that by faith in him who suffered on the cross
we may triumph in the power of his victory;
through Jesus Christ your Son our Lord,
who is alive and reigns with you,
in the unity of the Holy Spirit,
one God, now and for ever.

Psalms **40**, 125 *or* **78.1-39***
Jeremiah 23.9-32
John 12.12-19

Jeremiah 23.9-32

'... a hammer that breaks a rock in pieces' (v.29)

The verses in the first part of today's reading (vv.9-15) probably come from the earlier part of Jeremiah's life. There is nothing in them to suggest that the words were spoken close to the catastrophe of the Exile. But the verses that follow (vv.16-24) might be much closer in time to that disaster.

Nevertheless, the entire passage has a strong and critical message: there are bad prophets and there are faithful, good prophets. The bad prophets are those who speak wispy words of easy comfort. But prophets who stand close to the counsel of God and speak the truth are the ones who should be heard. The truth from God has a terrifying force: 'Is not my word like fire, says the Lord, and like a hammer that breaks a rock in pieces?'

At the heart of Jeremiah's book is the belief that God is utterly holy, a God of purity, a God of justice, a fearsome God; one who demands the highest standards of righteous behaviour from his people.

It is an idea that also finds a place in the New Testament. In the Epistle to the Hebrews occurs this: 'Therefore, since we are receiving a kingdom that cannot be shaken, let us give thanks, by which we offer to God an acceptable worship with reverence and awe; for indeed our God is a consuming fire' (Hebrews 12.28-29). They are the kind of words that Jeremiah might have written himself.

Gracious Father,
you gave up your Son
out of love for the world:
lead us to ponder the mysteries of his passion,
that we may know eternal peace
through the shedding of our Saviour's blood,
Jesus Christ our Lord.

COLLECT

Friday 15 April

Psalms **22**, 126 *or* **55**
Jeremiah 24
John 12.20-36a

Jeremiah 24

'... they shall be my people' (v.7)

If only we knew when this chapter was written ...

If it is an account of a vision of Jeremiah after the leaders had been sent into exile, we should read it as a remarkable and courageous statement – a statement suggesting that all those who remained in Jerusalem were dross, and those who had been exiled were the true people of God. It is not at all what we would expect Jeremiah to say after all the harsh things he had written about the leaders previously.

However, if this passage was written once the exiles had returned from Babylon to Jerusalem in 538 BC (and there are scholars who regard parts of the Book of Jeremiah as dating from this time), then we might read it as a piece of political propaganda created by the returning exiles, staking their claim to be the true Israel.

It really is not possible at this distance in time to distinguish with certainty between these two interpretations of the passage. Perhaps, in such circumstances, we ought to opt more strongly for the first interpretation, that is, that this account really does pre-date the exile. In that case, what we are reading is Jeremiah's conviction that God would not allow the Exile to prevent reconciliation with himself: 'they shall be my people and I will be their God' (v.7).

Can anything, as St Paul asked, ever separate us from God's love? Allow yourself this Lent to accept that God's love for you is unshakeable.

COLLECT

Most merciful God,
who by the death and resurrection of your Son Jesus Christ
delivered and saved the world:
grant that by faith in him who suffered on the cross
we may triumph in the power of his victory;
through Jesus Christ your Son our Lord,
who is alive and reigns with you,
in the unity of the Holy Spirit,
one God, now and for ever.

Psalms **23**, 127 *or* **76**, 79
Jeremiah 25.1-14
John 12.36b-end

Jeremiah 25.1-14

'I have spoken persistently to you, but you have not listened' (v.3)

This passage begins with a very precise date: the fourth year of Jehoiakim, the king of Judah. We can say with reasonable certainty that this was 604 BC. In the previous year, 605 BC, there had been a remarkably significant battle between the Babylonians on the one side and a combined Assyrian/Egyptian force on the other. The Babylonians won, and this marked the end of Assyrian hegemony in that part of the Middle East. A new balance of power came into being. Jehoiakim, king of Judah, therefore, who had been installed as a vassal king of Judah by the Egyptians, now changed sides and started to pay tribute to the Babylonians.

Meanwhile, Jeremiah used the moment of huge political change to summarize his previous 23 years of public prophecies. His message was that he had been bringing to his people the Word of the Lord, but they had refused to listen. They had continued to worship other gods; they had refused to pay proper allegiance to Yahweh. The result, he said, would be a terrible judgement; the Babylonians would be used by God to fulfil his will: 'I will bring them against this land and its inhabitants ... I will utterly destroy them' (v.9). But, the prophecy went on, eventually the Babylonians would be punished by God.

Jeremiah saw in the struggle for territorial power in the Middle East the workings of God. He believed that he was being used by God to speak the revelation of this truth to his generation. It was a tough assignment – but the discernment of truth, and the speaking of truth, in any age, cannot be achieved without great courage and tenacity, can it?

Gracious Father,
you gave up your Son
out of love for the world:
lead us to ponder the mysteries of his passion,
that we may know eternal peace
through the shedding of our Saviour's blood,
Jesus Christ our Lord.

COLLECT

Luke 22.1-23

'Now the festival of Unleavened Bread, which is called the Passover, was near' (v.1)

The setting of the Last Supper at the time of the Passover is significant. We are reminded of the great act of deliverance by which God rescued his people at the time of the Exodus. Luke has already spoken of Jesus accomplishing his Exodus in Jerusalem in the conversation with Moses and Elijah at the transfiguration (Luke 9.30).

As they gather for the meal, Jesus tells the disciples that this Passover, which he has been longing to share with them, will be the last Passover he will take part in until the kingdom of God comes. Then he takes bread and wine, as he would normally do as the host, and invests them with new meaning. When they share bread in future, it will be his body, his way of being present with them, and the wine will be his blood, the sign of the new covenant that will be inaugurated through his suffering.

All this is enacted against the background of the forces of evil mounting their attack on Jesus, through the religious leaders trying to find a way to get rid of him, and through Judas who provides them with the means to achieve their end. Jesus warns his disciples of impending betrayal. But they are unable to grasp his meaning, and wonder whom he means.

COLLECT

Almighty and everlasting God,
who in your tender love towards the human race
    sent your Son our Saviour Jesus Christ
to take upon him our flesh
and to suffer death upon the cross:
grant that we may follow the example of his patience and
    humility,
and also be made partakers of his resurrection;
through Jesus Christ your Son our Lord,
who is alive and reigns with you,
in the unity of the Holy Spirit,
one God, now and for ever.

Psalm 27
Lamentations 3.1-18
Luke 22.[24-38] 39-53

Tuesday of Holy Week

Luke 22.[24-38] 39-53

'... not my will but yours be done' (v.42)

Just when Jesus could have done with their support, the disciples get into an argument about which of them is the greatest, and Jesus has to remind them about his servant model of service. Peter (addressed as Simon, indicating that he is about to revert to his status before he was called Peter 'the rock') is warned that he will deny knowing Jesus, despite his protestations of loyalty. Do we get distracted like the disciples by trivial arguments, or refuse to face our own fragility?

Then comes the final choice for Jesus. He knows that God's will is that evil must be defeated, and that the only way to break its power is to face it, absorb it and not hit back. Humanly speaking, he can't bear the thought of what lies ahead: 'Father, if you are willing, remove this cup from me' (v.42). But he had come to be the agent of God's will, and in agony he makes his decision, and says: 'not my will but yours be done'. His decision is given God's seal of acceptance through the ministry of the angel who comes to strengthen him.

What follows is inevitable once he has made his choice. He is betrayed by a kiss, and it seems that darkness has won.

True and humble king,
hailed by the crowd as Messiah:
grant us the faith to know you and love you,
that we may be found beside you
on the way of the cross,
which is the path of glory.

COLLECT

123

Psalm 102 [or 102.1-18]
Jeremiah 11.18-20
Luke 22.54-end

Wednesday 20 April
Wednesday of Holy Week

Luke 22.54-end

'The Lord turned and looked at Peter' (v.61)

Peter has repeatedly said that he will not desert Jesus, in spite of all the warnings Jesus has given him. He does at least follow, albeit at a distance, as far as the courtyard of the high priest's house where Jesus had been taken. Here the challenge comes, and three times Peter denies any link with Jesus. Hardly has the third denial passed his lips than the cock crows. And the Lord turns and looks at Peter.

That look must have been one of compassion, rather than an 'I told you so' look. If it had been the latter, Peter would probably have got defensive. ('I know I said I would never forsake you, but I didn't think you'd go this far – I've got a wife and family to think of.') But that wasn't his response. Perhaps Peter remembered at that moment what Jesus had said earlier: 'Simon, Simon, listen! Satan has demanded to sift all of you like wheat, but I have prayed for you ['you' in the singular here] that your own faith may not fail; and you, when once you have turned back, strengthen your brothers' (Luke 22.31-32). Realizing that Jesus understood was enough to move him to tears.

Isn't it Jesus' compassion that moves us to repentance too?

COLLECT

Almighty and everlasting God,
who in your tender love towards the human race
   sent your Son our Saviour Jesus Christ
to take upon him our flesh
and to suffer death upon the cross:
grant that we may follow the example of his patience and
   humility,
and also be made partakers of his resurrection;
through Jesus Christ your Son our Lord,
who is alive and reigns with you,
in the unity of the Holy Spirit,
one God, now and for ever.

Psalms 42, 43
Leviticus 16.2-24
Luke 23.1-25

Thursday 21 April

Maundy Thursday

Luke 23.1-25

'I have found in him no ground for the sentence of death' (v.22)

The one thing Pilate couldn't stand was a shouting mob. When he took up his post in Jerusalem, he had marched into the city with Roman standards flying, and the people had rioted in protest. Pilate gave in, and the Roman symbols were removed. But the people had discovered his weak spot. Now, when they shouted for Jesus' death, his blood ran cold. He couldn't risk an uprising – it would be more than his job was worth.

He looked for loopholes. The man came from Galilee, which was not his responsibility, so he sent Jesus to Herod, who wanted to meet him anyway. But Herod, although he appreciated the friendly gesture by someone he had regarded as an enemy, failed to take responsibility, and Jesus came back to Pilate.

Pilate did try to get Jesus released, but the mob's shouting continued, and their voices prevailed. So, Jesus was condemned to death.

We are used to talking about sins of omission or commission. But there is a third category too: that of *permission*, the things we allow to happen because we haven't got the will or the courage to challenge them.

Which category do our sins fall into on the whole?

True and humble king,
hailed by the crowd as Messiah:
grant us the faith to know you and love you,
that we may be found beside you
on the way of the cross,
which is the path of glory.

COLLECT

Friday 22 April
Good Friday

Psalm 69
Genesis 22.1-18
John 19.38-end *or* Hebrews 10.1-10

Hebrews 10.1-10

'... we have been sanctified ... once for all' (v.10)

'Once, only once, and once for all
His precious life he gave;
Before the cross our spirits fall,
And own it strong to save.'

The words of William Bright's hymn develop the thoughts of the writer of the Letter to the Hebrews. The author refers back to the instructions in Leviticus 16 for the offering of sacrifice in atonement for sin. The elaborate ritual for the cleansing of God's people under the terms of the old covenant had to be repeated each year. More than one Old Testament writer, as time passed, had pointed out that God was not interested in sacrificial offerings that meant nothing if they were not accompanied by a change of heart: Psalm 40.6-8; Amos 5.21-24.

Jesus said the same, as the writer to the Hebrews says: 'in burnt-offerings and sin-offerings you have taken no pleasure' (v.6). By his self-offering, Jesus has inaugurated the new covenant sealed with his blood, and the old rituals can be dispensed with. Now everyone has the opportunity of being set free by God's forgiveness.

Small wonder, then, that when we gather for worship on this day and contemplate the cross, we often say:

'We adore you O Christ and we bless you,
Because by your cross and passion you have redeemed the world.'

COLLECT

Almighty Father,
look with mercy on this your family
for which our Lord Jesus Christ was content to be betrayed
    and given up into the hands of sinners
    and to suffer death upon the cross;
who is alive and glorified with you and the Holy Spirit,
one God, now and for ever.

John 2.18-22

'Destroy this temple, and in three days I will raise it up' (v.19)

Unlike the other Gospel-writers, John placed what we call the cleansing of the temple at the beginning of Jesus' ministry. Jesus' action understandably raised questions about his authority for acting in such a cavalier fashion. Jesus told his questioners: 'Destroy this temple, and in three days I will raise it up.' The Jews didn't understand – it had taken them 46 years to build the temple, so how could anyone rebuild it in three days? With hindsight, after the resurrection, his disciples remembered what he had said, and understood that he was referring to the temple of his own body, the dwelling place of God, and that he had indeed been raised on the third day.

The temple, because of the way the religious leaders had allowed it to become corrupted into a commercial enterprise rather than a place of prayer, had ceased to fulfil its proper function. Jesus would provide in himself the place where people could meet God. Paul would later develop the idea of each believer being the dwelling place of God (1 Corinthians 3.16-17, 6.19).

Are we fit for purpose as temples of God? Or do we need cleansing too?

Grant, Lord,
that we who are baptized into the death
of your Son our Saviour Jesus Christ
may continually put to death our evil desires
and be buried with him;
and that through the grave and gate of death
we may pass to our joyful resurrection;
through his merits,
who died and was buried and rose again for us,
your Son Jesus Christ our Lord.

COLLECT

Monday 25 April

Monday of Easter Week

Psalms 111, 117, 146
Song of Solomon 1.9 – 2.7
Mark 16.1-8

Mark 16.1-8

'Who will roll away the stone ...?' (v.3)

One of the strongest arguments for the truth of the resurrection is that all the Gospel-writers give a different account of what the disciples experienced. There is no attempt to get the stories to tally.

Mark's account is the earliest, and the shortest, possibly because the original ending to the book was lost. The women who went to the tomb were not expecting the resurrection. Their main concern was how they would get to Jesus' body to carry out the burial rites they had not had time for three days before. To say that they were surprised by what they saw and heard is an understatement. The stone had been rolled back; a messenger told them that Jesus was alive, and that they were to tell the disciples and Peter that Jesus would meet them in Galilee. The women were terrified and ran away, mute with fear.

They must have spoken eventually, though. Perhaps, as the shock subsided, they remembered that Jesus had said something about being raised from the dead. Their contribution to the interpretation of events was part of the growing conviction that Jesus really is alive.

COLLECT

Lord of all life and power,
who through the mighty resurrection of your Son
overcame the old order of sin and death
to make all things new in him:
grant that we, being dead to sin
and alive to you in Jesus Christ,
may reign with him in glory;
to whom with you and the Holy Spirit
be praise and honour, glory and might,
now and in all eternity.

Psalms 112, 147.1-12
Song of Solomon 2.8-end
Luke 24.1-12

Tuesday 26 April

Tuesday of Easter Week

Luke 24.1-12

'Why do you look for the living among the dead?' (v.5)

Luke's account of what happened gives a little more insight into the reaction of the women. There was fear and perplexity, but this time the messengers helped the women to remember and make connections. 'Why do you look for the living among the dead? ... Remember how he told you ... that the Son of Man must ... be crucified, and on the third day rise again.'

The women went and told the disciples about their experience. But women in their day were not regarded as credible witnesses, and so their words were dismissed as an idle tale.

In a verse which not all versions of the Gospel include, Luke tells us that Peter went off to the tomb to see for himself, and went home amazed at what had happened. Perhaps both Mark and Luke include special mention of Peter as an indication that, in spite of denying all knowledge of Jesus, he was still included among the disciples.

It was hard for Jesus' disciples to get their heads round what had happened. Dead men don't come back to life, do they? But gradually, through the experiences they had, the disciples realized that Jesus was very much alive, recognisable though no longer constrained by the limitations of a physical body. It was still a mystery, but they could not deny that they had experienced Jesus' presence with them.

God of glory,
by the raising of your Son
you have broken the chains of death and hell:
fill your Church with faith and hope;
for a new day has dawned
and the way to life stands open
in our Saviour Jesus Christ.

COLLECT

Psalms 113, 147.13-end
Song of Solomon 3
Matthew 28.16-end

Matthew 28.16-end

'I am with you always, to the end of the age' (v.20)

Much of what happens in Matthew's Gospel takes place on a mountain, and that is the setting for this event too. The disciples have obeyed the instruction to go to Galilee, but some of them are hesitant – whether their hesitation is about believing in the resurrection or about worshipping Jesus is not clear. Faith in Jesus doesn't always come easily, and it doesn't preclude doubt.

Jesus leaves them in no doubt about how he sees his own status, though: 'All authority in heaven and on earth has been given to me' (v.18). This echoes the vision in Daniel chapter 7, vv.13-14, when 'one like the Son of man' (Authorized Version) is given authority by the Ancient of days (a name for God in Aramaic) to hold sway over all the nations in a kingdom that won't be destroyed. The disciples are commissioned to go and proclaim that truth to all nations, and make disciples as they go. To be a disciple requires an act of commitment, baptism, and a willingness to go on growing in understanding through the apostles' teaching.

If that task seems daunting, Jesus promises to be with his followers always, to the end of the age. The Gospel ends as it had begun with the promise of Emmanuel, 'God with us'.

That promise is for us, too, as we witness to God's transforming power in our lives.

COLLECT

Lord of all life and power,
who through the mighty resurrection of your Son
overcame the old order of sin and death
to make all things new in him:
grant that we, being dead to sin
and alive to you in Jesus Christ,
may reign with him in glory;
to whom with you and the Holy Spirit
be praise and honour, glory and might,
now and in all eternity.

Psalms 114, 148
Song of Solomon 5.2 – 6.3
Luke 7.11-17

Luke 7.11-17

'When the Lord saw her, he had compassion for her' (v.13)

This, like the record of the events set for the next two days, is not about resurrection as Jesus experienced it and the disciples witnessed it. The widow's son, like Jairus' daughter and Lazarus, are called back to *this* life, and will one day die again.

As Luke records this event, he demonstrates God's healing love at work.

As Jesus meets the grieving mother, doubly bereaved, left completely unsupported through widowhood and the loss of her only son, compassion stirs within him. He halts the funeral procession, and tells the boy to get up. To everyone's surprise, he does so, and is restored to his overjoyed mother.

The bystanders are amazed. Jesus has done what prophets like Elijah and Elisha had done centuries before (1 Kings 17; 2 Kings 4). 'God has visited his people', they said; God has acted with his saving power.

There are times in life when everything seems to have come to a dead end. Then, inexplicably, things change, and life is possible again. Do we recognize God's hand at work in those circumstances? Or do we think they are just chance?

God does not wait for our death to work his transforming grace in us. Thank God for that!

God of glory,
by the raising of your Son
you have broken the chains of death and hell:
fill your Church with faith and hope;
for a new day has dawned
and the way to life stands open
in our Saviour Jesus Christ.

COLLECT

Friday 29 April

Friday of Easter Week

Psalms 115, 149
Song of Solomon 7.10 – 8.4
Luke 8.41-end

Luke 8.41-end

'Do not fear. Only believe' (v.50)

This passage contains two examples of Jesus' compassion issuing in life-giving action.

Tucked into his response to Jairus' request that Jesus should come to his daughter who was dying is the incident involving a woman with persistent bleeding. Debilitated by her condition, which no doctor had been able to alleviate (this is Luke the doctor speaking!), and shunned by society because of it, the woman has no sense of self-worth left. But summoning up courage to touch Jesus brought instant results. And Jesus knew that life-giving energy had left him. The woman hardly dared admit to her action. But Jesus commended her for having the faith to come to him, and sent her away at peace.

The delay meant that it was apparently too late to do anything for Jairus' daughter. But Jesus was not put off: 'Do not fear. Only believe,' he said, and continued his journey to the house. There, taking the girl by the hand, he told her to get up. She did, and Jesus, with his practical insight into human need, made sure that she was given some food.

In life and in death, the compassion of Jesus makes all the difference. Has that been our experience too?

COLLECT

Lord of all life and power,
who through the mighty resurrection of your Son
overcame the old order of sin and death
to make all things new in him:
grant that we, being dead to sin
and alive to you in Jesus Christ,
may reign with him in glory;
to whom with you and the Holy Spirit
be praise and honour, glory and might,
now and in all eternity.

Psalms 116, 150
Song of Solomon 8.5-7
John 11.17-44

Saturday of Easter Week

John 11.17-44

'Lord, I believe' (v.27)

The death of Lazarus touched Jesus more deeply, probably, than any other occasion when he encountered human suffering, for this was a family which had been a great support to him during his ministry. No wonder Jesus wept at the death of his friend.

Mary and Martha both regretted that Jesus hadn't arrived earlier: perhaps then Lazarus would have been spared death. But then they would also have missed the startling claim that Jesus made about himself. Jesus said to Martha that belief in resurrection at the end of time is a pale reflection of the living truth in front of her: 'I am the resurrection and the life' (v.25). Anyone who believes in Jesus will never ultimately be overcome by death.

Jesus always points to the bigger picture. This is not just about the fate of one man who has died, it is an occasion when the glory of God will be revealed. Jesus makes that clear as he publicly thanks God, who is always working with him, for demonstrating his glory, before he calls Lazarus from the tomb.

Lazarus will die again, and Jesus will die too. But it is because Jesus went through death and was raised victoriously to life that for Mary, Martha and Lazarus and for all of us, there is hope. Can we say, with Martha, 'Lord, I believe'?

God of glory,
by the raising of your Son
you have broken the chains of death and hell:
fill your Church with faith and hope;
for a new day has dawned
and the way to life stands open
in our Saviour Jesus Christ.

COLLECT

Monday 2 May

George, martyr, patron of England

Psalms 5, 146
Joshua 1.1-9
Ephesians 6.10-20

Ephesians 6.10-20

'Put on the whole armour of God' (v.10)

St George is not the easiest of patron saints to embrace in modern times. His association with the crusades makes many people uncomfortable, and, latterly, George and his cross have become associated with expressions of English patriotism that may seem jingoistic. The great irony for those who use his flag as a totem of exclusive English identity is that he is far better suited as a saint for an inclusive and multicultural society. Our sketchy knowledge of his life does at least confirm that he has no direct links with England; rather, he was a Turkish national who spent much of his life in Palestine fighting for the Roman army. He is patron saint of numerous places, from Greece to Georgia, Beirut to Barcelona.

Sharing St George with other nations undermines any attempt to use him in a xenophobic manner and challenges those who are narrowly patriotic to enlarge their vision. Indeed, he is the 'foreigner' whom we welcome as our brother in Christ, and we honour him for his steadfastness in the faith. It was because he put on the whole armour of God, not that of a Roman soldier, that he was able to remain faithful unto death. May we who don the same armour use it to proclaim a gospel of welcome and acceptance to all people.

COLLECT

God of hosts,
who so kindled the flame of love
in the heart of your servant George
that he bore witness to the risen Lord
by his life and by his death:
give us the same faith and power of love
that we who rejoice in his triumphs
may come to share with him the fullness of the resurrection;
through Jesus Christ your Son our Lord,
who is alive and reigns with you,
in the unity of the Holy Spirit,
one God, now and for ever.

Psalms 37.23-end, 148
Isaiah 62.6-10
Acts 12.25 – 13.13

Tuesday 3 May

Mark the Evangelist

Acts 12.25 – 13.13

'John ... left them and returned to Jerusalem' (13.13)

There is scant reference to John Mark in this passage, but what there is is significant.

He sets off as an assistant to Paul and Barnabas on the first missionary journey to Cyprus. Having travelled through the island, Paul and Barnabas plan to sail on to Pamphylia for the next leg of the journey. Mark, however, 'separates' from them and turns back to Jerusalem (13.13). No reason is given for this, but the verb used suggests more than a simple return home. His action is clearly regarded as a desertion by Paul and is a later source of conflict between Paul and Barnabas (15.36-39).

Something has happened in Cyprus to make John Mark bail out of the trip. It is pointless to speculate what this might have been: a reaction to the dramatic spiritual confrontation between Paul and Bar-Jesus-Elymas, or something else entirely? Whatever it was, when Barnabas wishes to include Mark on the second missionary journey, Paul refuses. Barnabas, 'son of encouragement' (Acts 4.36), aims to give Mark a second chance, but Paul is unyielding and the falling-out is 'sharp' (15.39).

As we remember Mark today, let us reflect on any disagreements we may have with other Christians about how and by whom the Gospel is best proclaimed.

Almighty God,
who enlightened your holy Church
through the inspired witness of your evangelist Saint Mark:
grant that we, being firmly grounded
in the truth of the gospel,
may be faithful to its teaching both in word and deed;
through Jesus Christ your Son our Lord,
who is alive and reigns with you,
in the unity of the Holy Spirit,
one God, now and for ever.

COLLECT

Wednesday 4 May

Philip and James, Apostles

James 1.1-12

'... whenever you face trials of any kind, consider it nothing but joy' (v.2)

It is a brave soul who can truly embrace the exhortation of James to face trials with 'all joy'. The zeitgeist encourages us, rather, to moan, complain and blame whenever difficulties arise. We know that testing is an essential part of the Christian faith and that, along with the saints who've gone before, it will happen to us. We know too that, like cabbage, it is good for us and helps us grow. Nevertheless, the phrase 'do not bring us to the time of trial' is possibly one of the more earnestly prayed lines of the Lord's Prayer.

When testing comes, it can help to remember the transformative effect of rejoicing in adversity. We have been given an opportunity to know and love Christ in a deeper way. The English Methodist preacher Leslie Weatherhead referred to this as a 'treasure of the darkness'. In 1956, he wrote: 'I have learned far more about God and life and myself in the darkness of fear and failure than I have ever learned in the sunshine. There are such things as the treasures of the darkness.' The lessons learned while walking through the valley of darkness are often the most lasting and precious, but it is not always possible to see this until we emerge on the other side.

COLLECT

Almighty Father,
whom truly to know is eternal life:
teach us to know your Son Jesus Christ
as the way, the truth, and the life;
that we may follow the steps
    of your holy apostles Philip and James,
and walk steadfastly in the way that leads to your glory;
through Jesus Christ your Son our Lord,
who is alive and reigns with you,
in the unity of the Holy Spirit,
one God, now and for ever.

Psalms **28**, 29 *or* 14, **15**, 16
Deuteronomy 4.1-14
John 21.1-14

John 21.1-14

'... that night they caught nothing' (v.3)

'I am going fishing': an innocent comment by Peter to the other disciples. Or is it? A central theme of John 21 is the restoration of Peter, the failed follower. Tomorrow we will hear the difficult conversation Jesus has to have with him, but today's reading sets this up. We are bound to ask why Peter, who is an ex-fisherman called away from his nets to become a 'fisher of men', is going back to his boat. Some scholars suggest that this indicates a desire to return to the security of his former way of life. Better to keep busy with the old trade than sit around wondering how this disciple business is going to pan out, especially given that threefold denial.

At daybreak, the hour of the cock-crow, Jesus appears on the bank. Despite the endearment 'Children', his question is pointed: 'you have no fish, have you?' The symbolism of the miraculous catch in the wake of a long night with no bites emphasizes the point that these are no longer fishermen, but men who have been given a new commission. Does Peter's impulsiveness (v.7), and the nervousness at breakfast ('no one dared'), further hint at some embarrassment? He has been caught out not following. Again.

Almighty Father,
you have given your only Son to die for our sins
and to rise again for our justification:
grant us so to put away the leaven of malice and wickedness
that we may always serve you
in pureness of living and truth;
through the merits of your Son Jesus Christ our Lord,
who is alive and reigns with you,
in the unity of the Holy Spirit,
one God, now and for ever.

COLLECT

John 21.15-19

'... do you love me?' (vv.15,16,17)

The rehabilitation of Peter is carefully done. On the surface level, Peter's threefold 'I do not know him' is matched with Jesus' threefold 'do you love me?', three being the number of completion. Complete denial must be matched with complete commitment.

Significantly, each time Jesus addresses Peter, he uses his full title, 'Simon son of John'. The only other use of this form is in 1.42 when Jesus names him Cephas. The role of tending sheep, like the name 'rock', will give Peter his particular identity within the Church. The message for Peter is that the motivation for his future ministry must find its origin in love for Christ. Jesus does not say 'Simon, son of John, do you love the sheep?' It is Peter's love for Jesus that will ensure that he perseveres. After all, the sheep are not always very lovable. In all that unfolds, Peter, through love, must be as much a follower of Christ as a leader of the flock. In doing so, he will eventually share a similar fate to the Good Shepherd.

Our motivations for Christian service can become very complex indeed. They are not always easily traced back to love for Jesus – and, for this reason, are worth regular scrutiny.

COLLECT

Almighty Father,
you have given your only Son to die for our sins
and to rise again for our justification:
grant us so to put away the leaven of malice and wickedness
that we may always serve you
in pureness of living and truth;
through the merits of your Son Jesus Christ our Lord,
who is alive and reigns with you,
in the unity of the Holy Spirit,
one God, now and for ever.

Psalms 63, **84** *or* 20, 21, **23**
Deuteronomy 4.32-40
John 21.20-end

John 21.20-end

'Lord, what about him?' (v.21)

On my first evening at theological college, the ordinands gathered
together in the common room to be addressed by the Principal. There
was a lot of looking around and sizing up of one another as we made
our introductions to the group. The Principal welcomed us and gave a
short talk about our training. We were each there, he explained, to
begin formation for the priesthood. We should focus on maturing in
our relationship with God, who had called us, through prayer, study
and the rigours of community living. Nevertheless, he added, very soon
our focus would likely wander. We would become extremely interested
in the formation of other people. We'd have views about what they
were up to and whether they would be good priests – better or worse
than ourselves; indeed, whether they were suitable for ministry at all!
'Do not spend your time looking around others,' he concluded. 'Look
to Christ.'

The question 'what about him?' is one we may be tempted to ask in
a variety of situations. For us, as for Peter, it is a distraction from what
we have been called to do ourselves. The likelihood is that we will
receive a similar reply from Jesus: 'What is that to you? Remember, he
is my disciple, not yours.'

Risen Christ,
for whom no door is locked, no entrance barred:
open the doors of our hearts,
that we may seek the good of others
and walk the joyful road of sacrifice and peace,
to the praise of God the Father.

COLLECT

Monday 9 May

Psalms **96**, 97 *or* 27, **30**
Deuteronomy 5.1-22
Ephesians 1.1-14

Ephesians 1.1-14

'Blessed ... in Christ with every spiritual blessing' (v.3)

Where is your favourite place? Somewhere you feel relaxed, safe and 'away from it all'? Or perhaps somewhere you are invigorated and find excitement and challenge?

As we begin Ephesians, we are immediately drawn into the favourite place of its author. That place is 'in Christ'. After the initial greeting in verses 1-2, we are plunged into a beautiful and complex prayer of blessing, which extends to verse 14. One of its most striking features, lost in translation, is that it is one continuous sentence in Greek. Even divided up, it is rather overwhelming to read, with its effusive and repetitive language encompassing the full sweep of salvation history. We have here a meditation that begins before the creation of the world, rejoices in the redemption gifted to us in the Beloved and anticipates the summation of all things in the fullness of time. In all that is written about predestination, adoption, wisdom and will, we are returned continually to that favourite place 'in Christ', which – with its variant, 'in him' – is used eleven times in this passage. It is in him that we are blessed, elected, redeemed, sealed and gathered up. It is the place of surest repose and ultimate challenge, to which we can always return, wherever we are actually located.

COLLECT

Almighty Father,
who in your great mercy gladdened the disciples
    with the sight of the risen Lord:
give us such knowledge of his presence with us,
that we may be strengthened and sustained by his risen life
and serve you continually in righteousness and truth;
through Jesus Christ your Son our Lord,
who is alive and reigns with you,
in the unity of the Holy Spirit,
one God, now and for ever.

Ephesians 1.15-end

'... a spirit of wisdom and revelation' (v.17)

'Get wisdom; get insight.' This exhortation from Proverbs 4.5 characterizes a book packed full of practical advice. The prayer in today's reading echoes the centrality of wisdom to well-being, but, rather than expounding it through a set of skills to be acquired and pitfalls to be avoided, it is sought as a gift from God. Wisdom, revelation, knowledge and illumination: all forms of understanding are encompassed here, but Paul's prayer is not that the Ephesians should be more intellectually alert or shrewd in their dealings; rather that the eyes of the heart may be enlightened (v.18). It's a strange phrase but very evocative – with the eyes of the heart open, the hope to which God has called us, and the greatness of his power, can readily be seen.

The role of the heart in acquiring wisdom is well testified in Scripture, which claims: 'The fear of the Lord is the beginning of wisdom' (Proverbs 9.10). This is a helpful reminder for those who live in a culture saturated with information. Knowledge of the deep things cannot be verified by that contemporary font of all wisdom, Wikipedia; rather, it is forged in the crucible of Christian discipleship – the application of the mind coupled with the yielding of the heart to God.

Risen Christ,
you filled your disciples with boldness and fresh hope:
strengthen us to proclaim your risen life
and fill us with your peace,
to the glory of God the Father.

COLLECT

Wednesday 11 May

Psalm 105 *or* 34
Deuteronomy 6
Ephesians 2.1-10

Ephesians 2.1-10

'... by grace you have been saved' (v.8)

Ephesians 2.8 has been called the jewel in the crown of the epistle: 'For by grace you have been saved through faith, and this is not your own doing; it is the gift of God.' Its power lies in the threefold emphasis on the initiative of God: by grace, which is to say, not your work, which is to say, God's gift. An unmerited gift is hard to receive, which is why the stark truth of the human condition is set out so forcefully: 'You were dead through ... trespasses and sins' (v.1).

Accepting our absolute dependence on grace is tremendously difficult. It is, fundamentally, a matter of pride. Am I really making no contribution whatsoever to my own salvation?, we wonder. It is almost impossible for us to believe that nothing we do helps God in the redemptive task or makes God love us more, so programmed are we with a works-based mentality. It is a truth that needs to be realized again and again throughout our Christian life. And, when we do come to know it, it is hugely liberating. We can stop beating ourselves up for not being 'good enough' Christians and simply rejoice at the amazing gift God has given us in Christ.

COLLECT

Almighty Father,
who in your great mercy gladdened the disciples
    with the sight of the risen Lord:
give us such knowledge of his presence with us,
that we may be strengthened and sustained by his risen life
and serve you continually in righteousness and truth;
through Jesus Christ your Son our Lord,
who is alive and reigns with you,
in the unity of the Holy Spirit,
one God, now and for ever.

Psalm **136** *or* **37***
Deuteronomy 7.1-11
Ephesians 2.11-end

Ephesians 2.11-end

'In him the whole structure is joined together' (v.21)

Today's reading concludes with a number of construction metaphors. Christ is the master builder. He demolishes an old dividing wall – here between Jew and Gentile, circumcised and uncircumcised – and in its place he builds one temple. Himself he lays as the cornerstone; the prophets and apostles form the foundation, and from the cornerstone the whole building is constructed.

Human beings like to build walls – it makes us feel safe. In modern times, we have rejoiced to see some torn down, but we are just as adept at constructing them. It was little more than a decade between the tearing down of the Berlin Wall in 1989 and the commencement of the Israeli separation barrier in 2002. Even within the Church, it seems to be our natural inclination to construct barriers against those from different Church traditions and with opposing views on biblical or moral principles. Ephesians reminds us that the dividing walls that we establish to help us feel safe and secure against 'the others' are futile. There are no walls within the body of Christ; indeed, we need no walls, for our security is found in him, who loves and values all equally. Let us ask Jesus to show us those walls we need to begin dismantling – and start today.

Risen Christ,
you filled your disciples with boldness and fresh hope:
strengthen us to proclaim your risen life
and fill us with your peace,
to the glory of God the Father.

COLLECT

Ephesians 3.1-13

'... the mystery hidden for ages in God' (v.9)

In common parlance, we are most likely to encounter the word 'mystery' in connection with detective fiction. What makes the murder mysteries of Agatha Christie so enjoyable is the way they engage our minds as we try to guess 'whodunnit' before Poirot summons everyone into the drawing room for the dénouement. The concept of mystery is important to Ephesians: the term occurs six times in the epistle, which is more than in any other New Testament book. However, this is not the type of mystery which can be solved by brainpower as we follow a trail of clues in the wake of some calamity; rather, it is revealed by God through an incredible act of love. The mystery can be found in Christ (v.4), who implements God's secret plan to unite all in his body. For Ephesians, it is an astonishing mystery that Jews and Gentiles are now one in Christ. Unable to be understood by human ingenuity, it has been revealed to the apostles by the Spirit and is now open to everyone to comprehend. 'To you', says Jesus to his uneducated disciples, 'it has been given to know the mysteries of the kingdom of God' (Luke 8.10). This mystery of profound unity with other Christians is ours to wonder at and live out.

COLLECT

Almighty Father,
who in your great mercy gladdened the disciples
    with the sight of the risen Lord:
give us such knowledge of his presence with us,
that we may be strengthened and sustained by his risen life
and serve you continually in righteousness and truth;
through Jesus Christ your Son our Lord,
who is alive and reigns with you,
in the unity of the Holy Spirit,
one God, now and for ever.

Psalms 16, 147.1-12
1 Samuel 2.27-35
Acts 2.37-end

Saturday 14 May

Matthias the Apostle

Acts 2.37-end

'... the promise is for you, for your children, and for all' (v.39)

Aside from that of reluctant preacher Jonah (input: five words, outcome: 120,000 penitents), Peter's speech at Pentecost is the most effective sermon in the Bible. His listeners are, literally, 'stung in the heart'. Peter finishes his speech with the words: 'let the entire house of Israel know with certainty that God has made him both Lord and Messiah, this Jesus whom you crucified'. God's chosen people have rejected God's chosen instrument. This moment of realization is dramatic, as evidenced by the urgency of their question: what should we do? The language of promise used by Peter (2.33,39) gives the hint that all is not lost. God will be faithful to his promise to Abraham, as he has been throughout salvation history. They can be 'saved' as a remnant (v.40), becoming part of God's restored people. All that is needed is for compunction to lead to repentance and baptism.

This narrative of restoration is fitting for the day on which we commemorate St Matthias. His election as a replacement for Judas restored the apostles to their full complement of twelve. It may sometimes seem that, following failure or faithlessness, a wholeness has been lost which cannot be repaired. With God, the 'heart-knower' (1.24), restoration to wholeness is always possible.

COLLECT

Almighty God,
who in the place of the traitor Judas
chose your faithful servant Matthias
to be of the number of the Twelve:
preserve your Church from false apostles
and, by the ministry of faithful pastors and teachers,
keep us steadfast in your truth;
through Jesus Christ your Son our Lord,
who is alive and reigns with you,
in the unity of the Holy Spirit,
one God, now and for ever.

Monday 16 May

Psalm **103** *or* **44**
Deuteronomy 9.1-21
Ephesians 4.1-16

Ephesians 4.1-16

'... grow up in every way into him who is the head' (v.15)

'Oh, grow up!' Many of us have had those words thrown at us at some point in our life – and they can be sobering to hear. Whether justified or not, they challenge us to assess our behaviour: do our words and deeds reveal us to be mature adults? What does it mean to be a real 'grown-up'?

Ephesians now turns itself to this question, addressing, in chapters 4 to 6, matters of practical Christian living. Contemporary approaches to spiritual development can tend towards the individualistic in a 'ten steps to full Christian maturity' manner. This passage shows us that growing up spiritually is anything but individualistic. The qualities mentioned in v.2 – humility, gentleness, patience – are for maintaining the unity of the Spirit. The gifts outlined in v.11 – evangelists, pastors, teachers – are for building up the body of Christ. Maturity itself – the measure of the full stature of Christ – is gained by knowledge of Jesus and coming to the unity of faith (v.13). As we grow up into him, we promote the body's growth (v.16). As the epistle begins this section on Christian behaviour, the definition of maturity could not be clearer. It's not about personal fulfilment; it is about corporate service.

COLLECT

Almighty God,
whose Son Jesus Christ is the resurrection and the life:
raise us, who trust in him,
from the death of sin to the life of righteousness,
that we may seek those things which are above,
where he reigns with you
in the unity of the Holy Spirit,
one God, now and for ever.

Psalms **139** *or* **48**, 52
Deuteronomy 9.23 – 10.5
Ephesians 4.17-end

Ephesians 4.17-end

'... clothe yourselves with the new self' (v.24)

If only assuming a Christian character was as easy as changing clothes – taking off the old set and putting on the new. Of course, old clothes are often very comfortable and new ones a bit stiff and scratchy until we are used to them. Ephesians uses the imagery of changing clothes to remind its readers not to return to the old garment of their former life, with its familiar but futile patterns of behaviour. Rather, they are urged to clothe themselves anew (v.24).

The passage begins by contrasting a life driven by desires which never fully satisfy (lust and greed) with the life they have learned in Christ, characterized by truth, righteousness and holiness. Lest this seems difficult to apply, four different occasions for sin, with their communal ramifications, are addressed. Lying, harbouring anger, stealing and gossiping maliciously are all activities that impair unity and damage the body. Conversely, speaking truthfully and working honestly build it up.

The final list of vices and virtues, a common feature of ethical writing in the ancient world, press home the point: the dark colours of the old garment – bitterness, malice, slander – are no longer suited to those who, through baptism, have been clothed in white (Revelation 3.4-5).

Risen Christ,
faithful shepherd of your Father's sheep:
teach us to hear your voice
and to follow your command,
that all your people may be gathered into one flock,
to the glory of God the Father.

COLLECT

Easter Season

Wednesday 18 May

Psalm **135** *or* **119.57-80**
Deuteronomy 10.12-end
Ephesians 5.1-14

Ephesians 5.1-14

'... now in the Lord you are light' (v.8)

The same Jesus who, speaking of himself, said 'I am the light' says to his followers: 'You are the light in your whole existence, provided you remain faithful to your calling. And since you are that light, you can no longer remain hidden, even if you want to.'

These are words written by Dietrich Bonhoeffer, the German Lutheran pastor who opposed Hitler. Bonhoeffer lived in the darkest of times, and it was his visibility as a beacon to Christ, the one true light, which led to his execution by the Nazis in 1945.

Today's passage is packed with the language of light and darkness. 'Once you were darkness, but now in the Lord you are light. Live as children of light', urges verse 8. Believers are enlightened people: as we are in Christ, so his light is within us. Its fruit is wholly positive and its glare is searing: darkness cannot conceal its fruitless, death-dealing works. The more our lives are given over to Christ, the more incandescent we become. We may not always feel like the greatest of luminaries, but can perhaps take heart from Bonhoeffer's words: it is simply by remaining faithful to our calling that the inevitable will happen. Hiding is impossible when, in Christ, we are the light in our whole existence.

COLLECT

Almighty God,
whose Son Jesus Christ is the resurrection and the life:
raise us, who trust in him,
from the death of sin to the life of righteousness,
that we may seek those things which are above,
where he reigns with you
in the unity of the Holy Spirit,
one God, now and for ever.

Psalms 118 *or* 56, 57 (63*)
Deuteronomy 11.8-end
Ephesians 5.15-end

Ephesians 5.15-end

'Be subject to one another ...' (v.21)

Today's reading introduces the 'Household Code'. As the basic unit of society, good management of the household was important, and such codes were common in the Greco-Roman world, providing advice to the paterfamilias (male head) about how to treat wives, children and slaves.

Such texts clearly reflect the social context of their day: in the same way that the injunction to slaves to obey their masters is now archaic, so the assumption of the inferior status of women reflected in verses 22-33 clearly belongs to an age in which women were considered the property of their husbands. The paterfamilias had absolute power over other members of the family, but Ephesians moderates this, setting the call for wifely submission after a command for both partners to be subject to one another.

Within a Christian household, the paterfamilias may not rule as an absolute dictator; instead there is an element of mutual accountability in Christ. This may seem like a very small redeeming feature of what has been deemed a largely oppressive text, but it was a radical reinterpretation of familial relations. What would it look like to be so radical now?

Risen Christ,
faithful shepherd of your Father's sheep:
teach us to hear your voice
and to follow your command,
that all your people may be gathered into one flock,
to the glory of God the Father.

COLLECT

Friday 20 May

Ephesians 6.1-9

'... masters ... stop threatening them' (v.9)

The final part of the Household Code refers to the relationship between slaves and masters. It's easy to skim over this section feeling that, with the abolition of the slave trade in Britain in 1807, such matters need not concern us. Slavery was one of the more heinous sins of our forefathers, and our enlightened society has rightly eschewed it.

Sadly, however, the story of slavery is far from over. Its modern equivalent – human trafficking for sexual or economic exploitation – is the fastest-growing criminal industry in the world. Today's slave 'sales' take place not in dusty African markets but in bars, basements and airports, where women and young men are sold into prostitution. Traffickers lure their victims by offering new opportunities and financial rewards in Europe and the USA. They are deceived, enslaved and transported across national borders, where they are abused and manipulated. Traumatized and dehumanized, they rarely manage to escape. This is the horrific reality of the slave trade of our day. In the light of this, the words 'Slaves, obey your earthly masters with fear and trembling' (v.5) are truly sickening. Our text should rather be, 'remember them that are in bonds, as bound with them' (Hebrews 13.3) as we work and pray for their liberty.

COLLECT

Almighty God,
whose Son Jesus Christ is the resurrection and the life:
raise us, who trust in him,
from the death of sin to the life of righteousness,
that we may seek those things which are above,
where he reigns with you
in the unity of the Holy Spirit,
one God, now and for ever.

Psalm **34** *or* **68**
Deuteronomy 15.1-18
Ephesians 6.10-end

Ephesians 6.10-end

'... stand against the wiles of the devil' (v.11)

Christians are not often noted for their stunning wardrobe, but in our final reading from Ephesians we are encouraged to don the most spectacular outfit imaginable. Belt, breastplate, shoes, shield, helmet, sword: these are serious clothes with serious accessories for serious warfare. The language is derived from motifs of God the Divine Warrior, who takes up his armour to judge human sin and injustice (Isaiah 11.5, 59.17). However, while the Divine Warrior is an avenging image, in Ephesians the armour is for defensive purposes: for 'standing against', 'withstanding' and 'standing firm' against the forces of darkness (vv.11,13). Christ has already won the victory and is seated above all powers and dominions (1.20ff.). In the strength of God's power, evil can be faced with confidence and courage. Moreover, as John Bunyan reminds us in *Pilgrim's Progress*, when pilgrim Christian meets an evil fiend face to face, he realizes why retreat is not an option: there is no armour provided for the back! Turning round would enable the enemy to shoot his darts into Christian's exposed rear. 'Therefore', concludes Bunyan, 'he resolved to venture and stand his ground.' Sometimes it is helpful to have one's options limited.

Risen Christ,
faithful shepherd of your Father's sheep:
teach us to hear your voice
and to follow your command,
that all your people may be gathered into one flock,
to the glory of God the Father.

COLLECT

1 Peter 1.1-12

'... he has given us a new birth into a living hope' (v.3)

The term 'born again' has rather fallen out of fashion lately. Although it has generally been more heavily associated with charismatic traditions within Christianity, it is a central concept for us all. The opening prayer of this Epistle begins by rejoicing in the new birth God has given us through Christ (v.3). Just as we receive our ethnic identity, citizenship, social class and biological determinants from our parents, so, as Christians, we receive a new identity and citizenship from God. These redefine our relationship with society and mould our character. As humans are born into the physical world, so Christians are born into two things: a hope and an inheritance. Hope is a predominant theme in 1 Peter, and its nature is introduced here: it is living because it has its ground in the ever-living Christ, rather than an animate object or futile delusion. Similarly, the Christian inheritance is characterized by eternal qualities of immortality, purity and beauty: it is untouched by death, unstained by evil and unimpaired by the ravages of time. These are God's gifts to those reborn in his Son. They are not 'privileges of birth', which may result in elitism and a sense of superiority over others. Rather, they are powerful incentives for thanksgiving and holy living.

COLLECT

Almighty God,
who through your only-begotten Son Jesus Christ
have overcome death and opened to us the gate
    of everlasting life:
grant that, as by your grace going before us
    you put into our minds good desires,
so by your continual help
we may bring them to good effect;
through Jesus Christ our risen Lord,
who is alive and reigns with you,
in the unity of the Holy Spirit,
one God, now and for ever.

1 Peter 1.13-end

'You shall be holy, for I am holy' (v.16)

'Gird up the loins of your mind.' This is the literal meaning of the beginning of v.13, which most Bibles will translate with the rather less colourful 'prepare your minds for action'. 'Gird up the loins' is a Semitic idiom which describes the act of tucking up a long robe into a belt so that the legs can move more freely. Commentators suggest the modern equivalent 'roll up your (mental) sleeves', which captures the sense, but not the associations, of the original phrase. The Israelites ate their first Passover with their loins girded, that is, ready to travel (Exodus 12.11). This opening verse therefore begins with a journey image evocative of the Exodus. The journey will require intellectual effort and disciplined living, and the destination is holiness. What is meant by holiness? Simply that believers should conform their thinking and behaviour to God's character. Christian holiness is utterly derivative: 'you shall be holy, as I am holy' (Leviticus 19.2). God's holiness is revealed in Christ, the Holy One who, in love, gives himself for the world. Similarly, Christian holiness is worked out by engaging with the world, not retreating into the safety of a churchy huddle.

Risen Christ,
your wounds declare your love for the world
and the wonder of your risen life:
give us compassion and courage
to risk ourselves for those we serve,
to the glory of God the Father.

COLLECT

Wednesday 25 May

1 Peter 2.1-10

'... let yourselves be built into a spiritual house' (v.5)

Within the Church, we are often encouraged not to focus too much on buildings. 'The Church is more than bricks and mortar', we say; 'it is the people who are important, not the building.' True enough, but in this passage the two conflate: the people are the building – a house made up of different 'living stones', built by God. I often imagine such a structure looking rather like a dry stone wall. If you have ever examined such a wall, you will appreciate what a complex and interesting creation it is. Dry stone walls are constructed without mortar and are held up purely by the interlocking of the stones. The builder uses every size and shape of stone, rock and chock to make the wall, placing each one carefully so that it fits snugly against the others and gives the structure stability. This is the sort of edifice we should allow ourselves be built into. It is the master builder who knows exactly where to put each stone for best effect to make the house strong and secure. If we sometimes feel we have ended up next to a living stone with a rather sharp edge, it is as well to reflect that we may have a similarly shaped one that fits rather neatly against it.

COLLECT

Almighty God,
who through your only-begotten Son Jesus Christ
have overcome death and opened to us the gate
    of everlasting life:
grant that, as by your grace going before us
    you put into our minds good desires,
so by your continual help
we may bring them to good effect;
through Jesus Christ our risen Lord,
who is alive and reigns with you,
in the unity of the Holy Spirit,
one God, now and for ever.

Psalms **57**, 148 *or* **78.1-39***
Deuteronomy 19
1 Peter 2.11-end

1 Peter 2.11-end

'Slaves, accept the authority of your masters with all deference' (v.18)

This must surely be one of the most awkward texts in the New Testament for modern readers. It seems to advocate cowering submission in the face of harsh oppression. How is this good news for anyone?

Within its historical context, we can understand this passage as an encouragement to slaves to interpret their sufferings in the light of Christ's and adopt a similar attitude of forbearance. As a letter written to believers in a particular situation, it instructs them how to live out their faith practically, rather than question the basic givens of society.

Understanding personal suffering in this way can be transformative, especially when there seems to be no escape from the cause. We learn to identify our own afflictions with those of Christ, to empathize with others and to offer them up to God. But such language can also be unhelpfully used to perpetuate abuses of power, with the vulnerable told they must accept damaging situations by submitting to those in authority. Sometimes resistance is right; indeed, it is the vocation of those who, as servants of God, are called to live as free people and to lead others into freedom. The challenge is discerning what we are called to in any given situation.

Risen Christ,
your wounds declare your love for the world
and the wonder of your risen life:
give us compassion and courage
to risk ourselves for those we serve,
to the glory of God the Father.

COLLECT

Friday 27 May

Psalms **138**, 149 *or* **55**
Deuteronomy 21.22 – 22.8
1 Peter 3.1-12

1 Peter 3.1-12

'... so that ... they may be won over without a word' (v.1)

The Christian wife of an unbelieving husband was in a difficult position in Greco-Roman society. Conversion, then as now, was life-changing and resulted in the realignment of personal relationships, with new loyalties emerging. This could be seen as dangerously subversive. A woman was expected to worship the gods of her husband, adopting his social circle rather than fostering her own. To do the latter would contravene the ideal of an orderly home, threatening the family and society. Furthermore, the husband may perceive his wife's worship of Jesus Christ as rebellious, or at the very least find that it caused social embarrassment, resulting in criticism of the way he managed his household.

This is the context the epistle addresses, and the advice is to yield to acceptable social norms for the sake of the gospel. Wives are not to challenge the harmony of the household, nor are they to call attention to themselves by gaudy outward apparel, as did the adherents of pagan cults. Rather, they should focus on cultivating holiness, evangelizing their husbands using inner qualities rather than outward speech or appearance. It is, of course, a far greater challenge, but genuine purity of spirit is deeply attractive – irresistible even – and far more effective than sermonizing.

COLLECT

Almighty God,
who through your only-begotten Son Jesus Christ
have overcome death and opened to us the gate
    of everlasting life:
grant that, as by your grace going before us
    you put into our minds good desires,
so by your continual help
we may bring them to good effect;
through Jesus Christ our risen Lord,
who is alive and reigns with you,
in the unity of the Holy Spirit,
one God, now and for ever.

1 Peter 3.13-end

'... yet do it with gentleness and reverence' (v.16)

To what extent are gentleness and reverence features of contemporary evangelism? Despite the clear command of 1 Peter, some evangelistic enterprises are anything but gentle. The wild-eyed style of the hellfire preacher may be viewed as comic and outdated, but the same content is often present in today's 'missions', where the central message of the gospel is presented as an emotional threat: 'turn or burn'. As a result, the World Council of Churches recently called on Christians to ensure that their evangelism is Christlike rather than domineering in its style and content, promoting peace not division.

For the original audience of this epistle, the advice of this passage was wise and practical. Do good, fear not, and be ready to 'give an account for the hope that is in you', with gentleness and reverence. The way they conducted their lives within a hostile environment was important. Making the best possible impression on outsiders would avoid persecution and draw in converts: there was no question of bullish evangelism. These days, the environments we live in are rarely violently hostile to Christianity, but the guidance remains pertinent. A reasoned defence of the faith, shared respectfully with genuine concern for others, is far more effective than any amount of crusading.

Risen Christ,
your wounds declare your love for the world
and the wonder of your risen life:
give us compassion and courage
to risk ourselves for those we serve,
to the glory of God the Father.

COLLECT

Monday 30 May

Psalms **65**, 67 or **80**, 82
Deuteronomy 26
I Peter 4.1-11

1 Peter 4.1-11

'... be serious and discipline yourselves for the sake of your prayers' (v.7)

I write this morning overlooking Lake Victoria from Bethany House in Entebbe, Uganda. Bethany House is named after the place where Mary and Martha showed Jesus such hospitality, and the hospitality here is glorious. I get to this part of the world whenever I can to bask in the glow of friends' smiles and hear stories of their vital ministries. Of course, I enjoy packed worship services. But I enjoy even more hearing about friends' ministries reconciling former enemies, caring and creating new options for commercial sex workers, planting trees and teaching people to grow and feast on traditional crops. These ministries are also done joyfully as well as prayerfully, and all have at their core the spiritual gift of hospitality, of creating space for new relationships of love and peace.

I think of my friends here whenever I read 1 Peter's admonition to discipline ourselves and 'be serious'. There are serious problems here to confront. But our text defines serious discipline as hospitality and love, speaking and serving as if it were God before us. That's true, after all; our relationships are with people made in God's image. Friends here know that serious problems call for serious and disciplined service – and also that such work is done best with joy. Serious Christianity teaches us how to smile, knowing that in serving one another we recognize God's image and bask in God's presence.

COLLECT

God our redeemer,
you have delivered us from the power of darkness
and brought us into the kingdom of your Son:
grant, that as by his death he has recalled us to life,
so by his continual presence in us he may raise us to eternal joy;
through Jesus Christ your Son our Lord,
who is alive and reigns with you,
in the unity of the Holy Spirit,
one God, now and for ever.

Psalms 85, 150
1 Samuel 2.1-10
Mark 3.31-end

**Visit of the Blessed Virgin Mary
to Elizabeth**

1 Samuel 2.1-10

'... those who were hungry are fat with spoil' (v.5)

This is good news. It's good news for everyone – it's what the world will look like when, as John the Baptist preached in the desert, 'all flesh shall see the salvation of God' (Luke 3.6).

But if we're rich, if we have enough to eat now, how is it good news for us? We're not going to stay on top for ever.

But the news we hear in Hannah's song is better than 'you'll always be on top'. When God is at the centre of our community, things change. The closer we are to the centre, the more likely we are to be pushed out to the margins. Being pushed out doesn't always feel good, and friction often doesn't feel good either. Have you ever watched a load of laundry in a machine with a clear door? All that movement can make you pretty dizzy. It's hard to maintain a sense of equilibrium in there, I'm sure. But, when Christ is truly at the centre, we will be spun around and sent out, and brought in, and sent out. And that's how the transformation happens, the transformation we long for in the deepest part of our being. The proud are humbled, the rich made poor, and the lowly are lifted up and gathered in, and all flesh will see the salvation of our God.

Including us. We all need that transformation, and we all need one another – and we need that agitation that originates with Christ – to see it. We need that more than we need to outrank others.

Mighty God,
by whose grace Elizabeth rejoiced with Mary
and greeted her as the mother of the Lord:
look with favour on your lowly servants
that, with Mary, we may magnify your holy name
and rejoice to acclaim her Son our Saviour,
who is alive and reigns with you,
in the unity of the Holy Spirit,
one God, now and for ever.

COLLECT

1 Peter 5

'Humble yourselves therefore under the mighty hand of God' (v.6)

Benjamin Franklin writes in his autobiography of his plan to master all of the virtues in turn; it was a smashing success until he had mastered all but the last one, humility. Proud as he was at that point of having mastered every other virtue, humility was no longer possible. He was joking, but he has a serious point. True humility is elusive, and part of the reason is that we define it incorrectly. Humility isn't trying to think of yourself as lesser; it involves thinking about yourself less.

Today's reading from 1 Peter makes use of that insight. With its exhortation to humility comes instruction to remain 'steadfast in your faith, for you know that your brothers and sisters throughout the world are undergoing the same kinds of suffering'. When we think of sisters and brothers suffering in other parts of our communities and our world, we're in a spiritually dangerous spot if we think of it as 'we must help those poor people'. When we help 'those people' without addressing the systemic issues that keep us in a position of privilege, we easily succumb to pride while continuing to exacerbate the circumstances that feed pride as well as injustice. 'They' are *we* – and the more we think in 'we' terms, the less 'I' terms will dominate and isolate our souls.

COLLECT

God our redeemer,
you have delivered us from the power of darkness
and brought us into the kingdom of your Son:
grant, that as by his death he has recalled us to life,
so by his continual presence in us he may raise us to eternal joy;
through Jesus Christ your Son our Lord,
who is alive and reigns with you,
in the unity of the Holy Spirit,
one God, now and for ever.

Hebrews 7.[11-25] 26-end

'... he has no need to offer sacrifices day after day' (v.27)

The word 'priest' – in Greek, *hieros* – isn't used of any of Jesus' followers in the New Testament. It is used here, though, of Jesus. The job of 'priests' (*hieroi*) is in the temple, not in the assembly, and their job is largely about shedding blood. First-century Jews believed as much as 21st-century ones that God is gracious and forgiving. They also believed that the primary mechanism through which forgiveness of sin happens is sacrifice. Pharisees taught that love is the sacrifice God most desires (Hosea 6.6) – but, until the Jerusalem temple fell, blood sacrifice still played a key role in the piety of many. Bloodshed indicated forgiveness, as blood shared indicated kinship. That's why men from other cultures practising circumcision still had to be cut to convert to Judaism – a drop of blood shed was enough to declare him a son of Israel.

For Christians, Jesus put an end to that. If blood is shed in war or terror, no blood needs to be shed as a precondition to reconciliation; Jesus' blood is enough. Nor do we need the same blood in our veins to be bound to one another as sister and brother; God has declared Jesus high priest for ever, as we are freed to live in peace as one family. The key 'priest' in our Eucharist is *on* the altar, not in front of it.

COLLECT

Grant, we pray, almighty God,
that as we believe your only-begotten Son
our Lord Jesus Christ
to have ascended into the heavens,
so we in heart and mind may also ascend
and with him continually dwell;
who is alive and reigns with you,
in the unity of the Holy Spirit,
one God, now and for ever.

Galatians 5.13-end

'... but through love become slaves to one another' (v.13)

Paul's language of slavery and freedom has caused a great deal of head-scratching. If we were slaves before, and Christ has redeemed us, then we're free now, right? But, if we're free, how is it that we're slaves to righteousness or, as Paul says in today's reading, slaves to one another? Also, a lot of people do not know that 'Lord' and 'Master' are the same word (*kyrios*) in Greek – when we call Jesus 'Lord', we are in at least one sense accepting status as slaves. Slavery is a great evil, so how can this be good news?

I think the good news that Jesus is Lord becomes clear from what Jesus says – that 'no slave can serve two masters'. A great many people and powers try to claim the title of 'Lord' in our lives. Political rulers, employers, modern-day slavers, and even family members, as well as forces such as greed, fear, individualism, racism and sexism, and countless others, sometimes contend to become masters – and our nature abhors a vacuum in that position. When we can say that the position of 'Lord' in our lives has already been filled, we can tell all other would-be masters of humanity that there's no vacancy for them. That's true freedom – the freedom to serve in a beloved community bearing fruit of the Spirit in all our relationships.

COLLECT

Grant, we pray, almighty God,
that as we believe your only-begotten Son our Lord Jesus Christ
to have ascended into the heavens,
so we in heart and mind may also ascend
and with him continually dwell;
who is alive and reigns with you,
in the unity of the Holy Spirit,
one God, now and for ever.

1 Corinthians 2

*'I decided to know nothing among you except Jesus Christ,
and him crucified' (v.2)*

The wealthiest Christians of Corinth heard not only from Paul but also from other Christian teachers, who found very willing audiences for their message that they (and anyone who followed them) were among the spiritual as well as the social elite, and their superior knowledge freed them from 'worldly' concerns such as making sure that the poor among them were both fed and heard.

So, Paul rather cleverly names the wealthy Corinthians as they'd wish: as the strong, spiritual people with superior knowledge. 'We have the mind of Christ', he writes, and it's easy to imagine the rich and educated nodding along in approval. They'll find themselves in a far less comfortable but far more compassionate position, though, if they come to understand that having the mind of Christ means using power as Christ uses his.

It's all too easy to take pride in being 'right' about the issues of the day. When people agree with us, it strengthens our conviction, and when they oppose us, we can tell ourselves we're being persecuted for our fidelity to the True Gospel. So, when I find myself thinking I'm right about something, I try also to ask myself when I last learned from someone else's perspective on the matter and what it was I learned. I don't know whether that helps me to be right, but it does keep me listening in community.

Risen Christ,
you have raised our human nature to the throne of heaven:
help us to seek and serve you,
that we may join you at the Father's side,
where you reign with the Spirit in glory,
now and for ever.

COLLECT

Monday 6 June

Psalms **93**, 96, 97 *or* **98**, 99, 101
Numbers 27.15-end
I Corinthians 3

1 Corinthians 3

'Do you not know that you are God's temple and that God's Spirit dwells in you?' (v.16)

The Saturday-morning cartoons I grew up with often had an antagonist chasing the hero so intently that he wouldn't notice when the cliff he was on crumbled, leaving him just one self-satisfied fraction of a second before he looked down to see where he was about to plummet.

That's where Paul puts the wealthy Corinthians in today's reading. They want to be thought of as strong. They think this means they can be independent from those whom they consider spiritually inferior. They want to see themselves as high priests – so, Paul shows them what the temple of God's Spirit really is. 'You are', he writes, using the plural form of the pronoun. Even without seeing that in Greek, we might tell that Paul is speaking of us collectively by what comes immediately before and after it in Paul's letter. The context in which Paul says 'you are God's temple' and 'God's Spirit dwells in you' is his criticism of division within the community. Separating oneself and like-minded others from the rest of the Church is, Paul argues, what defiles and destroys God's temple. Just as the spiritually 'strong' are congratulating themselves for having driven out those unspiritual others, Paul announces that the Spirit has, not coincidentally, left the building. Without those 'unspiritual' people, these 'strong' Christians can't escape a long, hard fall.

COLLECT

O God the King of glory,
you have exalted your only Son Jesus Christ
with great triumph to your kingdom in heaven:
we beseech you, leave us not comfortless,
but send your Holy Spirit to strengthen us
and exalt us to the place where our Saviour Christ is gone before,
who is alive and reigns with you,
in the unity of the Holy Spirit,
one God, now and for ever.

Psalms 98, **99**, 100 *or* **106*** (*or* 103)
1 Samuel 10.1-10
1 Corinthians 12.1-13

1 Corinthians 12.1-13

'... in the one Spirit we were all baptized into one body' (v.12)

Years ago, I attended a fellowship for young adults hosted by a wealthy parish that also had a programme feeding homeless people. One evening on my way to the fellowship, I saw outside the church a homeless friend who, like me, was a young adult. I told him about the fellowship meeting and started introducing him around inside. But one of the priests told my friend that he should leave and come back for the morning 'outreach' food. Fortunately, better sense prevailed, and my friend Charles had dinner with the rest of the young adult fellowship in the parish hall.

A lot of congregations have 'outreach' programmes for poor people and 'fellowship' programmes for 'members', the latter sharing greater wealth and status. It's an exceptionally unhelpful distinction. As Paul writes here, God's Spirit showers gifts on *all* people. God gives each of God's children gifts that we need to be Christ's Body, the temple in which the Holy Spirit dwells. For all that that wealthy parish knew, Charles had the gifts to be an excellent Sunday-school teacher or parish-board member. Wise Christians rejoice whenever they can engage God's mission to bring abundant, fruitful life to all – not because fewer of 'those poor people' will miss out what we enjoy, but because all of God's children benefit from each person's gifts used fully.

Risen, ascended Lord,
as we rejoice at your triumph,
fill your Church on earth with power and compassion,
that all who are estranged by sin
may find forgiveness and know your peace,
to the glory of God the Father.

COLLECT

165

Wednesday 8 June

Psalms 2, **29** *or* 110, **111**, 112
1 Kings 19.1-18
Matthew 3.13-end

Matthew 3.13-end

'... it is proper for us in this way to fulfil all righteousness' (v.15)

In the Gospel according to Mark, Jesus is baptized by John without question or explanation. The other Gospel-writers seem to have found this as puzzling as many Christians do today. If Jesus brought us the ultimate revelation of God's character and will, why would Jesus be baptized as the disciple of someone else, even someone as powerful a prophet as John? Matthew deals with it by inserting an explanation from Jesus: that John must baptize him 'to fulfil all righteousness'.

This explanation has been as puzzling to many as the puzzle it was supposed to solve. I find it helpful when wrestling with this text to think more about what 'righteousness' means. The Greek word usually translated as 'righteous' or 'just', namely *dikaios*, can be and perhaps would be clearer to us if translated as 'in right relationship'. Usually in Greek literature, it's used for people following cultural rules about status in how they treat others. But doesn't that just underscore the question of why Jesus would be baptized by John if Jesus is better? Not if you consider a central point of the gospel: that Jesus gives honour to the lowliest. In Jesus' way of life, being baptized by and recognizing John as a teacher is as appropriate as washing the feet of a disciple. It's even more challenging to follow Jesus than to figure him out.

COLLECT

O God the King of glory,
you have exalted your only Son Jesus Christ
with great triumph to your kingdom in heaven:
we beseech you, leave us not comfortless,
but send your Holy Spirit to strengthen us
and exalt us to the place where our Saviour Christ is gone before,
who is alive and reigns with you,
in the unity of the Holy Spirit,
one God, now and for ever.

Psalms **24**, 72 *or* 113, **115**
Ezekiel 11.14-20
Matthew 9.35 – 10.20

Matthew 9.35 – 10.20

'See, I am sending you out like sheep into the midst of wolves' (10.16)

The prospect of leaving behind all I know to work amid some distant, foreign culture is as nerve-wracking to me as it is to anyone else. Somehow, though, it becomes a lot more attractive when things get difficult for me where I am. Sure, I'd find the real thing to be far more difficult than daydreams. But imagine how much more appealing a call far away would be if I were facing arrest and death rather than mere annoyances at home!

So, when I hear Jesus tell the Twelve not to go to Gentiles and Samaritans, I try to keep reading even if my heart stops for a moment. It's true that this is strange to hear from Jesus, who healed the centurion's slave and drank from Samaritan wells. But then I read what circumstances the Twelve faced as they were sent to the house of Israel: arrest and trial, flogging or worse, and, perhaps most painful of all, being hauled off to face them by members of their own families. If I were among the Twelve, I'd start wondering what the climate in Samaria or Spain is like at this time of year. So, Jesus has to counsel the Twelve to face what they are fearing most, knowing that God is with them. Samaria will come soon enough, but all should be invited to the feast – even our most difficult neighbours.

Risen, ascended Lord,
as we rejoice at your triumph,
fill your Church on earth with power and compassion,
that all who are estranged by sin
may find forgiveness and know your peace,
to the glory of God the Father.

COLLECT

Friday 10 June

Psalms **28**, 30 *or* **139**
Ezekiel 36.22-28
Matthew 12.22-32

Matthew 12.22-32

'... if it is by the Spirit of God that I cast out demons, then the kingdom of God has come to you' (v.28)

I can say from experience that the loudest and longest quarrels are often between siblings. It takes contact to produce the friction that can spark an argument, and then it's much easier to keep it going when each person quarrelling thinks the others are so maddeningly close to being right that just a bit more pressure might persuade them.

The Pharisees and Jesus clashed not because they were so far apart, but because they were so close. Jesus agreed with the Pharisees that Isaiah should be read as Scripture, that the Torah was given for everyone's instruction but needed reinterpretation as circumstances change, that God would raise the righteous from the dead, that Israel is called to reach out to and be a blessing for all nations, and that a dinner table could be as holy as anywhere in the temple. A lot of other movements within Judaism disagreed with them on these points. Jesus and the Pharisees also agreed that there are angels and demons in the world, and that demons can be cast out with spiritual power. They're just differing here about *which* spiritual power. And so, theological cousins start calling each other blasphemers and agents of Beelzebub. Perhaps, next time we start to hear such strong language in Church quarrels, we should ask ourselves whom our shouting leaves mute and whether we might instead join together to ask the Holy Spirit to help them – and us.

COLLECT

O God the King of glory,
you have exalted your only Son Jesus Christ
with great triumph to your kingdom in heaven:
we beseech you, leave us not comfortless,
but send your Holy Spirit to strengthen us
and exalt us to the place where our Saviour Christ is gone before,
who is alive and reigns with you,
in the unity of the Holy Spirit,
one God, now and for ever.

Saturday 11 June

Barnabas the Apostle

Acts 4.32-end

'... for as many as owned lands or houses sold them' (v.34)

I hope you're sitting down as you read this, because I have shocking news: it is probable that your Bible is missing a word at the beginning of Acts 4.34. The word is 'for'.

I know this probably doesn't sound like earth-shattering news, but it should affect how we read this passage, and also how we 'test the spirits' to see which are operating in God's Church globally. Acts tells us that Jesus' followers held all things in common and that the apostles testified with great power while grace rested upon the whole community, *FOR* there was not a needy person among them, because whenever there was need, someone with resources would sell them to provide for poorer members. 'Sell your land' may not sound like a great strategy for Church growth, and in one sense it isn't. But today's reading tells us that there is a direct relationship between the power with which we can testify to new life in Christ, the extent to which we can experience true, deep grace, and the readiness with which we see that the resources that we have go to those most in need. St Barnabas, whom we celebrate today, is an icon of that generosity; I pray that the powerful testimony of this 'son of encouragement' (v.36) can encourage us today to end poverty.

Bountiful God, giver of all gifts,
who poured your Spirit upon your servant Barnabas
and gave him grace to encourage others:
help us, by his example,
to be generous in our judgements
and unselfish in our service;
through Jesus Christ your Son our Lord,
who is alive and reigns with you,
in the unity of the Holy Spirit,
one God, now and for ever.

COLLECT

Monday 13 June

Romans 1.1-17

'… I am longing to see you' (v.11)

The letters of Paul can be difficult to read. They can be even more difficult to read out loud – but that can be a good way to help understand them. Paul pours out huge long sentences. The first sentence of this letter is a good example, running on for several lines. Reading a passage from a letter out loud forces us to think about how Paul's ideas join up. It can be an excellent way to work out what he means.

From this opening passage of Romans, we get a sense of why his sentences charge on at such a pace: Paul loves the Roman Christians. He wants to see them face to face, but has often been prevented (v.13). Having them in mind, and wanting to encourage them (vv.11-12), he falls over himself to tell them about Jesus and salvation.

Over the next fortnight, we may sometimes find Paul forbidding – and sometimes hard to understand. Today, we can take two ideas that may help us: first, that reading Paul out loud can help when he is confusing, and second, that however severe Paul might sound, at root his motivation is always one of love.

COLLECT

O Lord, from whom all good things come:
grant to us your humble servants,
that by your holy inspiration
we may think those things that are good,
and by your merciful guiding may perform the same;
through our Lord Jesus Christ,
who is alive and reigns with you,
in the unity of the Holy Spirit,
one God, now and for ever.

Psalms **132**, 133
2 Chronicles 18.1-27
Romans 1.18-end

Tuesday 14 June

Romans 1.18-end

'... the wrath of God is revealed from heaven against all ungodliness' (v.18)

As we saw yesterday, St Paul's thought often traces a long arc. Sentences run on for lines, and ideas for pages. We do well to bear this in mind with the second half of Romans 1, which has become a battleground in one of the most provocative debates in the contemporary Church. Towards the end of a long list that includes the envious, gossips and many more, Paul makes a strongly worded condemnation of 'unnatural' homosexual acts. For some Christians, this poses few problems; it puts others off Paul altogether, as it does many outside the faith.

If we approach this half-chapter thinking about how Paul writes, we recognize that he is in mid-span. His overarching point is that all humanity stands estranged from God. Paul is not singling out one group for unique condemnation. That means his wider argument stands, whether or not we decide that his sense of what is and is not natural stands in need of some modification.

It also means that everyone is in his sights in this chapter. Straight people are not let off, let the conservative remember. But neither are gay people, however much the liberal might demur from Paul's moral assessment.

Finally, taking the long view of Paul's writing shows us that all this judgement is not there for its own sake. With his message of sin, he is preparing the backdrop for a message of grace.

O Lord, from whom all good things come:
grant to us your humble servants,
that by your holy inspiration
we may think those things that are good,
and by your merciful guiding may perform the same;
through our Lord Jesus Christ,
who is alive and reigns with you,
in the unity of the Holy Spirit,
one God, now and for ever.

COLLECT

Romans 2.1-16

'... do you despise the riches?' (v.4)

Romans is a many-layered book. For tidy-minded theologians down the ages, it has been admired for the clarity with which it spells out the central message of the Gospel. Paul has built a solid edifice, with clear lines and strong angles. And yet, as today's reading shows us, that building is covered with some intriguing detail.

Immediately after yesterday's words of judgement comes Paul's condemnation of those who judge. In a letter famous for teaching that salvation is by grace and not by works, we read today that God 'will repay … those doing good' with 'eternal life'. On Friday, we will read a catalogue of evidence for the depravity of humankind; today we read that the Gentiles 'do instinctively what the law requires' and that 'their conflicting thoughts' may 'perhaps excuse them' on the day of judgement.

Details like these make the epistles an endless treasure trove for reflection. They speak anew down the ages and over the course of any particular reader's life. When they frustrate us, we might wish that the apostles had left neater treatises. It is better that they did not. The epistles we have are far less likely ever to go stale.

COLLECT

O Lord, from whom all good things come:
grant to us your humble servants,
that by your holy inspiration
we may think those things that are good,
and by your merciful guiding may perform the same;
through our Lord Jesus Christ,
who is alive and reigns with you,
in the unity of the Holy Spirit,
one God, now and for ever.

Psalms **143**, 146
2 Chronicles 20.1-23
Romans 2.17-end

Romans 2.17-end

'... real circumcision is a matter of the heart' (v.29)

At the end of yesterday's reading, Paul introduced the idea of parity between Jew and Gentile: 'God shows no partiality' (v.11). Today's passage develops this theme. The emphasis is on human beings brought to the same level by sin. There is a parity of fallenness. There are also hints today of a solidarity in doing good, whether that person is taught by the Jewish law or by the promptings of conscience (vv.25-29). In the days to come, we will encounter the truest basis for equality and solidarity: the grace of God, offered to any and all as a free gift.

In Paul's writings, an idea of extraordinary power dawned on the world – a sense of universality that transcends every barrier, whether between Jew and Gentile, Greek and barbarian, man and woman, or slave and free. People of all countries could enter the most truly universal community – the Church.

Almost 2,000 years before globalization, Paul announced the coming of a community that would span the globe and eclipse every human division. The nearest thing to it was Roman citizenship, but, on the other hand, nothing could be more different from Roman citizenship. That was a privilege for the few; in the Church there is a place for anyone, and for all side by side.

O Lord, from whom all good things come:
grant to us your humble servants,
that by your holy inspiration
we may think those things that are good,
and by your merciful guiding may perform the same;
through our Lord Jesus Christ,
who is alive and reigns with you,
in the unity of the Holy Spirit,
one God, now and for ever.

COLLECT

Friday 17 June

Psalms 142, 144
2 Chronicles 22.10 – 23.end
Romans 3.1-20

Romans 3.1-20

'... no human being will be justified in his sight' (v.20)

In our reading today, we find a chain (or 'catena') of verses. They come from different books of the Old Testament and are run together into a continuous passage. It is a favourite way for New Testament authors to provide quotations. Paul uses it to make a powerful point: human beings have no cause for pride or confidence in standing before God.

Paul is not teaching Calvinist 'total depravity'. He is not saying that everyone is as bad as it is conceivable for a person to be. It is enough that no one is as good as they ought to be.

Paul is in mid-sweep of a large argument. Everyone alike depends upon the grace of God, whether Jew or Gentile. He has made this point one way, and he will make it in another. Today his angle is that absolutely no one can make him- or herself righteous before God.

Paul is painting in a background. It is now as dark as he wants it to be. Tomorrow comes the light. Paul has laid our sins before us 'that every mouth may be silenced'. He has our attention. All is quiet. Tomorrow comes the good news.

COLLECT

O Lord, from whom all good things come:
grant to us your humble servants,
that by your holy inspiration
we may think those things that are good,
and by your merciful guiding may perform the same;
through our Lord Jesus Christ,
who is alive and reigns with you,
in the unity of the Holy Spirit,
one God, now and for ever.

Psalm 147
2 Chronicles 24.1-22
Romans 3.21-end

Romans 3.21-end

'... they are now justified by his grace as a gift' (v.24)

Everything we have encountered in Romans so far has been leading up to this moment: the levelling of Jews and Gentiles, the stripping-away of mistaken confidence in our own goodness. With this passage, announced by Paul's 'But now', the light dawns.

Paul has shown us that everyone is on the same level, so that everyone will recognize his or her need. He has stripped us of whatever we might claim as our own, to free our hands to receive the gift God wishes to give us in his grace.

Grace is the centre of Paul's theology. It is the sun around which the other ideas in thought orbit. Grace is the gift of God. We have a useful connection between 'gift' and 'grace' in English: a gift is something gratuitous.

A gift is something that could not be required. It is something over and above what we could expect. There is a 'redemption that is in Christ Jesus' over and above law, works, condemnation or deserving. 'Irrespective of law', and irrespective of our goodness or sin, our merit or demerit, God offers to put things right (to 'justify' us) by his own initiative.

O Lord, from whom all good things come:
grant to us your humble servants,
that by your holy inspiration
we may think those things that are good,
and by your merciful guiding may perform the same;
through our Lord Jesus Christ,
who is alive and reigns with you,
in the unity of the Holy Spirit,
one God, now and for ever.

COLLECT

Monday 20 June

Romans 4.1-12

'Abraham believed God, and it was reckoned to him as righteousness' (v.3)

Paul clinches his argument with a concrete example. For Paul's readers, Abraham was a hero: the man to whom God revealed himself, the man who left idolatry behind and followed the true God.

Abraham is the archetypal righteous person. Yet, as Paul points out, he is commended in Genesis not for his *deeds* but rather for his *faith*: 'And he believed the Lord; and the Lord reckoned it to him as righteousness' (Genesis 15.6).

For Paul, this demonstrates that righteousness does not come from the law. Moses received the law. Abraham came before Moses and therefore before the law. Abraham was righteous before there was a law to be righteous by, because Abraham was righteous by faith.

What part does faith play in this? It would be a mistake to see faith as some human effort. That makes faith our 'work', fusing faith and works together. It is equally mistaken to prise faith and actions apart. By faith we accept the gift God offers, and believing involves all of us – both our minds and our bodies, our actions as well as our thoughts.

Abraham is commended for his faith, but, as we know from Genesis, this faith was a practical matter. Abraham bound his son Isaac and was willing to raise the knife. Before that, he had packed up and left the city of Ur. Faith always involves action.

COLLECT

Almighty and everlasting God,
you have given us your servants grace,
by the confession of a true faith,
to acknowledge the glory of the eternal Trinity
and in the power of the divine majesty to worship the Unity:
keep us steadfast in this faith,
that we may evermore be defended from all adversities;
through Jesus Christ your Son our Lord,
who is alive and reigns with you,
in the unity of the Holy Spirit,
one God, now and for ever.

Psalms **5**, 6 (8)
2 Chronicles 28
Romans 4.13-end

Romans 4.13-end

*'God ... gives life to the dead and calls into existence the things
that do not exist' (v.17)*

Paul looks for images to describe the grace of God. It is like raising the
dead, he says; it is like the creation of the world.

God's grace is more than we could have imagined – is it also more
than we can believe? God gives us what we do not deserve – is that
too good to be true? Paul bolsters our faith by pointing to creation
and the resurrection of Christ.

God is the great giver, and his first and primordial gift is creation.
Through and through, creation is a matter of grace. God did not create
us because we deserved to be created. Before God made the world,
there was no one to deserve anything.

If we want reassurance that God is gracious, we need therefore only
turn to creation. Salvation burst upon the world with all the novelty of
the big bang. It brings us up short, just like Paul's other example – the
resurrection of Christ – overwhelmed the first apostles. That happy
ending to the Easter story was for them a 'sudden and miraculous
grace', to use a wonderful phrase from J. R. R. Tolkien. God's grace is
sure, and yet it should never cease to amaze us.

Holy God,
faithful and unchanging:
enlarge our minds with the knowledge of your truth,
and draw us more deeply into the mystery of your love,
that we may truly worship you,
Father, Son and Holy Spirit,
one God, now and for ever.

Wednesday 22 June

Psalm 119.1-32
2 Chronicles 29.1-19
Romans 5.1-11

Romans 5.1-11

'God proves his love for us in that while we still were sinners Christ died for us' (v.8)

Paul's task in the first few chapters of the Epistle to the Romans has been to strip away every reason for human self-confidence before God: confidence in our own works, in our own goodness, in the power of the law to make us just. Then came his message about the grace of God, and a right standing before him that rests on Christ and is his gift. With that in place, Paul returns to the topic of confidence. He now offers his readers a different sort of confidence before God and before the world. It is as sturdy as their prior self-confidence was flimsy.

Our confidence rests on what God has given us. Since it rests on God and not on ourselves, our confidence can be as secure as the grace of God is lavish.

Where we once had a confidence based on works, we now have a confidence based on faith. That brings us back to the role faith plays. Our confidence is not confidence in the strength of our own faith but confidence in the strength of the one in whom our faith is placed. We may have a confidence based on faith – but it is not confidence in our own faith; it is confidence in the faithfulness of God.

COLLECT

Almighty and everlasting God,
you have given us your servants grace,
by the confession of a true faith,
to acknowledge the glory of the eternal Trinity
and in the power of the divine majesty to worship the Unity:
keep us steadfast in this faith,
that we may evermore be defended from all adversities;
through Jesus Christ your Son our Lord,
who is alive and reigns with you,
in the unity of the Holy Spirit,
one God, now and for ever.

Psalm 147
Deuteronomy 8.2-16
1 Corinthians 10.1-17

Thursday 23 June

Day of Thanksgiving for the Institution of Holy Communion (Corpus Christi)

1 Corinthians 10.1-17

'For they drank from the spiritual rock that followed them, and the rock was Christ' (v.4)

The Israelites drank from a rock and it 'was Christ'. This is one of Paul's more extraordinary statements. His point is to ground all of God's dealings with us in Christ. Whether in the desert thousands of years ago, or in Rome in Paul's own day, or in our own place and time, God's grace comes to us through Christ. Paul has a point to stress: it is all about Jesus.

We are fed by word and sacrament. Today's commemoration of Corpus Christi celebrates that foundational Christian act – the Eucharist – which includes both. All of God's grace comes to us through Christ. This is Paul's point. That is what we should remember as we approach word and sacrament. We can hardly honour the Scriptures too much, so long as we honour them as the place where we meet Christ. Neither can we honour the Eucharistic elements too much, so long as we honour them as the place where we meet Christ.

Upon us, Paul says, 'the ends of the ages have come'. These are apocalyptic words, but we need not fear. In his word and sacrament, Christ's promise is fulfilled: 'And remember, I am with you always, to the end of the age' (Matthew 28.20).

Lord Jesus Christ,
we thank you that in this wonderful sacrament
you have given us the memorial of your passion:
grant us so to reverence the sacred mysteries
of your body and blood
that we may know within ourselves
and show forth in our lives
the fruits of your redemption;
for you are alive and reign with the Father
in the unity of the Holy Spirit,
one God, now and for ever.

COLLECT

179

Friday 24 June

The Birth of John the Baptist

Psalms 50, 149
Ecclesiasticus 48.1-10
or Malachi 3.1-6
Luke 3.1-17

Luke 3.1-17

*'... when Pontius Pilate was governor of Judea,
and Herod was ruler of Galilee' (v.1)*

Our reading holds together two extremes: the specific and the general, the local and the universal, the particular and the all-embracing. It begins with the specific. It situates John the Baptist exactly – we are given a time, a place and a context. The list of civil and religious leaders drives home that our salvation took place in history, at a particular time, and at a particular place. At the other pole, our reading goes on to make a broad, universal claim: 'all flesh shall see the salvation of God' (v.6), just as *every* valley shall be filled and *every* hill shall be made low.

The Christian faith takes in both poles, the particular and the universal. All people can be saved, and the whole cosmos made new, but this happens because of one man, Jesus, and because of what took place in a particular place at a particular time.

Into the setting defined by those listed rulers – almost all of them men with misdeeds recorded in the Gospels – comes John, preaching salvation and the forgiveness of sins. This forgiveness and this salvation are offered to all, but they are offered to each of us individually, and to each of us it falls to respond or to fail to respond. Every time the Gospel is preached, the universal and the particular intersect once again.

COLLECT

Almighty God,
by whose providence your servant John the Baptist
 was wonderfully born,
and sent to prepare the way of your Son our Saviour
by the preaching of repentance:
lead us to repent according to his preaching
and, after his example,
constantly to speak the truth, boldly to rebuke vice,
and patiently to suffer for the truth's sake;
through Jesus Christ your Son our Lord,
who is alive and reigns with you,
in the unity of the Holy Spirit,
one God, now and for ever.

Psalms 20, 21, **23**
2 Chronicles 32.1-22
Romans 6.15-end

Romans 6.15-end

'... you are slaves of the one whom you obey, either of sin, which leads to death, or of obedience, which leads to righteousness' (v.16)

The last two feast days have interrupted our readings from Romans. We have missed one of Paul's great rhetorical questions: shall we carry on sinning so that grace may abound? Now we have a similar question: since we have been delivered from the law, does that make us free to sin?

Paul casts his answer in terms of slavery. Perfect human independence is a myth. We always serve something; we always align ourselves with something bigger than we are. Even the person who cultivates a wilfully erratic outlook for the sake of independence becomes a slave to independence.

Paul invites us to be honest about the dynamics of the moral life. 'Grow up!', Paul is saying, 'snap out of it!' You have to obey someone, so obey the God who loves you – this is Paul's point. Sin was a tyrannous slavery, compared to which the 'servitude' of righteousness is a light yoke: do you really want to go back? Take an honest look at where the two options lead you in the end. All noble motives aside, even the pragmatic weighing of where the ultimate 'advantage' lies will lead us in the right direction.

Almighty and everlasting God,
you have given us your servants grace,
by the confession of a true faith,
to acknowledge the glory of the eternal Trinity
and in the power of the divine majesty to worship the Unity:
keep us steadfast in this faith,
that we may evermore be defended from all adversities;
through Jesus Christ your Son our Lord,
who is alive and reigns with you,
in the unity of the Holy Spirit,
one God, now and for ever.

COLLECT

Monday 27 June

Romans 7.1-6

'But now we are discharged from the law, dead to that which held us captive' (v.6)

Having dealt in chapter 6 with the Christian's freedom from the reign of sin, Paul now turns his attention to freedom from the reign of the law of Moses. If you're left confused by the analogy in verses 1 to 3, be encouraged by the knowledge that you're not alone! What Paul seems to be trying to say is that marriage to the law is never going to result in a happy, fruitful relationship. The law is demanding, faultless and, above all, inflexible. Trying to live up to its demands will result in failure, unhappiness and, ultimately, despair. Imagine waking up each day to a 'to do' list which is not only never-ending but also allows no flexibility, no understanding that you're under the weather that day, no possibilities of creative time-management. If God's blessing depends on us keeping to that list of demands come hell or high water, we may as well give up now.

But marriage to Christ is altogether different. It's a relationship where love reigns. It offers possibilities of spontaneity and flexibility, and a freedom to live creatively within boundaries acknowledged freely and respected as being life-giving in their own right. We do God's will not because an inflexible and demanding set of laws is forcing us to do so, but because we want to please the one who loves us and who has done so much to set us free.

COLLECT

O God,
the strength of all those who put their trust in you,
mercifully accept our prayers
and, because through the weakness of our mortal nature
we can do no good thing without you,
grant us the help of your grace,
that in the keeping of your commandments
we may please you both in will and deed;
through Jesus Christ your Son our Lord,
who is alive and reigns with you,
in the unity of the Holy Spirit,
one God, now and for ever.

182

Psalms 32, **36**
2 Chronicles 34.1-18
Romans 7.7-end

Romans 7.7-end

'I do not do what I want, but I do the very thing I hate' (v.15)

New Testament scholars seem to be in general agreement that if Paul was clear about what he wanted to say in the rest of this chapter, he failed in his attempts to make it clear to the rest of us! Following on from his teaching in yesterday's passage, Paul is quick to point out that he is not for one minute suggesting that the law is sinful in its own right. He may be quite clear about the inadequacies of the law, but he maintains a deep respect for it. The law is good and true in that it helps us to understand God and God's ways. But it all goes wrong when we depend solely on our ability to keep to the rules and regulations in order to receive God's blessing.

Paul then goes on to describe that all-too-familiar dilemma faced by us all. We understand what God wants of us. We know what we *want* to do, what we *ought* to do. But we somehow find ourselves doing the very opposite, and spend much of our time giving ourselves a hearty kick for being such failures at living up to God's standards. Thank God for Jesus. We may still get it wrong. We may still be defeated in many a daily battle. But ultimately, thanks to his death and resurrection, the war is won.

God of truth,
help us to keep your law of love
and to walk in ways of wisdom,
that we may find true life
in Jesus Christ your Son.

COLLECT

183

Wednesday 29 June

Peter the Apostle

Psalms 71, 113
Isaiah 49.1-6
Acts 11.1-18

Acts 11.1-18

'... nothing profane or unclean has ever entered my mouth' (v.8)

Peter was a good Jew. He knew in the very depths of his soul what it meant to be one of God's chosen people. He could recite at length the law of Moses which detailed how the people of Israel were to live, so that their very lives witnessed to their special status in God's eyes. He knew that four-footed animals were profane or unclean, and therefore off limits for a Jew.

And now a voice from God: 'Get up Peter; kill and eat' (v.7). Is God putting him to the test? Is he playing with him, teasing him, like a cat with a mouse? Is God seeing just how strong and faithful Peter can be? Has God remembered Peter's earlier denial of Jesus after all? His reply is robust and indignant. 'By no means, Lord.' No way.

But God isn't testing him. God means what he says. God is about to do something new, and Peter is to lead the way. The old laws, the old rules and regulations, with all their safety and sense of security, are out. Jesus has ushered in a new way of being through his death and resurrection, and Peter is to demonstrate this new life by stepping out and doing what he never thought he would be asked to do.

God is willing to do a new thing. Are we?

COLLECT

Almighty God,
who inspired your apostle Saint Peter
to confess Jesus as Christ and Son of the living God:
build up your Church upon this rock,
that in unity and peace it may proclaim one truth
and follow one Lord, your Son our Saviour Christ,
who is alive and reigns with you,
in the unity of the Holy Spirit,
one God, now and for ever.

Psalm **37***
2 Chronicles 35.1-19
Romans 8.12-17

Romans 8.12-17
'Abba! Father!' (v.15)

Why suddenly insert an Aramaic word in a letter to those who spoke no Aramaic? There must be only one explanation. The word 'Abba' must have become well known and much used in Christian circles. And, like the Hebrew 'Amen', it has stood the test of time, failing to be airbrushed out by the translators' pen.

'Abba' has its roots in the Hebrew word 'Ab', meaning 'father'. It developed into the Aramaic word as a term of affection and endearment, closest in our language to 'daddy'. It was the word Jesus used when he talked with God in the intimacy and agony of the Garden of Gethsemane that first Maundy Thursday. It was not the usual term used in religious circles when addressing God, and so it shows us something of that unique relationship Jesus enjoyed with his Father. The use of 'Abba' by those first Christians shows that they too were now a part of that special relationship. One of the family.

What does it mean to you to be an adopted son or an adopted daughter of God? It is only when we really stop to ponder and let the truth sink in that its significance hits us. Not a slave, but a son. Not a servant, but a daughter. And, in the same way that adopted children so often take on the mannerisms, speech patterns, behaviour and facial expressions of their adoptive parents, in the fullness of time our intimate relationship with our Father should cause others to see in us the likeness of God.

O God,
the strength of all those who put their trust in you,
mercifully accept our prayers
and, because through the weakness of our mortal nature
we can do no good thing without you,
grant us the help of your grace,
that in the keeping of your commandments
we may please you both in will and deed;
through Jesus Christ your Son our Lord,
who is alive and reigns with you,
in the unity of the Holy Spirit,
one God, now and for ever.

COLLECT

Romans 8.18-30

*'We know that all things work together for good for those
who love God' (v.28)*

These last few verses of Chapter 8 are the moment when we step back, having examined individually all the pieces of the jigsaw, to admire and reflect upon the completed picture. 'Change and decay in all around I see' – but, for the Christian, the promise holds fast that God does indeed abide with us, and a glorious inheritance awaits us. No matter how perplexing, how depressing, how confusing everything may seem, for those who love and trust in God, sharing in Christ's death involves sharing in his resurrection. I was once told by a journalist: 'The problem with you Christians is that you want to have your cake and eat it.' Well, yes!

It's as well every now and then to spend an hour or two going back over our lives and tracing their pattern, charting the significant moments, both positive and seemingly negative. It can be quite humbling to realize that things we considered at the time to be disappointments or disasters have turned out to have contained, if not blessings, then something that has shaped our character and brought us to where we are today.

We can't always help what happens to us, but we can always control how we respond. When lightning strikes, do we give in and crumble and accept defeat? Or do we know that, in loving and trusting God, we can find a way forward, knowing that one day we may well look back and see that it was meant to be?

COLLECT

O God,
the strength of all those who put their trust in you,
mercifully accept our prayers
and, because through the weakness of our mortal nature
we can do no good thing without you,
grant us the help of your grace,
that in the keeping of your commandments
we may please you both in will and deed;
through Jesus Christ your Son our Lord,
who is alive and reigns with you,
in the unity of the Holy Spirit,
one God, now and for ever.

Psalms 41, **42**, 43
2 Chronicles 36.11-end
Romans 8.31-end

Romans 8.31-end

*'For I am convinced that neither death, nor life,
nor angels, nor rulers, nor things present, nor things to come,
nor powers, nor height, nor depth, nor anything else in all creation,
will be able to separate us from the love of God in Christ Jesus
our Lord' (vv.38-39)*

Christians can't expect never to have to suffer. It brings us up short to see some who've been churchgoers all their life, stumble and fall at the first big hurdle they encounter. Their prayers to God remain polite and correct. But inside they're seething that God has allowed them to endure pain, be it emotional, mental or physical – and their faith begins to waver.

We're not immune to suffering. But we do know that the final outcome, no matter what happens, will be positive. And that confidence and assurance can give us the strength and hope we need to gather up all our resources and to face head-on whatever life throws at us. This is one of those passages we should commit to memory, to draw upon when lonely or afraid.

Long before it became quite so popular, I put up on the wall of my study the big red wartime poster bearing the slogan: 'Keep calm and carry on.' No matter how bloody the battle, we continue to put one foot in front of another, and walk steadily on, tenaciously confident that *nothing* in all creation can separate us from God's love.

God of truth,
help us to keep your law of love
and to walk in ways of wisdom,
that we may find true life
in Jesus Christ your Son.

COLLECT

Monday 4 July

Thomas the Apostle

Psalms 92, 146
2 Samuel 15.17-21
or Ecclesiasticus 2
John 11.1-16

John 11.1-16

*'Thomas … said to his fellow-disciples,
"Let us also go, that we may die with him"' (v.16)*

In this familiar story, Jesus hears the cries of his good friends Mary and Martha, but waits before moving to help. The raising of Lazarus from the dead will be a significant opportunity to speak of death and resurrection. And Jesus shows once again that he always hears and always acts – but in his own time and in his own way. Our timetable and our 'to do' list doesn't always coincide with his.

Thomas the Apostle plays a significant part in the story. The same Thomas who will always be known as 'the Doubter' is seen here as Thomas 'the Determined'. While the other disciples fret and try to dissuade Jesus from his seemingly foolish plan to return to Judea, Thomas expresses a dogged loyalty. Jesus seems to know what he's doing, even if it doesn't immediately make sense to his followers. Thomas will follow, no matter what the cost.

Following Jesus, even when our own plans seem far more practical and sensible, is shown by Thomas to be the right course of action.

COLLECT

Almighty and eternal God,
who, for the firmer foundation of our faith,
allowed your holy apostle Thomas
    to doubt the resurrection of your Son
till word and sight convinced him:
grant to us, who have not seen, that we also may believe
and so confess Christ as our Lord and our God;
who is alive and reigns with you,
in the unity of the Holy Spirit,
one God, now and for ever.

Psalms **48**, 52
Ezra 3
Romans 9.19-end

Ezra 3

'But many … wept with a loud voice when they saw this house,
though many shouted aloud for joy' (v.12)

The long, long years in exile in Babylonia caused God's people to think long and hard about who and what they were. They had plenty of time to consider their calling, deprived as they were of the outward trappings of temple and territory. And now King Cyrus of Persia has said they can go home. It's comfortable where they are. Why bother to move? Why go through all that upheaval? But some hear God's call, pack their bags and return to their homeland. Their first task is to rebuild 'the temple of the Lord'. And so they make a start.

The building of the foundations for the second temple is a cause for celebration. But, for some, the pain is too great. They remember how things were – the golden age when the first temple represented their hopes and dreams. And so they weep. And the shouts of joy and the cries of anguish blend into each other so that they are indistinguishable (v.13).

Growth means change. New ways of doing things. Listening out for God's direction. There will always be those who are willing to push ahead and do a new thing. There will always be those who mourn and long for what has passed and for how things were. The healthiest community is one where those who mourn are comforted and those who pioneer are encouraged. And where each is prepared to learn from the other.

Lord, you have taught us
that all our doings without love are nothing worth:
send your Holy Spirit
and pour into our hearts that most excellent gift of love,
the true bond of peace and of all virtues,
without which whoever lives is counted dead before you.
Grant this for your only Son Jesus Christ's sake,
who is alive and reigns with you,
in the unity of the Holy Spirit,
one God, now and for ever.

COLLECT

Wednesday 6 July

Psalm 119.57-80
Ezra 4.1-5
Romans 10.1-10

Ezra 4.1-5

*'Then the people of the land discouraged the people of Judah,
and made them afraid to build' (v.4)*

Just when everything seems to be going to plan with the rebuilding of
the temple, the conflict begins. The offer of help seems innocent
enough but is met with harsh rejection. The Judean leaders are aware
that these are their adversaries, and their offer of help is interpreted as
a way of infiltrating their ranks and derailing the building project. The
offer is declined, with the result that local antagonism hardens into
active opposition. The building project is stalled. Nothing much will
happen for the next 16 years.

Anyone who has braved an extension or a reordering of their church
building will find this familiar territory! But opposition to the
construction – not just of physical buildings but of anything related to
the building of God's kingdom – is likely to result in antagonism in the
form of discouragement and subtle sneers – and even intimidation
and threats. If we are confident that what we are doing is in
accordance with God's will, are we brave enough to keep going? Or
is such opposition a good excuse for us to put things on hold and delay
what may feel like a difficult and costly task?

COLLECT

Lord, you have taught us
that all our doings without love are nothing worth:
send your Holy Spirit
and pour into our hearts that most excellent gift of love,
the true bond of peace and of all virtues,
without which whoever lives is counted dead before you.
Grant this for your only Son Jesus Christ's sake,
who is alive and reigns with you,
in the unity of the Holy Spirit,
one God, now and for ever.

Psalms 56, **57** (63*)
Ezra 4.7-end
Romans 10.11-end

Ezra 4.7-end

'… this is a rebellious city, hurtful to kings and provinces' (v.15)

Today's verses refer to a later period but are included here to show that the opposition to the rebuilding of the temple and to the reconstruction of Jerusalem was bitter and sustained. In this episode, the king is encouraged to dig back into the past for evidence of wrong-doing. The opponents slander the Jews and worry the king. Planting the seeds of a potential threat to both his power and his wealth is a clever tactic – certain to make him feel insecure, and guaranteed to work. King Artaxerxes is convinced. He sends an order for the work to be stopped 'until I make a decree' (v.21).

Well, nothing more to be done then. An order from the king is an order from the king, and the work must stop. But some commentators point us to the prophet Haggai for a different take on this episode. Haggai (1.3) tells us that God chided his people for not building his house while spending much time and energy on improving and renovating their own comfortable dwellings. The opposition had worn them down, and they had simply given up. They turned their back on the temple and got on with their own lives.

How often in our own lives do we let procrastination win the day?

Faithful Creator,
whose mercy never fails:
deepen our faithfulness to you
and to your living Word,
Jesus Christ our Lord.

COLLECT

191

Friday 8 July

Psalms 51, 54
Ezra 5
Romans 11.1-12

Ezra 5

'... this work is being done diligently and prospers in their hands' (v.8)

Sixteen years pass. The temple remains unfinished. Enter the prophets Haggai, the straight talker, and Zechariah, the visionary. They stir up the people and remind them of their task. They encourage them to shake off their cynicism and despair over the long-abandoned project, and the work begins anew. But of course, the renewed activity on the building site attracts attention, and the dormant opposition to the building is shaken out of its slumber. The officials are prompted to start asking questions and to report back to King Darius. Memories of 'a great king of Israel' (v.11) are a cause for anxiety and a potential threat to the political stability.

It's interesting to note that it is the activity on the *building* that attracts attention and causes concern. It's the sheer size of the stone, the care with which the timber is laid in the walls and the diligence of the workers that raise the alarm. This is no ordinary building. This is something special – and it demands a response.

So often, our inherited church buildings can feel like a heavy burden with the care, expense and attention they demand. Wouldn't we be better off without them? But our church buildings attract attention. They have been built with the best materials, constructed with great care. They are serious buildings that demand a response. If we keep them open and allow the curious to enter, the walls can speak more loudly than we dare imagine.

COLLECT

Lord, you have taught us
that all our doings without love are nothing worth:
send your Holy Spirit
and pour into our hearts that most excellent gift of love,
the true bond of peace and of all virtues,
without which whoever lives is counted dead before you.
Grant this for your only Son Jesus Christ's sake,
who is alive and reigns with you,
in the unity of the Holy Spirit,
one God, now and for ever.

Psalm **68**
Ezra 6
Romans 11.13-24

Ezra 6

'The people of Israel … celebrated the dedication of this house of God with joy' (v.16)

Today's chapter neatly concludes the first 20 or so years of the return from Exile with the completion of the second temple. Far from bringing the project to a halt, the complaints and concerns of Tattenai the governor serve only to convince King Darius that the temple should be completed – and what's more, Tattenai and his accomplices are to lend a hand, stop interfering and foot the bill. The celebrations to mark the completion of the building are lavish and extensive. God has kept his promise, and the future is looking rosy.

The role of Haggai and Zechariah, the prophets, cannot be underestimated. They held on to the vision for what God had planned. They refused to give in to the apathy and despair that had gripped God's people when, time and time again, their plans were thwarted. They spoke plainly, they doled out encouragement, and they refused to give in until the task was completed.

Sometimes the effort of starting again simply feels too great. The taste of failure lingers and discourages us from stepping back out into the firing line. Much easier to retreat, to dawdle, to opt for an easier life. But, when God calls us to a task, he expects us to complete it. He sends encouragement, if we're prepared to accept it, from the most unlikely of sources. And with completion comes celebration and fulfilment. Procrastination and excuses have no place in the kingdom of God.

Faithful Creator,
whose mercy never fails:
deepen our faithfulness to you
and to your living Word,
Jesus Christ our Lord.

COLLECT

Ezra 7

'For Ezra had set his heart to study the law of the Lord' (v.10)

We jump ahead nearly 60 years, and at last meet the scholar and priest after whom the book is named. Chapter 7 begins with a description of Ezra, the man, and then outlines his commission from the king that sends him to Judah. The five verses of genealogy reassure us of his priestly credentials. In Jewish tradition, Ezra's importance is such that he came to be seen as a second Moses.

What was it about Ezra that made him great? Perhaps it was that he committed himself enthusiastically – heart, mind and soul – to God. He studied the Scriptures and committed them to heart; he lived out what he had gleaned from God's Word, and then he taught others what he himself had learned. The Old Testament scholar Derek Kidner comments that, with study, conduct and teaching put in the correct order in this way, each could function properly at its best: 'Study was saved from unreality, conduct from uncertainty, and teaching from insincerity and shallowness' (*Ezra and Nehemiah,* Inter-Varsity Press, 1979).

The stage, then, is set for Ezra to lead an expedition of Jews from Babylon to Jerusalem. It is not enough for God's people to worship in a shiny new temple. They must also understand how it is that God wants them to live.

COLLECT

Almighty God,
you have broken the tyranny of sin
and have sent the Spirit of your Son into our hearts
    whereby we call you Father:
give us grace to dedicate our freedom to your service,
that we and all creation may be brought
    to the glorious liberty of the children of God;
through Jesus Christ your Son our Lord,
who is alive and reigns with you,
in the unity of the Holy Spirit,
one God, now and for ever.

Psalm **73**
Ezra 8.15-end
Romans 12.1-8

Ezra 8.15-end

'The total was counted and weighed, and the weight of everything was recorded' (v.34)

It would seem that around 5,000 men, women and children followed Ezra from Babylonia to Jerusalem – a journey of about 800 miles. The journey would have been hazardous, not least because of all the precious metals they were carrying – but Ezra refuses the offer of royal protection, preferring instead to put his trust in God's care for his pilgrim people. Four months later, they arrive safely in Jerusalem and set about offering sacrifices to God in thanks for a different kind of royal protection.

Ezra may have refused a military escort, but he made sure that structures were in place and lines of accountability were organized so that the precious metals would arrive in Jerusalem intact. Everything was counted and weighed at the beginning of the journey. Everything was counted and weighed again at the end. Ezra was not blind to the temptations that entice frail human beings, and they were left in little doubt that any theft would be noticed.

Trust in God doesn't mean blind trust. Trusting in God doesn't mean being naive when it comes to day-to-day living. Ezra would have fully understood Jesus' requirement of his followers to be 'wise as serpents and innocent as doves' (Matthew 10.16).

God our saviour,
look on this wounded world
in pity and in power;
hold us fast to your promises of peace
won for us by your Son,
our Saviour Jesus Christ.

COLLECT

195

Wednesday 13 July

Ezra 9

*'O my God, I am too ashamed and embarrassed to lift my face
to you' (v.6)*

To our modern ears, chapter 9 sounds strange. But in Ezra's day, intermarriage was strictly forbidden, following the teaching of the Book of Deuteronomy (7.1-4). It was said to be wrong because it was felt that foreign husbands and wives would cause a distraction and dilute the faith handed down from generation to generation. To Ezra's ears, the news that the priests and the Levites, the leaders and the rulers, have also sinned in this way is truly horrifying. He sits in a state of shock and mourns the backsliding of God's people. After a period of fasting, Ezra offers a lengthy and heartfelt prayer of confession.

'Twas ever thus. God delights in giving us good things. God goes before us in our journey through life. God provides for us and shows us the best way to live. And we throw it back in his face. We think we know best. And then we wonder why when it all goes wrong. As Christians, we know the power of God's forgiveness through Jesus' death and resurrection. But that doesn't mean that we should treat confession lightly. How often do we actually physically fast? How often do we take time truly to examine our consciousnesses rather than skipping lightly and thoughtlessly through the words of the general confession? Do we take God's forgiveness for granted?

COLLECT

Almighty God,
you have broken the tyranny of sin
and have sent the Spirit of your Son into our hearts
    whereby we call you Father:
give us grace to dedicate our freedom to your service,
that we and all creation may be brought
    to the glorious liberty of the children of God;
through Jesus Christ your Son our Lord,
who is alive and reigns with you,
in the unity of the Holy Spirit,
one God, now and for ever.

Ezra 10.1-17

*'... let us make a covenant with our God to send away all these
wives and their children' (v.3)*

This passage offends us at so many levels. The people had done
wrong, no doubt about that. But was breaking up all those families –
divorcing all those wives, making fatherless all those children – really
the best way forward? We know that God – and humankind – finds
divorce extremely difficult. Would God really want his people to go to
such extremes to prove their sorrow at disobeying him? Which would
God hate most – the original sin or the attempts to put things right?

The cost of human sin and failure is not inconsequential. The ultimate
cost was paid on the cross by God's own son. Maybe this passage can
do little more than remind us of the price that was paid to put us right
with God. Maybe we will bring it to mind when tempted to do
something that we know goes against God's plans for us. Perhaps it
can remind us that, although God's forgiveness is assured when we are
truly sorry, the consequences of our actions may take longer to heal.
Restoration, though entirely possible, can be both costly and painful.

On this difficult and sombre note, we take leave of Ezra and wait for
Nehemiah to take up the story.

God our saviour,
look on this wounded world
in pity and in power;
hold us fast to your promises of peace
won for us by your Son,
our Saviour Jesus Christ.

COLLECT

Friday 15 July

Psalm **55**
Nehemiah 1
Romans 13.8-end

Nehemiah 1

'I sat down and wept, and mourned for days, fasting and praying'
(v.4)

Ezra has taken us through the physical restoration of the temple to a sombre attempt at spiritual restoration. Now the first seven chapters of Nehemiah take us back to more physical restoration – this time of Jerusalem's city wall. The name Nehemiah means 'the Lord comforts' – and Nehemiah finds himself moved to go to Jerusalem to bring comfort and support to downtrodden Jews living in Judah at a time thought to be around 13 years since we last heard from Ezra. Nehemiah is not a priest like Ezra, nor is he a prophet in the usual sense. As cupbearer to the king (v.11), Nehemiah is a dedicated layperson who hears God's call and obeys.

Faced with the reports of the distress of the Jews in Jerusalem, Nehemiah first and foremost prays. For days. The temptation must surely have been to get on with creating and executing an action plan. He'd need a strategy, a schedule, a budget, a 'to do' list, so that he could have the satisfaction of ticking off each task as it was completed. But no, he prays. He lays the problems before God, and he asks God what God wants to happen. He brings to mind God's past actions. He makes his confession. He prays with others. He asks for God's help. Only then does he swing into action.

COLLECT

Almighty God,
you have broken the tyranny of sin
and have sent the Spirit of your Son into our hearts
     whereby we call you Father:
give us grace to dedicate our freedom to your service,
that we and all creation may be brought
     to the glorious liberty of the children of God;
through Jesus Christ your Son our Lord,
who is alive and reigns with you,
in the unity of the Holy Spirit,
one God, now and for ever.

Psalms **76**, 79
Nehemiah 2
Romans 14.1-12

Nehemiah 2

'Why is your face sad, since you are not sick? This can only be sadness of the heart' (v.2)

Since hearing the news of the plight of the Jews in Jerusalem, Nehemiah has been praying and pondering, and eventually – inevitably – the strain begins to show on his face. As he goes about his daily work as cupbearer, the king – possibly prompted by the queen, who, we're told, is sitting beside him at the time (v.6) – asks him what's wrong. The stage is set for Nehemiah to unveil his vision for Jerusalem. He takes a deep breath and tells the king of his hopes and plans. And, to his immense relief, the king listens, understands, and writes the necessary letters.

The king notices Nehemiah's distress because it is unusual for his cupbearer to be downbeat in his presence. Nehemiah is not a whinger. He doesn't continually moan and groan. He is usually one of life's 'radiators' rather than one of those dreary 'drains' whose company we'd prefer to avoid. And so, when he has a genuine anxiety, the king notices and is prepared to listen.

We all know those who complain so often that, in the end, we're left with little choice other than to ignore them. How much better to work on being one of those who try to see the positive side, who look for solutions instead of problems. In that way, when things genuinely get tough, those around us will sit up and listen.

God our saviour,
look on this wounded world
in pity and in power;
hold us fast to your promises of peace
won for us by your Son,
our Saviour Jesus Christ.

COLLECT

Monday 18 July

Nehemiah 4

'... turn their taunt back on their own heads' (v.4)

There's one thing to be said for Nehemiah's prayer: it's honest. Just when everything seems to be going well, Sanballat and Tobiah the Ammonite turn up, like bad pennies, and launch into a verbal attack, hoping to discourage the Jews, by their taunts and ridicule, from building the wall. The wall clearly is a threat, and the two men do what most people do when they're feeling threatened. They attack.

Nehemiah is undaunted. Instead of wasting precious energy getting into useless arguments with his enemies, he pours out his heart to God. The actual words may cause us to feel uncomfortable, but we can learn much from this prayer, which has echoes in some of the psalms. Nehemiah's prayer is angry, indignant and, above all, real. His relationship with God is a confident one, built up over many years of constant contact through all life's ups and downs. He has no need to use polite phrases to God, as one would to a distant acquaintance. He tells it as it is, knowing that God will hear and understand. And, having got it all out of his system, and knowing that – despite what his enemies might say – he is doing what God wants him to do, he gets on with it.

'So we rebuilt the wall' (v.6).

COLLECT

O God, the protector of all who trust in you,
without whom nothing is strong, nothing is holy:
increase and multiply upon us your mercy;
that with you as our ruler and guide
we may so pass through things temporal
that we lose not our hold on things eternal;
grant this, heavenly Father,
for our Lord Jesus Christ's sake,
who is alive and reigns with you,
in the unity of the Holy Spirit,
one God, now and for ever.

Psalms 87, **89.1-18**
Nehemiah 5
Romans 15.1-13

Nehemiah 5

'.. there was a great outcry of the people and of their wives against their Jewish kin' (v.1)

'It's all very well putting all our resources into building a wall, but we can't eat a wall' is the gist of the complaint. Having dealt with those from outside who would derail the project if they could, Nehemiah now has to turn his attention to the internal squabbling and grumbling. Hunger and exploitation are causing a greater threat than that posed to the wall. This time, the structure of the very community itself is at risk. Success is once again followed by the threat of attack. Building God's kingdom can involve us in a subtle war.

Nehemiah's strategy for dealing with the complainants has much to teach us. The most effective leaders are those who make the time to *listen*, and who listen openly and seriously to complaints. Effective leaders don't react immediately, pinging off angry e-mails in response. They take time to *think* things through. Effective leaders *confront* the problem directly and speak to the actual people concerned. And effective leaders are willing to be *open* about their own mistakes. They are willing to say 'I was wrong'.

How does your leadership style, be it at home or at work, measure up?

Gracious Father,
by the obedience of Jesus
you brought salvation to our wayward world:
draw us into harmony with your will,
that we may find all things restored in him,
our Saviour Jesus Christ.

COLLECT

Nehemiah 6.1 – 7.4

'I am doing a great work and I cannot come down' (v.3)

And just when he thought things couldn't get any worse … Nehemiah has dealt forcefully with those who would threaten the rebuilding of the walls. He has dealt fairly with those who would threaten the stability of the community. And now his enemies turn on him. The attacks become personal. Intimidation, threats, a hostile open letter, even potential threats to Nehemiah's safety – all are deployed to try to throw him off course and make him give up his task. All fail.

Some of us may face such openly hostile threats in attempts to try to make us give up on what we know God wants us to do. Others of us may instead be seduced by flattery and encouraged to take on more than we can properly manage, so that our effectiveness is diluted and our attention distracted. Nehemiah reminds us that staying effective and focused may also involve saying 'no' (v.3). He also models a courageous way of dealing with personal attacks when those attacks contain no truth. He issues a simple rebuttal and then gets on with his task. Not for Nehemiah any slanging match or squandering precious energy on excuses, counter-attacks and elaborate denials. He trusts that the truth with eventually prevail. And so the wall was built.

COLLECT

O God, the protector of all who trust in you,
without whom nothing is strong, nothing is holy:
increase and multiply upon us your mercy;
that with you as our ruler and guide
we may so pass through things temporal
that we lose not our hold on things eternal;
grant this, heavenly Father,
for our Lord Jesus Christ's sake,
who is alive and reigns with you,
in the unity of the Holy Spirit,
one God, now and for ever.

Psalms 90, **92**
Nehemiah 7.73b – 8.end
Romans 15.22-end

Nehemiah 7.73b – 8.end

*'... all the people gathered together into the square before the
Water Gate' (8.1)*

The wall is built, the gates are finally in place – and, after such a long
silence, Ezra returns on the scene. Nehemiah has dealt with rebuilding
the physical wall. Ezra will deal with rebuilding a spiritual people. His
first task is to read 'the book of the law of Moses' out loud to the
assembled throng, which he does for about six hours. The people
interject with the occasional 'Amen' as they listen with enthusiasm
and wholeness of heart. And we complain when the sermon lasts
more than ten minutes!

The Levites work hard to explain the passages read by Ezra. The people
are not left to listen dutifully and then to carry on with their lives
unaffected. They are encouraged to interact with the Scriptures, to
engage with them fully and to apply what they learn to their daily
living. Furthermore, this reading and teaching takes place not in the
temple court but at one of the focal points of city life.

What can we do to ensure that Scripture is taken seriously? How do
we encourage one another to engage with the texts at whatever level
is most appropriate for us, and apply its teaching to our daily lives?
And how can we best use modern means of communication to ensure
that the message of the Gospel is heard in memorable and everyday
language?

Gracious Father,
by the obedience of Jesus
you brought salvation to our wayward world:
draw us into harmony with your will,
that we may find all things restored in him,
our Saviour Jesus Christ.

COLLECT

Friday 22 July

Mary Magdalene

Luke 8.1-3

'The Twelve were with him, as well as some women who had been cured of evil spirits and infirmities' (vv.1-2)

These women – the ones who had been 'cured of evil spirits' – what are they doing on the road? Shouldn't they be at home? In fact, don't they have a *duty* to be at home, where they have a well-defined role, instead of wandering along with an itinerant preacher and a motley bunch of disciples?

You can imagine the gossiping, the tittle-tattle, the finger-pointing and the head-wagging that accompanied Mary Magdalene and her sisters on their travels. But they were undeterred. They tagged along behind the disciples, and, when the disciples fell away, they stood at the foot of the cross, prepared themselves to anoint Jesus' body for burial, and witnessed the resurrection.

That's what can happen when we catch a glimpse of God and his purpose for our lives. We can be asked to go where we'd never expected to go; do what we'd never expect to do. We may be asked to put up with the disapproval of those who'd prefer us to be a little more conventional.

But, after all, only dead fish go with the flow.

COLLECT

Almighty God,
whose Son restored Mary Magdalene to health of mind and body
and called her to be a witness to his resurrection:
forgive our sins and heal us by your grace,
that we may serve you in the power of his risen life;
who is alive and reigns with you,
in the unity of the Holy Spirit,
one God, now and for ever.

Nehemiah 9.24-end

'... you have dealt faithfully and we have acted wickedly' (v.33)

We missed the first half of chapter 9 in order to celebrate Mary Magdalene, and so today we come back to Nehemiah halfway through an elaborate recounting of biblical history going right back to God's creative beginnings. The people have gathered together to make their confession. They have fasted. They wear sackcloth. They are serious about putting things right with God. They recount openly the ways in which they have failed God. But they tell too of God's redeeming ways and amazing grace.

In a similar way, when we gather for Holy Communion, we recount God's saving actions. We make present for ourselves in the here and now what Jesus did for us that first Easter. We remember and rejoice in God's unconditional love, and we go out prepared to live new lives, cleansed, restored and forgiven.

How seriously do we prepare to receive Holy Communion? Do we turn up at the last minute, and mumble our way through the confession, barely registering the words of absolution? Or do we take seriously the need to examine our lives on a regular basis, arriving prepared to confess our shortcomings? Perhaps only then will we fully appreciate what God has done for us through his Son.

O God, the protector of all who trust in you,
without whom nothing is strong, nothing is holy:
increase and multiply upon us your mercy;
that with you as our ruler and guide
we may so pass through things temporal
that we lose not our hold on things eternal;
grant this, heavenly Father,
for our Lord Jesus Christ's sake,
who is alive and reigns with you,
in the unity of the Holy Spirit,
one God, now and for ever.

COLLECT

Monday 25 July

James the Apostle

Psalms 7, 29, 117
2 Kings 1.9-15
Luke 9.46-56

Luke 9.46-56

'... they said, "Lord, do you want us to command fire to come down from heaven and consume them?" ' (v.54)

A little over a year ago, I was working at a music store where most of my colleagues were young men with little knowledge of Christianity. In their experience, Christians were people who liked to yell about how bad everyone else was. When they got the impression that the Christians had shifted their attention from yelling at non-Christians to fighting among themselves, they were puzzled but relieved to have escaped their attention.

Perhaps my music colleagues had met James and John on one of their worse days. 'Sons of thunder', Jesus called them, and we can see why in today's reading. They're really good with the rebuking and are eager to watch a good heavenly smiting. Jesus – not so much. Even today, there are a lot of 'sons of thunder' about who await the day Jesus stops the difficult, painful and sometimes seriously annoying work of reconciliation and instead lets loose as 'the Christinator', a fearsome and unstoppable machine of retribution against the wicked. They've got disappointment ahead of them.

If we want to see Jesus, we need to go to the least and learn from them. Those who know Jesus best see the world through their eyes. When you know poverty and oppression, it isn't hard to tell who is with you; it's the people who work and walk alongside you, sharing your pain and knowing your hope.

COLLECT

Merciful God,
whose holy apostle Saint James,
leaving his father and all that he had,
was obedient to the calling of your Son Jesus Christ
and followed him even to death:
help us, forsaking the false attractions of the world,
to be ready at all times to answer your call without delay;
through Jesus Christ your Son our Lord,
who is alive and reigns with you,
in the unity of the Holy Spirit,
one God, now and for ever.

Psalm **106*** (*or* 103)
Nehemiah 13.1-14
2 Corinthians 1.15 – 2.4

Nehemiah 13.1-14

'... it was found written that no Ammonite or Moabite should ever enter the assembly of God' (v.1)

In today's reading, the gathered Israelites read from the law, and 'it was found' that foreigners should not enter the assembly. How was it found? We don't know. We're told that it's because they met the Israelites with a curse instead of with bread and water, but we're not told anything about how this relates to the Torah. Similarly, we are told that when the people heard from the law, they separated from Israel all those of foreign descent (v.3), casting out foreign wives and the children they had with those women.

Somehow, I don't think Jesus had this in mind when he said that of those who had left 'mother or children … will receive a hundredfold' (Matthew 19.29). What of those women and children left with nothing because their husbands and fathers feared that their own conscience was not strong enough to withstand any negative influence? For that matter, what about the numerous instances in which the Torah commands Israel not to mistreat foreigners, as the Israelites themselves were foreigners in Egypt?

Almighty and everlasting God,
by whose Spirit the whole body of the Church
is governed and sanctified:
hear our prayer which we offer for all your faithful people,
that in their vocation and ministry
they may serve you in holiness and truth
to the glory of your name;
through our Lord and Saviour Jesus Christ,
who is alive and reigns with you,
in the unity of the Holy Spirit,
one God, now and for ever.

COLLECT

Wednesday 27 July

Psalms 110, 111, 112
Nehemiah 13.15-end
2 Corinthians 2.5-end

Nehemiah 13.15-end

'Shall we then listen to you ...?' (v.27)

Nehemiah goes for an interesting form of law enforcement: when people went against his edict, he 'contended with them and cursed them and beat some of them and pulled out their hair' (v.25). The hair-pulling is a strike against the offender's honour; Nehemiah takes their non-compliance with his reading as a swipe at his own authority as a governor and a man.

He does at least seem to soften his earlier directives for men to cast aside their foreign wives and children from those marriages, now only instructing those who have not already married to vow that they will marry Israelites. But he's treading in very dangerous spiritual territory when he identifies his wishes with God's wishes and his reading of the Torah with the Torah itself. We would do well to take sabbath-keeping seriously, as Nehemiah counsels and the Torah instructs repeatedly, including in the Ten Commandments. But Nehemiah's way of honouring that commandment involves sending Levites to work on the sabbath to make sure that others don't.

It's worth seeking counsel and pausing for prayerful and thoughtful reconsideration, in my opinion, whenever I find myself thinking that the problems of the world would be solved if only everyone else was more like me. Nehemiah's desire to preserve his people's language and culture, distinct among the nations, is commendable. His unwavering belief that he knew the mind of God and would please God most by punishing those who didn't is less helpful.

COLLECT

Almighty and everlasting God,
by whose Spirit the whole body of the Church
    is governed and sanctified:
hear our prayer which we offer for all your faithful people,
that in their vocation and ministry
they may serve you in holiness and truth
to the glory of your name;
through our Lord and Saviour Jesus Christ,
who is alive and reigns with you,
in the unity of the Holy Spirit,
one God, now and for ever.

Psalms 113, 115
Esther 1
2 Corinthians 3

Esther 1

'... every man should be master in his own house' (v.22)

Women should be available for display at male command, and otherwise should remain invisibly at the ready. This is the message that pleased 'the king and his [male] officials' (v.21), and the decree that King Ahasuerus sent out to that effect, meant to declare clearly and unalterably that this is what it means to give honour to authority, and that authority over all women, 'high and low', belongs to men. Men can be rather silly in that regard – and, for that matter, so can women.

As we shall see in this story, when people make grand declarations such as this, God has other plans. In this story, Esther will claim her authority and use it to far greater effect than the king used his. And her authority does not come from being prettier than the queen she replaced, or because she had powerful men or long-standing tradition behind her; it comes from God. You can tell that because of how she uses it: to benefit others, not herself, and not to consolidate or increase her position, but at great personal risk. She might have lost not only the privilege she held as queen, but also her life. The king and his advisers find out what decrees and courtly standing amount to, and it's nothing compared to Esther's unprecedented, unwarranted and even unwanted voice.

Almighty God,
send down upon your Church
the riches of your Spirit,
and kindle in all who minister the gospel
your countless gifts of grace;
through Jesus Christ our Lord.

COLLECT

Friday 29 July

Psalm **139**
Esther 2
2 Corinthians 4

Esther 2

*'Now Esther had not revealed her kindred or her people,
as Mordecai had charged her' (v.20)*

In this chapter, we begin to see in outline what and whom the pontificators of the previous chapter want to render invisible. Esther is seen only to the extent to which she does what others wish; she obeys the king's word, does as the eunuch in charge of the harem prescribes, and obeys Mordecai's charge to keep her ethnicity and her identity secret. As one outside the gates, Mordecai is positioned to hear the plots of other outsiders, but even as an informant he seems to remain invisible. When he hears of a plot against the king, he tells Esther, who reports it 'in Mordecai's name', but the king seems surprised when he later reads that it was Mordecai who had saved him.

Why did Mordecai charge Esther not to reveal her identity as a Jew or his identity as her adoptive father? Would a courtier to the king have proposed wiping out Mordecai's people had he known that his enemy was the queen's kin as well as the king's protector? The text is silent. Fortunately, Esther and Mordecai will not co-operate with mandates of silence and invisibility for ever. But what kinds of silence and invisibility do we foist upon others or collude in by our action or inaction – and what deadly consequences can result from them?

COLLECT

Almighty and everlasting God,
by whose Spirit the whole body of the Church
　　is governed and sanctified:
hear our prayer which we offer for all your faithful people,
that in their vocation and ministry
they may serve you in holiness and truth
to the glory of your name;
through our Lord and Saviour Jesus Christ,
who is alive and reigns with you,
in the unity of the Holy Spirit,
one God, now and for ever.

Psalms 120, **121**, 122
Esther 3
2 Corinthians 5

Saturday 30 July

Esther 3

'There is a certain people ...' (v.8)

Here the plots thicken, only this time they are against the whole Jewish people, not against one man, the king. To be sure, it is one man – namely, Mordecai – who angers Haman, but Haman's response goes beyond personal vengeance to government-funded genocide. In the light of more recent genocides, such as the hundred days in Rwanda following the shooting-down of its president's aeroplane in 1994, one cannot help but wonder whether the recently exposed plot against the king helped to foment a climate of suspicion and fear conducive to the mass murder that Haman proposes and the king approves.

Ironically, Haman's proposal to annihilate Mordecai's people may have found a more willing accomplice in the king specifically because of the plot that Mordecai foiled. And even as they are targeted for destruction, the Jews remain invisible, named as Jews by the narrator but named only as a different, disobedient and therefore dangerous people by Haman in his petition to the king. Did Mordecai spark an attempted genocide by refusing to bow to Haman? I think a better case can be made that equating diversity with danger and insisting that minorities remain silent and invisible began the spiral of violence to follow.

Almighty God,
send down upon your Church
the riches of your Spirit,
and kindle in all who minister the gospel
your countless gifts of grace;
through Jesus Christ our Lord.

COLLECT

Monday 1 August

Psalms 123, 124, 125, **126**
Esther 4
2 Corinthians 6.1 – 7.1

Esther 4

'Perhaps you have come to royal dignity for just such a time as this' (v.14)

At the end of chapter 3, the king sits with Haman to drink in their citadel as the city around them starts to burn. The crisis will finally force an end to silence, but first Mordecai has a decision to make. Amid his people's tears and ashes, will he continue to charge Esther with secrecy, hoping that she will be seen only as the queen? Or will he encourage Esther to speak for her people and assume the risks of making her ethnic difference visible? He chooses the latter, recognizing that continued secrecy would mean death for her and her 'father's family'.

The text remains silent as to whether anything remains of her 'father's family' beyond Mordecai; if Esther has further kin, they are nameless in this story. And perhaps most interestingly, Mordecai's report of the situation could be read as ambiguous about the source of the threat that Esther now faces. He says that someone else will help the Jews if Esther does not. Are her own people and/or their rescuers the ones whom Mordecai sees as the danger to Esther?

In any case, if Esther maintains the silence expected of her as a woman and the invisibility imposed upon her as a Jew, she and others will die. Arguably, though, that silence and invisibility, however brightly crowned by earthly powers, had already been a kind of death for her and her family.

COLLECT

Merciful God,
you have prepared for those who love you
such good things as pass our understanding:
pour into our hearts such love toward you
that we, loving you in all things and above all things,
may obtain your promises,
which exceed all that we can desire;
through Jesus Christ your Son our Lord,
who is alive and reigns with you,
in the unity of the Holy Spirit,
one God, now and for ever.

Psalms **132**, 133
Esther 5
2 Corinthians 7.2-end

Esther 5

'... all this does me no good so long as I see the Jew Mordecai sitting at the king's gate' (v.15)

Survey after survey shows that most people in the Western world think that more money and prestige would make them happy, and a lot more would make them a lot happier. Studies also demonstrate that this is not the case. Partly, this is due to what psychologists call the 'anhedonic response': we become accustomed very quickly to what we have, and our ideas of how much is enough and how much is good shift in that process.

And partly, my experience suggests, we aren't happier with more wealth or greater social status because these things don't do what we subconsciously hope they will. They don't resolve our insecurities. They don't improve our relationships. And they don't make us or those we love invulnerable, immortal or capable of making a good world. I think those of us who are wealthy (and, in a world where a billion people live or die on less than a dollar a day, most of us reading this are wealthy) tend to avoid direct exposure to the poor, the sick and the prisoners because they remind us of our inescapable vulnerability as human beings. They remind us that we're not God.

What did Haman want? He thought it was wealth, sons and a place of honour in the king's court. But, when he had those things, he still was not content. He wanted to have absolute control over his world, and the presence of even one person who challenged his assumption of that privilege was enough to make him miserable. Can we ever be content? Only if we accept our place as human beings can we accept gracefully the gifts that God offers graciously.

Creator God,
you made us all in your image:
may we discern you in all that we see,
and serve you in all that we do;
through Jesus Christ our Lord.

COLLECT

Wednesday 3 August

Psalm 119.153-end
Esther 6.1-13
2 Corinthians 8.1-15

Esther 6.1-13

'Haman said to himself, "Whom would the king wish to honour more than me?" ' (v.6)

Esther's tale begins with powerful men trying to defend and enhance their privilege while Mordecai counsels invisibility and secrecy. In the last chapter, Mordecai realized the danger of his earlier counsel. Now it is time for Haman's lesson: the reward of seeking one's own honour rather than honouring the outsiders blessed by God. Haman cannot imagine who other than himself has better handled power and is more worthy to receive recognition, so he proposes lavish honours for himself, which instead go to the outsider whom he chose to make an enemy, while even his wife and advisers predict his downfall with impeccable hindsight.

It's easy to point fingers at Haman – but how different are we? Our culture surrounds us with messages that with power, money and privilege come security and joy. When we get more and find ourselves anxious about losing it, we imagine that the problem is that we just haven't acquired enough. It's a classic example of the definition of insanity as doing the same thing over and over expecting different results. Wouldn't those of us who are privileged people in privileged nations do better by releasing our grip on privilege and working for justice for those outside it? Or will we choose Haman's course instead, looking for the blessing of earthly authorities and the trappings of what we call 'success'?

COLLECT

Merciful God,
you have prepared for those who love you
such good things as pass our understanding:
pour into our hearts such love toward you
that we, loving you in all things and above all things,
may obtain your promises,
which exceed all that we can desire;
through Jesus Christ your Son our Lord,
who is alive and reigns with you,
in the unity of the Holy Spirit,
one God, now and for ever.

Psalms 143, 146
Esther 6.14 – 7.end
2 Corinthians 8.16 – 9.5

Esther 6.14 – 7.end

*' "Look, the very gallows that Haman has prepared for Mordecai" ...
And the king said, "Hang [Haman] on that" ' (7.9)*

In today's reading, we see Esther fully claim her identity and her voice. While the king may have extended his sceptre to her as a queen, she speaks from the fullness of her identity as a woman, a daughter and a Jew, shining at last with the eloquence that she had up to this point concealed at the behest of the men around her. She speaks finally and fully, not for 'those people' but for 'my people'. With her bold speech, her people are saved.

Haman, however, comes to see the downside of recognition. He gets full credit for his genocidal designs, and is hanged from the gallows he constructed for his enemy. That's one of the problems of building gallows. What we persecute in others is often a projection of what we hate and fear but refuse to recognize in ourselves, so the gallows that we build for them are likely to fit us better.

For the most part, we would recognize where we are in Esther's story as a happy ending: Esther is now recognized not only as an eloquent woman, but as her people's saviour; the king recognizes the horror of his earlier edict, so we can expect him to revoke it.

Is this a satisfying ending to you? If there is to be more (which there is) and this story were new to you, what would you expect the rest of the text to say?

Creator God,
you made us all in your image:
may we discern you in all that we see,
and serve you in all that we do;
through Jesus Christ our Lord.

COLLECT

215

Friday 5 August

Psalms 142, **144**
Esther 8
2 Corinthians 9.6-end

Esther 8

'... to destroy, to kill, and to annihilate' (v.11)

At this point, Haman's position is vacant, so Esther gives it to Mordecai. And Esther goes before the king to ask that a new edict be issued reversing his earlier one. He agrees, and hands responsibility for crafting it to Esther and Mordecai. That's good. If only the story ended there.

Esther and Mordecai, given power to do as they wish 'with regard to the Jews', write something almost exactly like Haman's edict, only this time it is the Jews who are not only to 'defend their lives' against those who might attack them, but also to 'destroy, to kill, and to annihilate ... their children and women, and to plunder their goods'. Terror strikes the kingdom: 'many of the peoples of the country professed to be Jews, because the fear of the Jews had fallen upon them'. A new set of people are crafting the edicts, but the result is still genocide and terror, with those of ethnicities different from the rulers choosing invisibility to increase their chances and their children's to survive. The next chapter of the story tells us that Jews killed 75,300 others on a single day, though they chose not to plunder.

Such cycles of violence seem to be the way of the world, so perhaps it's best that the text of the book never mentions God. It challenges us readers to ask where God is throughout the story, whether saving, encouraging or weeping. How would you answer that question?

COLLECT

Merciful God,
you have prepared for those who love you
such good things as pass our understanding:
pour into our hearts such love toward you
that we, loving you in all things and above all things,
may obtain your promises,
which exceed all that we can desire;
through Jesus Christ your Son our Lord,
who is alive and reigns with you,
in the unity of the Holy Spirit,
one God, now and for ever.

Psalms 27, 150
Ecclesiasticus 48.1-10
or 1 Kings 19.1-16
1 John 3.1-3

The Transfiguration of Our Lord

1 Kings 19.1-16

'... after the fire a sound of sheer silence' (v.12)

Elijah is in exile, having fled Queen Jezebel lest she take revenge for Elijah's slaughter in the previous chapter of 450 prophets of her ancestral God Baal. Elijah had killed these people to avenge Jezebel's slaughtering prophets of the Hebrews' God. Do these spirals of violence never end? Not yet, alas.

But we do see an instructive moment in Elijah's experience in the wilderness. There is an excellent piece of advice to avoid making major decisions in circumstances covered by the acronym 'HALT' – namely, when one is hungry, angry, lonely or tired. Before Elijah hears God, he finds circumstances as close as he can find to peace and comfort despite the turmoil and violence that has driven him out of the city. He gets distance from those he rightly fears. Adrenaline subsides, and hunger and exhaustion kick in. God knows (literally) this is not the time for fasting, and sends angels to see that Elijah is fed and can rest.

Once he is rested, God calls him to the mountain to listen for God's voice. It comes not in spectacular and fearsome displays of earthquake, fire or wind. In the midst of such things, the most appropriate kind of question to ask is where to find shelter, not whom God calls to shape the fate of a nation. Decisions of great importance are best made in the place where Elijah hears from God: in a moment of sheer silence.

COLLECT

Father in heaven,
whose Son Jesus Christ was wonderfully transfigured
before chosen witnesses upon the holy mountain,
and spoke of the exodus he would accomplish at Jerusalem:
give us strength so to hear his voice and bear our cross
that in the world to come we may see him as he is;
who is alive and reigns with you,
in the unity of the Holy Spirit,
one God, now and for ever.

Monday 8 August

2 Corinthians 11.1-15

'... if you receive a different spirit from the one you received' (v.4)

'Does the grain run true?' Grain that doesn't run true in a trunk or branch is grain that knots or doubles back on itself so that, when wood is prepared or planed for use, the very internal make-up of the plank makes it hard to shape and, therefore, to build with. It is sometimes hard to tell from the outside, looking at bark, for example, whether or not the grain is true on the inside. In other words, Paul is saying that we can be easily deceived by ourselves or by some forms of evil. As Jesus said, it is possible to exclaim 'Lord, Lord' outwardly but not to be a true-grained disciple in reality within (Matthew 7.21-23).

It is possible for religious people to offer worship ceremonies and rites but to lack heart on the inside so that no compassion leads to no care for others. God is the God of the whole of life and of the whole person.

But no grain is wholly 'true' in the strict sense, for there is always some 'knottiness' – and so we pray, echoing that lovely prayer, 'Oh Jesus, master carpenter of Nazareth, who on the cross through wood and nails didst work *our* whole salvation: wield well thy tools in this thy workshop; that we who come to thee rough-hewn may by thy hand be fashioned to a truer beauty and a greater usefulness; for the honour of thy holy name.' Christ can even carve rotten wood, thank goodness.

COLLECT

Lord of all power and might,
the author and giver of all good things:
graft in our hearts the love of your name,
increase in us true religion,
nourish us with all goodness,
and of your great mercy keep us in the same;
through Jesus Christ your Son our Lord,
who is alive and reigns with you,
in the unity of the Holy Spirit,
one God, now and for ever.

Tuesday 9 August

2 Corinthians 11.16-end

'For you gladly put up with fools ...' (v.19)

One of the most poignant, complex and sometimes tragic dilemmas of modern relationships is framed in questions such as 'Should I leave this marriage? Or end this relationship?' The questions often arise because there may seem to be too much to bear, whether in terms of incompatibility, different values systems, or abuse.

Paul says, in effect, that it is a very rare and special kind of graced strength in relationships that puts up with foolishness, slavery, predatory behaviour, being used, or being patronized and insulted. Paul asks the Corinthians to accept him as foolish because, ironically, they have shown that they can bear with fools, having put up with all kinds of extreme wrong from apostles who intrude.

Even when we may seek to be thoughtful and caring, we may still miss the mark at times in our own relationships. So we ask colleagues, friends and loved ones to bear with us on an everyday basis. This is part of the secret of abiding, growing and maturing love. However, this cannot mean putting up with abuse or being a doormat. The people of Israel could only endure slavery for so long, until God sent Moses for their liberation. How much should you put up with? Seek guidance from the God of Paul and Moses.

Generous God,
you give us gifts and make them grow:
though our faith is small as mustard seed,
make it grow to your glory
and the flourishing of your kingdom;
through Jesus Christ our Lord.

COLLECT

Wednesday 10 August

2 Corinthians 12

*'My grace is sufficient for you, for power is made perfect
in weakness' (v.9)*

Why wear an instrument of torture, a cross, around your neck? The
cross speaks of a power that overcomes torture and death – of a
power that, by God's good will towards all humankind, by grace,
makes the cross empty. Christ crucified and risen is the true power of
God. Christ was crucified in weakness and seemed to be defeated by
the power of oppression and death. But God's power raised him from
death and makes that death-defying power alive in us. And so we can
boast of 'weakness' as Paul does (v.5), so that the grace, which
overcomes the world, can work through and with our weaknesses to
overcome the insults, the hardships, the persecutions and calamities,
for the sake of Christ (v.10).

We are like earthen vessels, made of common clay with its cracks and
grit, but have placed within us the immeasurable riches of Christ, so
that even if the pottery vessel is chipped or breaks, the treasure holds
its worth. This is the beautiful truth about ourselves.

This does not mean wallowing in weakness or becoming lethargic
because we ourselves are weak, but, rather, letting the beauty, light
and power of the treasure course through us in prayer and sacrament,
to make us strong, to rise up and walk in God's ways of justice and
righteousness.

COLLECT

Lord of all power and might,
the author and giver of all good things:
graft in our hearts the love of your name,
increase in us true religion,
nourish us with all goodness,
and of your great mercy keep us in the same;
through Jesus Christ your Son our Lord,
who is alive and reigns with you,
in the unity of the Holy Spirit,
one God, now and for ever.

Psalms 14, **15**, 16
Jeremiah 30.1-11
2 Corinthians 13

Thursday 11 August

2 Corinthians 13

*'Examine yourselves to see whether you are living in the faith.
Test yourselves' (v.5)*

How do you deal with those against whom you have a case? Paul seems to be saying that, if possible, we should call for self-testing by them because this has a better chance of evoking repentance, enlightenment and spiritual development. This cannot mean judging or condemning, which belong solely to God. Perhaps we could use the discipline of self-testing ourselves before we ask others to audit their lives and behaviours. When you point the finger at someone, there are always three more pointing back at you. Someone once said: 'to sit alone with my conscience would be judgement enough for me.'

Paul is also honest about the fact that the Christian community can experience radical differences in discernment. From a God's-eye view, goodness and truth, surely, are not found only on one side of the argument. We need the wisdom and justice of Solomon to see what makes for the greatest good for all parties. In the end, it is how differences are handled that matters, as much as the outcome.

According to Acts 15, a careful process of listening and humble receptivity to what God is saying through everyone is crucial to a healthy and inclusive outcome. To understand is to 'stand under', to keep close to the ground – the humus, which is from where we get the meaning of humility.

Generous God,
you give us gifts and make them grow:
though our faith is small as mustard seed,
make it grow to your glory
and the flourishing of your kingdom;
through Jesus Christ our Lord.

COLLECT

Psalms 17, 19
Jeremiah 30.12-22
James 1.1-11

James 1.1-11

'... the testing of your faith produces endurance' (v.3)

Some Christians put crucial texts on the inside of the sun visor of their car. Today's reading could well be one of those. 'Whenever you face trials of any kind, consider it nothing but joy, because you know that the testing of your faith produces endurance; and let endurance have its full effect, so that you may be mature and complete, lacking in nothing.' The Hebrews kept a small saying from the Torah in a little case strapped to their foreheads, or some saying sewn into their hems.

Why do this? Because we forget the wisdom of God that is available to us. In the face of trials, our bird brain can take over, leading us to fight or flight, leading us to prejudice or aggression, leading us to ignorance and blindness. This is like the wave of the sea, driven and tossed by the sea, as Paul said it would be for those who doubt the goodness and justice of God and God's capacity to reign in and through the trials. This flies in the face of a pleasure-loving society which thinks that suffering is evil and tries to medicate or immunize against trials. Faith is never free from trial or test but matures through endurance. This is life in God's real world, and – even in the tribulation – it can bring a peace the world cannot give.

COLLECT

Lord of all power and might,
the author and giver of all good things:
graft in our hearts the love of your name,
increase in us true religion,
nourish us with all goodness,
and of your great mercy keep us in the same;
through Jesus Christ your Son our Lord,
who is alive and reigns with you,
in the unity of the Holy Spirit,
one God, now and for ever.

Psalms 20, 21, **23**
Jeremiah 31.1-22
James 1.12-end

James 1.12-end

'... look into the perfect law, the law of liberty' (v.25)

How do you live in the real world? What is the real world anyway? Is the bottom line, in reality, 'do to others before they do to you?' – a first-strike policy? Therefore, should Christians get real and leave humility and meekness behind, following the path of pre-emptive aggression by which we might create real security and defence? Certainly, some paths of the commercial and political world would tell Christians to 'Get real' in this way.

But James is uncompromisingly clear in his claim that the real world comes from the Father of lights, who purposed to give us birth by the word of truth (vv.17-18). Reality is made up of deep listening, wise speaking, great patience, compassionate action and honest self-reflection. The real world involves caring for the marginalized and distressed without being contaminated by 'the world'. The world in this case is the way things are arranged by Caesar, whose commercial and militarist world view dehumanized and commodified thousands of human beings.

So, James says 'don't forget who you are': do not look at yourself as in a mirror, but look to the law of freedom in God and look to walking in humility and acting with justice. These are the real wheels that turn the world in the end, not the lords and governors.

Generous God,
you give us gifts and make them grow:
though our faith is small as mustard seed,
make it grow to your glory
and the flourishing of your kingdom;
through Jesus Christ our Lord.

COLLECT

Monday 15 August

The Blessed Virgin Mary

Psalms 98, 138, 147.1-12
Isaiah 7.10-15
Luke 11.27-28

Isaiah 7.10-15

'... the Lord himself will give you a sign' (v.14)

The phrase 'take me to your leader', or 'I want to see the boss', suggests that we want to go where the action and power is in order to get something done for us. It suggests that there is no point in messing with minor officials or lowly minions, but to get to the chief, the brains of the outfit. In Isaiah 7, the leader, the boss, the brains, is described as 'the Lord himself', the God of all the cosmos. It would be natural in this first testament then to see the power, the glory and the majesty of the Lord described. Unexpectedly, and centuries before the birth of Jesus, we see that the sign of the Lord is to be a young woman with a child, called Emmanuel, whose discernment between good and evil will change the world in every way.

The royal power lies in pregnancy and birth, and are a sign of God's concern for God's people, even within their international politics and the dangers of warfare. This is not a feel-good sentimental message such as you might see on some commercially produced Christmas cards, but the picture of a God who comes through in birthing, mothering and profound wisdom. This is what ultimately rules the world; it is the only reason we are here at all. Let us live by this power.

COLLECT

Almighty God,
who looked upon the lowliness of the Blessed Virgin Mary
and chose her to be the mother of your only Son:
grant that we who are redeemed by his blood
may share with her in the glory of your eternal kingdom;
through Jesus Christ your Son our Lord,
who is alive and reigns with you,
in the unity of the Holy Spirit,
one God, now and for ever.

Psalms 32, **36**
Jeremiah 32.1-15
James 2.14-end

James 2.14-end

'... faith by itself, if it has no works, is dead' (v.17)

Have you ever felt embarrassed or wary of some ragged person in church and been concerned about the effect they might have on the congregation? Have you noticed a resistance in yourself to TV adverts of people in famine? Have you ever been reluctant to open your heart and your space for those who are radically different? I have. James' challenge is to overcome the embarrassment, resistance and reluctance and to put our faith where our mouth is, because faith without works is dead, as the body is dead without the spirit.

Faith for James is like a fountain of justice, like a wellspring of love, like streams in the desert. It does not dam up inside a person; it is, rather, a reservoir that can then irrigate, flowing over the hard and crusty ground.

The language of Jesus and his first disciples, Aramaic, was verb-orientated. This meant that they saw things in terms of happening and events and actions, more than static definitions and philosophies. So, when John's disciples ask Jesus if he is the Messiah, he says not 'I am' but 'Tell John that the blind see, the lame walk, the deaf hear and the poor have good news preached to them'. He is saying to look to the action. God is a verb. We are called to practise, not to navel-gaze.

Almighty Lord and everlasting God,
we beseech you to direct, sanctify and govern
both our hearts and bodies
in the ways of your laws and the works of your commandments;
that through your most mighty protection, both here and ever,
we may be preserved in body and soul;
through our Lord and Saviour Jesus Christ,
who is alive and reigns with you,
in the unity of the Holy Spirit,
one God, now and for ever.

COLLECT

Wednesday 17 August

James 3

'Does a spring pour forth from the same opening both fresh and brackish water?' (v.11)

If Jesus had only a few seconds to speak of the kingdom that was coming through and around him, many scholars think he would say something like 'It is not what goes into a person that defines them, but what comes out of them ... for out of the heart comes good and evil.' Jesus is recorded as saying this kind of thing in all three synoptic gospels, and it seems to be at the heart of his message.

James, his disciple, in this passage is picking up this central point by commending us to guard our heart, have a care for what comes out of us, to use our mouths to elevate, not desecrate, to build up, not to tear down. There is no point in having a reformation of structures and a revolution in politics if what comes out of the mouths of people continues to be prejudicial, or cruel or malicious. We are called to an internal reformation, a revolution of the heart that brings forth a new way of thinking or speaking.

We are called to be transformed by the renewal of our minds, as Paul said. Then, the renewal of structures becomes viable. It can go something like this: love, then justice, then peace, although they are all totally interdependent in a holistic gospel. Jesus brings in a new creation through our hearts and minds.

COLLECT

Almighty Lord and everlasting God,
we beseech you to direct, sanctify and govern
    both our hearts and bodies
in the ways of your laws and the works of your commandments;
that through your most mighty protection, both here and ever,
we may be preserved in body and soul;
through our Lord and Saviour Jesus Christ,
who is alive and reigns with you,
in the unity of the Holy Spirit,
one God, now and for ever.

Psalm **37***
Jeremiah 33.14-end
James 4.1-12

James 4.1-12

'God opposes the proud, but gives grace to the humble' (v.6)

Every Christian wears an invisible sign around their necks, which reads 'work in progress' or 'be patient with me, God has not finished with me yet', or 'you should have seen what I was like before'. James reminds us that conversion is an ongoing evolution as we are transformed spiritually. This is not a super-religious, pious activity, but a day-by-day growing in integrity, faithfulness and hope. We are always growing out of the ways of the world and always growing into the ways of God. There is some ambiguity in this that every Christian learns to understand and work with. We have been saved, we are being saved, we shall be saved.

Each little victory over the ways of the world such as gluttony, aggression or hardness of heart is a possibility of growth in God. By contrast, James' description of envy, leading to murder, is the most dramatic of all the New Testament, challenging us to be so careful with the state of our emotions. We are called to see ourselves as learners in 'the way' by paying deep attention to the state of our heart and by shaping what we feel and think with consistent, attentive prayer, so that we are guided by the light within us rather than the shadows around us.

Lord God,
your Son left the riches of heaven
and became poor for our sake:
when we prosper save us from pride,
when we are needy save us from despair,
that we may trust in you alone;
through Jesus Christ our Lord.

COLLECT

227

Friday 19 August

James 4.13 – 5.6

'Yet you do not even know what tomorrow will bring' (4.14)

There is a story of a pious Scottish minister who, when asked by a parishioner if he would be at a particular meeting the following morning, said: 'Yes, I'll be there, if I'm spared in the night!' This is, perhaps, an extreme example that James is making when he says: 'If the Lord wishes, we will live and do this or that' (4.15). James is encouraging us to live our lives in complete interdependence with the grace and purpose of God in every moment and every happening. We are not called to live as if we are here for ever, and as if money and our travels in business govern the course of everything.

Rather, we should find our treasures in the treasure trove of the kingdom of God, which are the fruits and gifts of the Spirit, which are righteousness and justice. This means honouring the wages or labourers, dealing in equity and fairness. God wills this kind of even-handedness. So, the will of God is not to do with a safe place in heaven as an individual, but is to do with a good place on earth for you and everyone else. 'Your kingdom come on earth as it is in heaven' is not a graduation prize for being good, but the offer of wholeness for every one and every thing God has made. This is a vision of your true wealth and worth.

COLLECT

Almighty Lord and everlasting God,
we beseech you to direct, sanctify and govern
    both our hearts and bodies
in the ways of your laws and the works of your commandments;
that through your most mighty protection, both here and ever,
we may be preserved in body and soul;
through our Lord and Saviour Jesus Christ,
who is alive and reigns with you,
in the unity of the Holy Spirit,
one God, now and for ever.

Psalms 41, **42**, 43
Jeremiah 36.1-18
James 5.7-end

Saturday 20 August

James 5.7-end

'The farmer waits for the precious crop from the earth' (v.7)

The answer lies in the soil. This phrase could well have been the catch-cry of many New Testament preachers. They loved to use horticultural, agricultural and viticultural imagery when talking about the kingdom of God. James begins today's reading with a farmer waiting for a precious crop from the earth, exercising great patience and hope, with farmer and field and crop being so dependent on the gift of early and late rain showers. This is not the dynamics of warfare or ruthless competition or cut-throat market economies, but a dynamic of interdependence, of the natural grace of the goodness of time and the time of the seasons. It is about people's hard work in harmony with nature as a gift, not something to be fought or squandered with impatience and lust.

And so James goes on to say that we must be patient, strong-hearted, not grumbling, showing endurance, remembering the compassion and mercy of God, trusting that the redeeming of things is always coming through, even when there is little evidence. James talks about the prayer of faith, which really means praying in hopefulness and trust. As the contemporary poet Nadia Colburn said: 'Giving up on hope is always wrong. Even in the place of what we can calculate to be certain destruction. Because it cuts us off from ourselves and our own humanity, privileging the head over the heart, the mind over the body.'

Lord God,
your Son left the riches of heaven
and became poor for our sake:
when we prosper save us from pride,
when we are needy save us from despair,
that we may trust in you alone;
through Jesus Christ our Lord.

COLLECT

229

Monday 22 August

Psalm **44**
Jeremiah 36.19-end
Mark 1.1-13

Mark 1.1-13

'The beginning of the good news' (v.1)

Strange though it may seem, Mark feels compelled to tell us in the opening sentence that this is the beginning. Most translations of Mark render his opening words '*the* beginning of the good news ...'. But Mark doesn't even bother to use the word 'the'; he starts with 'beginning ...'. We are, in other words, straight into it. And, of course, if you turn to the end of Mark's Gospel, you'll also see that it has no proper ending either – it is all a bit ragged.

An abrupt beginning and an abrupt ending point to several themes that occur throughout Mark's Gospel. Readers don't get a gentle introduction to Jesus. The good news is here, now. And it requires your attention, and a response. Here, now. The end is the same. There is no neat finish. You have to write that yourself, with your life as a disciple.

So there is no room for the armchair critic in Mark's opening remarks. You are not offered an easy introduction to Jesus – his genealogy, for example (see Luke and Matthew) – but are invited straight away to deal with the challenging presence of John the Baptist. It is his call to repent, be baptized and follow Jesus that forms the heart of Mark's Gospel. So, the tone of abruptness in the message of Mark is also his theme. There is no time to cogitate and deliberate. Choose Jesus. Drop everything you are doing, and follow him. Now.

COLLECT

Almighty God,
who sent your Holy Spirit
to be the life and light of your Church:
open our hearts to the riches of your grace,
that we may bring forth the fruit of the Spirit
in love and joy and peace;
through Jesus Christ your Son our Lord,
who is alive and reigns with you,
in the unity of the Holy Spirit,
one God, now and for ever.

Psalms **48**, 52
Jeremiah 37
Mark 1.14-20

Mark 1.14-20

'Jesus came to Galilee, proclaiming the good news' (v.14)

The breakneck speed at which Jesus calls and gathers his first disciples should not surprise us. Mark's Gospel is the shortest and, to some extent, a kind of shorthand account of Jesus' ministry. It is reasonable to assume that Jesus had much more to say to the crowds than: 'The time is fulfilled, and the kingdom of God has come near; repent, and believe in the good news' (v.15). One can imagine long, eloquent sermons, parables and lively exchanges, even from the outset.

So, Mark, in summarizing the essence of Jesus' early teaching, is trying to say something about the urgency and immediate impact of the preacher from Galilee. That Jesus' teaching also resonated with that of John is clearly important. Although we know little about the content of John's teaching, we can speculate that the message of repentance and baptism was spoken into a complex cultural context that longed for change and salvation.

Yet, what is so intriguing about Jesus is the range of people he chose to share in this work. It included women and men – and not all of great repute – along with fishermen, tax-collectors and others. The ensemble was hardly at the cutting edge of scholarship, leadership and eloquence. Yet this is where the 'Jesus Project' is born. In choosing widely, Jesus gives us a foretaste of what the kingdom will be like and what the Church might become: a place both of diversity and unity, and a true home for all. Though many, one body.

Gracious Father,
revive your Church in our day,
and make her holy, strong and faithful,
for your glory's sake
in Jesus Christ our Lord.

COLLECT

Wednesday 24 August

Bartholomew the Apostle

Psalms 86, 117
Genesis 28.10-17
John 1.43-end

John 1.43-end

'You will see greater things than these' (v.50)

Matthew, Mark and Luke always mention Bartholomew in the company of Philip. The two of them are part of the original twelve disciples called by Jesus. So, it is possible that John's reference to Nathanael in today's reading is meant to imply Bartholomew. We cannot be sure. But that is hardly the point, for today sees the celebration of one the great saints of the Church, on whom the New Testament is mostly silent.

The tradition surrounding Bartholomew is that he brought the gospel to Armenia (where is patron saint) and died a particularly gruesome death. Martyred, he was skinned alive before being beheaded. Christian art often pictures him in heaven, holding his own skin. And his patronage is also linked with hospitals and healing.

But what I most enjoy about Bartholomew is that we know almost nothing about him from Scripture. It is as though the Bible is saying to us, loudly, that not all the disciples who follow Jesus will gain in reputation. Remember what John the Baptist says: 'He must increase, but I must decrease' (John 3.30). So, Bartholomew is called, named – and then vanishes into service and discipleship, and eventually martyrdom.

We can't all be like Bartholomew. Yet, we must remember that all saints are basically normal folk. They just give their lives over to God, and watch God make the ordinary into the extraordinary. There is no better way to live.

COLLECT

Almighty and everlasting God,
who gave to your apostle Bartholomew grace
    truly to believe and to preach your word:
grant that your Church
may love that word which he believed
and may faithfully preach and receive the same;
through Jesus Christ your Son our Lord,
who is alive and reigns with you,
in the unity of the Holy Spirit,
one God, now and for ever.

Psalms 56, **57** (63*)
Jeremiah 38.14-end
Mark 1.29-end

Mark 1.29-end

*'He came and took her by the hand and lifted her up.
Then the fever left her' (v.31)*

The healings of Jesus are radical for at least two reasons. First, they are miraculous. And second, they almost always go to people with no name, status, power or obvious religious reputation.

Moreover, Jesus was interested not just in healing, but also in how people had been classed as 'ill' in the first place, and what or who kept them there. He was, I suppose, in the modern idiom, tough on illness, and tough on the causes of illness.

We also need to remember that, when Jesus heals the leper, he makes himself unclean by touching a source of impurity. The radical demand of Jesus is that the Church is required to assume the pain and impurity of the excluded, the demonized and the (allegedly) impure. That's why the Church often works with the most marginalized in our communities – in hospitals, prisons and asylum centres, for example. It is just carrying on the job of Jesus, namely looking for the lost, rejected, marginalized and fallen, and trying, with the love of God, to bring them back into the fold of society and the arms of God.

Jesus, the friend of tax-collectors, prostitutes and other undesirables – but that's not how the Church portrays Christ. And I guess that's the trouble with Christians; we regard only ourselves as honorary sinners, and the Church as a haven for the saved and secure. Yet, it is for the lost and the loveless, the place for the unplaced, the home for the homeless.

COLLECT

Almighty God,
who sent your Holy Spirit
to be the life and light of your Church:
open our hearts to the riches of your grace,
that we may bring forth the fruit of the Spirit
in love and joy and peace;
through Jesus Christ your Son our Lord,
who is alive and reigns with you,
in the unity of the Holy Spirit,
one God, now and for ever.

Friday 26 August

Mark 2.1-12

*'So many gathered around that there was no longer room for them,
not even in front of the door' (v.2)*

So, Jesus heals a paralytic. But why one among so many? There are
many reasons, no doubt. But at least three come to mind in relation to
Jesus' teaching on the kingdom of God.

First, there is the urgency of the kingdom – a key concern for Mark. The
roof has to be removed so that the paralytic man can be brought to
Jesus. 'If there is no way through to Jesus, then we'll just have to go up
and over.' Mark is telling us that the effort to get to Jesus will be worth
it. Don't count the cost; just do it.

Second, Jesus often puts the ill person at the centre of his ministry and
therefore at the centre of the crowd. The sick and diseased are not a
miraculous sideshow for the wonder-preacher from Galilee. Jesus is
saying that, if we put our most dispossessed and disabled at the centre
of our lives, we will all be transformed.

Third, Jesus touches. He seems willing and able to take on the associated
stain, stigmas and taboos of his society by getting his own body and
soul 'dirty'. He has no fear of touching, embracing and healing people
whose bodies are leaking sin, sickness and pollution, for which they
would have been excluded from mainstream society.

So, the healer is the one who becomes tainted. Jesus heals, to be sure.
But, in doing so, he not only heals the individual – he also transforms the
way we now look at the world: 'thy kingdom come'.

COLLECT

Almighty God,
who sent your Holy Spirit
to be the life and light of your Church:
open our hearts to the riches of your grace,
that we may bring forth the fruit of the Spirit
in love and joy and peace;
through Jesus Christ your Son our Lord,
who is alive and reigns with you,
in the unity of the Holy Spirit,
one God, now and for ever.

Psalm **68**
Jeremiah 40
Mark 2.13-22

Mark 2.13-22

'... and [Jesus] said to [Levi], "Follow me."
And he got up and followed him' (v.14)

If I had to be reincarnated as an animal, I would like to come back as a St Bernard dog. I have my reasons. First, I aspire to be more of a saint, and this is about as close as I'll get. Second, everyone loves a good dog, so there is a chance of being both liked and gainfully employed – and you can rarely do both of these in the Church. Third, I believe in searching for the lost.

One of the more famous quotes from another saint of the same era as Bernard is from Benedict's Rule: 'Before all things and above all things, care must be taken of the sick; so that the brethren shall minister to them as they would to Christ himself ...'. Benedict had read his Gospels, and he would have known that Jesus went not only to the sick, but also to the despised and lonely, to the hated and ostracized.

Benedict would have also read Mark and known of the call of Levi. Here, Jesus deliberately seeks out the lost. And some of the ones he found and who followed him actually ended up with quite important roles in the new kingdom he was ushering in. Jesus was, to his critics, lacking in discernment and poor at discriminating. Yet to us, this is precisely the challenge, for he shows love beyond measure to those who are hated most and trusted least.

Gracious Father,
revive your Church in our day,
and make her holy, strong and faithful,
for your glory's sake
in Jesus Christ our Lord.

COLLECT

Mark 2.23 – 3.6

'Look, why are they doing what is not lawful on the sabbath?' (2.24)

To what extent do we know this 'gentle Jesus, meek and mild ...'? Not very well, according to Mark. For here in this rather breathless narrative, we meet Jesus the radical, Jesus the lawbreaker, Jesus the challenger and disturber of tradition. This is the Jesus who will not be an easy, passive member of your average congregation. He's a nuisance. And it is early days in so far as his ministry goes. Lord knows how it will end – though you can begin to see quite early on why so many would turn against him at the end.

In today's reading, Jesus first of all breaks a common and customary interpretation of the sabbath with almost casual determination. Just like Gandhi making salt from the sea and defying the British Empire salt tax in 1930, Jesus simply breaks the law to point out its absurdity. But it does not stop there. For next, he goes into the synagogue on the sabbath and breaks the law again by healing a man with a withered hand.

What do these gestures tell us about Jesus and the law? That Jesus is intent on redefining the relationship between humanity and the law. And that, in the new kingdom, the law must live under the love of God and with the compassion that God has for all humanity. A religious tradition that cannot feed and heal others, because of its compliance to an apparently divinely inspired code of ethics, has rather lost the plot.

COLLECT

Let your merciful ears, O Lord,
be open to the prayers of your humble servants;
and that they may obtain their petitions
make them to ask such things as shall please you;
through Jesus Christ your Son our Lord,
who is alive and reigns with you,
in the unity of the Holy Spirit,
one God, now and for ever.

Mark 3.7-19a

'... and a great multitude from Galilee followed him' (v.7)

Inevitably, perhaps, the crowds follow Jesus. A faith that is full of compassion, love and mercy for those who are neglected and marginalized, and puts the needs of others first, will not want for followers. And a faith that puts strictness and zeal first – in both behaviour and belief – will also find followers. And this is one of the major tussles that Mark presents us with. The crowds prefer the first kind of faith; the Pharisees and Sadducees the second.

These are the early days of Jesus' ministry – the honeymoon period, as it were. The crowds follow; they are amazed; and they are moved. The carpenter's son speaks their language and meets them at their points of need. And he also finds fresh and original ways of indicting the clergy of the day, who lurk in the shadows and slowly begin their plotting.

But, for now, the ministry of Jesus is in its expansive phase. Twelve are called. Many others follow. The ragtag army of disciples and followers is on the march, and it seems as though the Galilean will sweep all before him. Even the demons flee. Yet Mark is careful, even here, to point to the bitter-sweet ending of this tale. The disciples are not listed by profession, or alphabetically, or by region. It seems almost haphazard, until you realize that the last disciple to be named by Mark is 'Judas Iscariot, who betrayed him' (v.19). 'Let the reader understand', as Mark will later comment (Mark 13.14).

Lord of heaven and earth,
as Jesus taught his disciples to be persistent in prayer,
give us patience and courage never to lose hope,
but always to bring our prayers before you;
through Jesus Christ our Lord.

COLLECT

237

Mark 3.19b-end

'Who are my mother and my brothers?' (v.33)

'Then he went home ...'; but they all came together again the next day. And it is amazing what a night's sleep does for the minds of all the witnesses. After the amazement and awe of the first miracles, the questions start to come thick and fast. How is all this possible? Could this be Satanic trickery? Like a politician campaigning on the stump, Jesus suddenly finds himself having to give detailed answers to detailed questions. A crowd that was wholly impressed with yesterday is now restless for some answers today. Some even say 'he is mad'.

Jesus responds calmly, and with compassion. And his appeal, interestingly, is not to himself, but to the fruits of what the crowd have witnessed. If all that has been said and done is good – truly good – how can it be of Satan? To be sure, this is no trickery. The fruit of the kingdom is now before them, and evil is being served notice by Jesus. The work of the Holy Spirit is known through the fruits of what the crowd can see and hear.

It is no surprise, then, that the debate turns to family origins. If this Jesus is good, then surely there must be a natural lineage of goodness? Yet Jesus is careful to sidestep the implications of this argument. Goodness is not something inherited, but rather something received, given and practised under God. The crowd are told, firmly but gently, that God's playing field is completely level in this respect. Whoever does the will of God is the brother and sister of Jesus. Home, then, which is where this Gospel reading started, is where God's will dwells and under the only law that matters, which is of supreme love.

COLLECT

Let your merciful ears, O Lord,
be open to the prayers of your humble servants;
and that they may obtain their petitions
make them to ask such things as shall please you;
through Jesus Christ your Son our Lord,
who is alive and reigns with you,
in the unity of the Holy Spirit,
one God, now and for ever.

Psalm **78.1-39***
Jeremiah 44.1-14
Mark 4.1-20

Mark 4.1-20

'He began to teach them many things in parables' (v.2)

One of my favourite children's stories is Mick Inkpen's *Jasper's Beanstalk*. The hero, a cat, plants a bean. But, after no apparent growth from one day to the next, he tosses it away – only to find that, after leaving it alone to germinate, it does just fine.

It seems to me that the two great besetting sins of the Church these days are impatience and procrastination. Either the Church moves too quickly and then regrets the unforeseen consequences, or it moves too slowly or not at all, with all the activity and energy of a hibernating tortoise. And many churches and ministers often move between action and inaction, impatience and procrastination. So, you'd think that the art of ministry is all about striking the right note of compromise. But it really isn't.

Good ministry is, in the end, not finding the middle ground between action and inaction, or decision and indecision. It is not about compromising between extremes; it is about living authentically in the midst of the place where God has set you.

The parable of the sower teaches many things, but two particularly stand out. First, there is a lesson about patience and action. Second, we are taught that some grounds are better than others: some seeds do better in some soils than others. We need to value each other's ministries. Some work in lush, fertile, soft soil; others have ministries that are tougher – and only some things will grow there.

Lord of heaven and earth,
as Jesus taught his disciples to be persistent in prayer,
give us patience and courage never to lose hope,
but always to bring our prayers before you;
through Jesus Christ our Lord.

COLLECT

Friday 2 September

Psalm **55**
Jeremiah 44.15-end
Mark 4.21-34

Mark 4.21-34

'It is like a mustard seed' (v.31)

When Jesus reaches for metaphors that describe the kingdom of God, he often uses untidy images. 'I am the vine, you are the branches' comes to mind (John 15.5). No stately cedar tree of Lebanon here – or even an English oak. Jesus chooses a sprawling, knotted plant that requires patience and careful husbandry. And one that is hardly pretty to look at either. Actually, it is bug ugly to look at – but taste the fruit of the vine, and don't judge on appearances.

In another short parable today, he compares the kingdom of heaven to a mustard seed – one of the smallest seeds that grows into 'the greatest of all shrubs, and puts forth large branches' (v.32). The image is ironic, and possibly even satirical. One has every right to expect the kingdom of God to be compared to the tallest and strongest of trees. But Jesus likens the Church to something that sprouts up quite quickly from almost nothing, and then develops into an ungainly sprawling shrub that barely holds up a bird's nest.

Churches, then, can take some comfort from the lips of Jesus. Like the mustard seed, a church can be an untidy sprawling shrub. Like a vine, it can be knotted and gnarled. Neither plant is much to look at. But Jesus was saying something quite profound about the nature of the Church: it will be rambling, extensive and just a tad jumbled. And that's the point. Jesus seems to understand that it often isn't easy to find your place in neat and tidy systems. And maybe you'll feel alienated and displaced for a while. But, in a messy and slightly disorderly Church, and in an unordered and rather rumpled institution, all may find a home.

COLLECT

Let your merciful ears, O Lord,
be open to the prayers of your humble servants;
and that they may obtain their petitions
make them to ask such things as shall please you;
through Jesus Christ your Son our Lord,
who is alive and reigns with you,
in the unity of the Holy Spirit,
one God, now and for ever.

Saturday 3 September

Mark 4.35-end

'Teacher, do you not care that we are perishing?' (v.38)

One of my favourite Woody Allen lines is this. If you want to make God laugh, tell him your future plans. The story of the stilling of the storm is hardly a barrel of laughs, but, for anyone with faith, it ought at least to raise a wry smile. The disciples – not for the first time – find that their plans are about as stable as the sea that threatens to engulf them. And, confronted by chaos, they quickly lose their faith. They even question the mindfulness and love of Jesus: 'do you not *care* that we are perishing?'

But all of this gives Jesus an opportunity to say two profound things in the face of apparent annihilation: 'Peace! Be still!' and 'Why are you afraid?' Sometimes we all find ourselves in the midst of what seem like great storms. We fear we will be engulfed. Even winds and waves are against us. Yet, we sometimes need to hear the words of Jesus that invite us out of fear and into peace. Sometimes what we need to do is reach out. Our salvation is nearer than we thought; it is within sight. Just not what we expected or thought.

The Scottish 20th-century philosopher John Macmurray tells us that the maxim of illusory religion runs like this: 'Fear not; trust in God and he will see that none of the things you fear will happen to you' (*Persons in Relation*, 1961 Gifford Lectures). But that of real religion is quite contrary: 'Fear not; the things you are afraid of are quite likely to happen to you – but they are nothing to be afraid of'. Peace be with you.

Lord of heaven and earth,
as Jesus taught his disciples to be persistent in prayer,
give us patience and courage never to lose hope,
but always to bring our prayers before you;
through Jesus Christ our Lord.

COLLECT

241

Mark 5.1-20

*'Go home to your friends, and tell them how much the Lord
has done for you' (v.19)*

An alienated man of terrifying strength, shackled by ungodly inner
turmoil, is, surprisingly, *drawn towards* Jesus, who takes immediate
and clear authority over *'Legion'*, over everything that works against
the fullness of life that God wants for this man, for us all.

Stunned swineherds watch as their herd surges to a sudden, squealing
death. The villagers crowd to see the outcast, now sane and safe in the
peaceful strength of Jesus. But, faced with the holiness of God
radiating through Jesus, they struggle with the unsettling mix of awe
and terror and beg Jesus to leave their territory.

Instead, Jesus' heart is turned towards the strengthening of
community, and he gives the man something simple and wonderful to
do: to tell the story of his restoration – to family, to friends, to all who
will listen. As he does this, the man will claim and deepen the truth of
his healing, and *others will be drawn* to the Love which enlivens the
universe and heals the most fractured soul.

This task is ours too, today. How do we share our God-story with those
with whom we live and work, and those for whom we pray?

COLLECT

O God, you declare your almighty power
most chiefly in showing mercy and pity:
mercifully grant to us such a measure of your grace,
that we, running the way of your commandments,
may receive your gracious promises,
and be made partakers of your heavenly treasure;
through Jesus Christ your Son our Lord,
who is alive and reigns with you,
in the unity of the Holy Spirit,
one God, now and for ever.

Psalms 87, **89.1-18**
Micah 2
Mark 5.21-34

Mark 5.21-34

'Daughter ...' (v.34)

Two distressed people enter our minds and hearts today: a father, repeatedly, publicly, pleading for his daughter's life, and a woman, privately, desperately, seeking an end to her suffering. As a religious leader, Jairus might have expected Jesus to 'drop everything' and answer his need without delay. Instead he feels the hope for his child fading as Jesus takes time out to meet and talk with a woman who dares to approach Jesus, contravening convention, risking everything.

What must Jairus have thought as Jesus stops, turns, asks, searches, waits ...?

How he must have longed to urge Jesus on – but Jesus is listening now to this woman, giving her the time to tell 'the whole truth'. Years of struggle and shame are shared and she is healed, not just physically but socially and emotionally too, as Jesus affirms her worth with words of relationship and healing: 'Daughter, your faith has made you well ...'

'Daughter' – what an irony. We can sense the tension in Jairus, can imagine him yelling at Jesus: 'But what about *my* daughter?' Jesus seems to be ignoring him.

Have you, like Jairus, ever felt overlooked or let down by God? Perhaps it's time to bring the pain of that disappointment to prayer, to share it with Jesus as honestly as you can.

God of glory,
the end of our searching,
help us to lay aside
all that prevents us from seeking your kingdom,
and to give all that we have
to gain the pearl beyond all price,
through our Saviour Jesus Christ.

COLLECT

Mark 5.35-end

'"Talitha cum", which means, "Little girl, get up!"' (v.41)

'Your daughter is dead.' This barren statement is overheard by Jesus, who, dismissing despair, bids Jairus make, in a matter of minutes, that life-long journey from fear to trust, from doubt to faith.

Stomach-churning loss is touched by a tiny, tentative hope. Curious crowds are turned away. The chosen few walk with Jesus towards the mystery of resurrection, so bright and certain in Jesus' mind. Wailing crowds are evicted. The parents and the expectant disciples accompany Jesus into the stillness of death and hear him speak two Aramaic words – clear, authoritative, calling the child back to life.

Jesus then, surprisingly, wisely, requests discretion, wary of those who would manipulate the girl's experience for their own purposes, or try to turn Jesus into something he was not and never would be – a man-made celebrity serving powers not of God.

As the emotional whirlpool begins to bubble with unimaginable joy, Jesus kindly suggests a practical task that will anchor the recovered child in the world of the living and reconnect her with her family. Through the comforting ritual of food shared with her loved ones, *her* new life can begin.

Today, Jesus invites *us* to 'get up' and reconnect with those we love, to open ourselves to his fullness so *our* new life can begin. How will we respond?

COLLECT

O God, you declare your almighty power
most chiefly in showing mercy and pity:
mercifully grant to us such a measure of your grace,
that we, running the way of your commandments,
may receive your gracious promises,
and be made partakers of your heavenly treasure;
through Jesus Christ your Son our Lord,
who is alive and reigns with you,
in the unity of the Holy Spirit,
one God, now and for ever.

Psalms 90, **92**
Micah 4.1 – 5.1
Mark 6.1-13

Mark 6.1-13

'He ordered them to take nothing for their journey ...' (v.8)

People who have seen us grow up can struggle to accept us in our adulthood. Jesus meets this dynamic when he returns to his home town and finds initial approval turning into outright denigration. Where he might reasonably have hoped for understanding, even joy in his vocation, he encounters such resistance that his capacity to draw people towards their healing is compromised. How it must have pained his spirit to have those whom he had known all his life reject who he has become and all he has to offer.

The Twelve, however, welcome the truth of his becoming, and take the risk of setting out with nothing more than a staff for support on the road. Because Jesus trusts them with this mission; because he inspires them to believe that they can be his hands and eyes and voice to those they meet, bringing new life and hope to the hurting, they respond with a leap of faith, a confidence that they can 'do all things through Christ'.

Where are we up to in *our* becoming in Christ? Would we be as fearless, as trusting, as these disciples, I wonder? Imagine leaving home without credit cards, keys or mobile phone, and then ask the question: 'In what do I put my security?'

God of glory,
the end of our searching,
help us to lay aside
all that prevents us from seeking your kingdom,
and to give all that we have
to gain the pearl beyond all price,
through our Saviour Jesus Christ.

COLLECT

245

Mark 6.14-29

*'Herod feared John, knowing that he was a righteous and holy man,
and he protected him' (v.20)*

What a sudden, shocking end to John the Baptist's life. This uncompromising prophet falls victim to a fatal combination: a conniving woman, the seduction of fleshly attraction, and the moral weakness of a man more interested in maintaining his image in front of his influential guests than in listening to the whisper of truth in his heart.

How easy it is for us to want to look good in front of others, even though this may mean that we go against what we know is right. The unacknowledged fear of 'what other people might think' can shape much of our behaviour, paralyse the person God has created us to be, and drive us down a path that leads to diminution and death.

John was free from that fear. Years spent living in the unforgiving conditions of the desert and listening to the Spirit in the wilderness had formed in him a deep sense of identity in God. John knew who he was and was committed to living out his vocation, to 'prepare the way of the Lord' even when he knew it put him at odds with the authorities and could cost him everything.

How free are *we* to live true to the person whom God has created each of us to be?

COLLECT

O God, you declare your almighty power
most chiefly in showing mercy and pity:
mercifully grant to us such a measure of your grace,
that we, running the way of your commandments,
may receive your gracious promises,
and be made partakers of your heavenly treasure;
through Jesus Christ your Son our Lord,
who is alive and reigns with you,
in the unity of the Holy Spirit,
one God, now and for ever.

Psalms 96, **97**, 100
Micah 6
Mark 6.30-44

Mark 6.30-44

'You give them something to eat ...' (v.37)

Two complementary fundamentals of the Christian life surface in this passage: contemplation, and compassionate action.

Jesus invites his disciples, so busy they haven't time to eat, to rest and, we can reasonably assume, to pray. For Jesus knows that from *contemplation* – that deep, sustained openness to the voice of the Spirit – will emerge the focus, confidence and emotional stamina the disciples need to serve others without succumbing to exhaustion or misunderstanding their call.

Compassionate action takes shape when Jesus, moved by the crowd's need, issues a challenge to his disciples to find a way of feeding the thousands who have followed him, looking for a miracle. They get one of course, the wonder of the multiplication of limited physical resources, an outward sign of the invisible Spirit at work. But the disciples get something more – they experience the reality of contemplation giving birth to compassionate action; they become part of the *outworking* of Jesus' power, perfected in silence and prayer. No longer simply observers or consumers, they *know* what happens when the ready spirit, enriched by deep prayer, meets and responds to human need.

How often do we take time to rest, pray *and listen* to God, *before* we undertake our daily tasks, big or small?

God of glory,
the end of our searching,
help us to lay aside
all that prevents us from seeking your kingdom,
and to give all that we have
to gain the pearl beyond all price,
through our Saviour Jesus Christ.

COLLECT

Mark 6.45-end

'Take heart, it is I; do not be afraid' (v.50)

The disciples, exhausted from rowing against the heavy swell, suddenly see Jesus *walking on the water.* Understandable anxiety about their battle with the elements immediately escalates into fear of the supernatural, and they cry out in terror.

Surely, fresh from seeing the multiplication of the loaves and fishes, the disciples would have understood Jesus' nature by now and, seeing him pass by, even at a distance, would have gained sufficient confidence to reach safe shore? But no – they were overwhelmed by their situation and *lost sight* of their recent experience of divine power at work. They clearly had still not internalized the truth that, in Jesus, someone of unique presence and power was among them.

Thankfully, grace-fully, when Jesus sees their panic, his first words are not words of chastisement but of encouragement, shouted through the storm, reminding them of his true identity, sending peace billowing across the wild waves.

We too can so easily lose sight of our experience of God when we are afraid or overwhelmed. But God in Jesus is only ever a prayer away. When we turn to him, even with shouts of terror, we can trust that his heartening words and peace-full presence *will* calm life's storms.

COLLECT

Almighty and everlasting God,
you are always more ready to hear than we to pray
and to give more than either we desire or deserve:
pour down upon us the abundance of your mercy,
forgiving us those things of which our conscience is afraid
and giving us those good things which we are not worthy to ask
but through the merits and mediation
of Jesus Christ your Son our Lord,
who is alive and reigns with you,
in the unity of the Holy Spirit,
one God, now and for ever.

Psalms **106*** (*or* 103)
Micah 7.8-end
Mark 7.1-13

Mark 7.1-13

'In vain do they worship me, teaching human precepts as doctrines'
(v.7)

What made these Pharisees undertake the hard journey from Jerusalem to Galilee? Was it indignation, curiosity, genuine interest, or even an unconscious wistfulness for something they could not quite name, a longing for something of the love of God hidden beneath their efforts to ensure that the law as they knew it was kept to the letter?

Whatever their motives, they would have been taken aback when, in response to their first question about his disciples' behaviour, Jesus condemns the way the religious leadership has subverted the principles of the law of Moses by favouring man-made 'traditions', even in relation to the fundamental obligations of children to care for their ageing parents.

Some traditions are life-giving, linking us with our forebears and the way our faith has been expressed for centuries. But some traditions serve our self-interest, or risk boxing in the creative Spirit of God, thwarting God's intention to shape new life among us. 'We've always done it this way' can be a common but life-denying response to proposed change in any relationship or institution, including the Church.

How wedded are we to our religious routines and liturgical preferences? How open are we to the challenging possibilities that God may want to bring into being through us?

God of constant mercy,
who sent your Son to save us:
remind us of your goodness,
increase your grace within us,
that our thankfulness may grow,
through Jesus Christ our Lord.

COLLECT

Wednesday 14 September

Holy Cross Day

Psalms 2, 8, 146
Genesis 3.1-15
John 12.27-36a

John 12.27-36a

'Now my heart is troubled ...' (v.27, NIV)

Jesus is dealing with the same human emotions as anyone facing impending death. However, rather than being paralysed by anguish or panic, he brings his feelings to his Father in honest prayer. His focus is restored; he stays faithful to the call of the God who loves him, transcends the fear, and looks beyond to the greater purposes of God: the work of the cross, the mystery of drawing *all people* to himself.

Power of
Prayer...

Through a divine dynamic far above our understanding, Jesus took upon himself then – and continues to take upon himself today – the pain and sinfulness of the world. In each individual human life, Jesus is ready and willing to bear for us the wounds that afflict us, freeing us to serve God with lightness of heart and mind.

However, Jesus can free us in this way *only* if we will first acknowledge our pain, if we name it for what it is before God, rather than trying to hide our woundedness behind masks of role, competence, religiosity or self-sufficiency.   *LEWIS's DENTIST*

Jesus is willing to bear our wounds *if* we will let him. If your 'heart is troubled', will you risk letting Jesus see your pain or hurt today? Will you bring it to him for healing and release?

COLLECT

Almighty God,
who in the passion of your blessed Son
made an instrument of painful death
to be for us the means of life and peace:
grant us so to glory in the cross of Christ
that we may gladly suffer for his sake;
who is alive and reigns with you,
in the unity of the Holy Spirit,
one God, now and for ever.

Psalms 113, 115
Habakkuk 1.12 – 2.5
Mark 7.24-30

Mark 7.24-30

'Sir, even the dogs under the table eat the children's crumbs' (v.28)

A feisty, foreign woman argues with Jesus. We applaud her persistence, wit and guts, but we can also see the inner struggle of Jesus as he explores the expansion of his vocation to include the Gentiles.

▷ INTERESTING..

Jesus naturally feels drawn to minister among the 'chosen people' of God – but, instead of welcoming him, the Jewish religious leaders are suspicious, confrontational. In this encounter, we can almost hear Jesus wrestling with the paradox: he longs to bring to the 'children' the good news of God's grace, but his *actual* experience repeatedly tells him that those who grasp his divine uniqueness, who are open to his loving message, are often *not* the Jews but the 'others', those deemed 'outsiders' because of their gender, race, traditions or illness, or those whose work evokes public censure. *EG TAX COLLECTORS*

While Jesus' words to the woman might seem harsh to us initially, in this interaction she helps us to see the pivotal moment when part of old Simeon's prophecy (Luke 2.29-32) takes flesh. Jesus becomes for the desperate woman 'a light for revelation to the Gentiles ...' as he shares with her something of his divinity, pronounces longed-for healing for her child, and consciously embraces both Gentile and Jew.

How have you seen the call of God on *your* life change and expand in unexpected ways?

Friday 16 September

Mark 7.31-end

'And immediately his ears were opened, his tongue was released, and he spoke plainly' (v.35)

How respectfully Jesus meets this unnamed man. We see Jesus stop and immediately understand the man's need of privacy for his healing. This man who has heard no sound, who has been unable to make himself understood without embarrassment, will need to be introduced to the wonder of hearing quietly, his first efforts at speech witnessed by Jesus alone.

This man is healed not by a long-distance miracle but in an intensely personal encounter with Jesus, who takes his time, who touches gently the deafened ears, who mysteriously uses his own saliva to salve the man's tight tongue. Acknowledging the depth of healing needed, a profound sigh comes from Jesus' lips. The pain of the man's limited life dissolves in the single sweet command, 'Be opened'.

Sounds from outside begin to filter through *the man's* unblocked ears. His first efforts at speech fall on *Jesus'* ears – we can imagine Jesus encouraging him as words begin to tumble through loosened lips – perhaps they laugh – and cry – together as the journey from isolation to community begins and a whole new life comes to birth.

What impediments to communication with those you love, or with God, are you experiencing?

In what part of your life do you need to hear Jesus' words: 'Be opened'?

COLLECT

Almighty and everlasting God,
you are always more ready to hear than we to pray
and to give more than either we desire or deserve:
pour down upon us the abundance of your mercy,
forgiving us those things of which our conscience is afraid
and giving us those good things which we are not worthy to ask
but through the merits and mediation
of Jesus Christ your Son our Lord,
who is alive and reigns with you,
in the unity of the Holy Spirit,
one God, now and for ever.

Psalms 120, 121, 122
Habakkuk 3.2-19a
Mark 8.1-10

Saturday 17 September

Mark 8.1-10

'I have compassion for the crowd, because they have been with me now for three days ...' (v.2)

Again Jesus' deep compassion finds expression in an act of amazing provision, this time for 4,000 people who, for *three days*, have been listening to Jesus, walking with him, watching him work wonders in unlikely places for unlikely people. Something about him has proved so engaging that they are continually drawn to him, and he, in turn, meets and fulfils their needs – not simply their physical need for nourishment, but also their longing for healing, for a deep sense of community, for inner freedom, for real and lasting joy.

What would it be like for them – for us – to spend three days in Jesus' company? Surely there would be enough time for little deaths and resurrections to happen in their lives, and in ours: the ego's plea for attention quietened; family squabbles and anxious thoughts dissolved in the warmth of his presence; hopelessness exchanged for a future; exhaustion replaced by new energy.

If you long for deep healing, for food which is eternal, why not spend 'three days' on retreat with Jesus? In the warm silence of God, experience for yourself the dynamic of letting go, of waiting, then of emerging to new life, held safe in the presence of Christ who can work wonders in our unlikely lives.

God of constant mercy,
who sent your Son to save us:
remind us of your goodness,
increase your grace within us,
that our thankfulness may grow,
through Jesus Christ our Lord.

COLLECT

Monday 19 September

Psalms 123, 124, 125, **126**
Haggai 1.1-11
Mark 8.11-21

Mark 8.11-21

'Then he said to them, "Do you not yet understand?"' (v.21)

The Pharisees want proof of Jesus' God-given uniqueness. But Jesus recognizes that a sign would make no difference, for their approach to God is through minds that are chained to analysis, to debating fine points of interpretation of the Torah. The God who seeks loving relationship with his people seems beyond their understanding. How frustrating for Jesus to find religious leaders who simply cannot 'see' him, because they want to unpick every word of Scripture to test its truth while the Word, the Truth stands before them, sighing.

[handwritten: I's THIS ALL BAD?]

How sad for Jesus that the disciples who have been part of recent, exceptional events among the hungry crowds, and have daily witnessed 'signs and wonders', seem forgetful, not only of their need for bread, but also of the spiritual implications of what they have seen Jesus do and be. Locked in their practical, literal world, they struggle to grasp the broader, symbolic meaning of Jesus' words and actions.

[handwritten: DISCIPLES ARE MODERN-ISTS!]

Do *we* frustrate and sadden our Lord too? Are we so fascinated by *studying* Scripture that we forget to *pray* with Scripture and so build our relationship with him? Do we forget moments of graced encounter with God, because we are locked in the land of the literal and cannot grasp that we are the delight of God's heart?

COLLECT

Almighty God,
who called your Church to bear witness
that you were in Christ reconciling the world to yourself:
help us to proclaim the good news of your love,
that all who hear it may be drawn to you;
through him who was lifted up on the cross,
and reigns with you in the unity of the Holy Spirit,
one God, now and for ever.

Psalms **132**, 133
Haggai 1.12 – 2.9
Mark 8.22-26

Mark 8.22-26

*'Some people brought a blind man to him and begged him
to touch him' (v.22)*

How *we* long for those *we* love, who may seem 'blind' to the journey of faith, to connect with Jesus. AMEN.

How can we share the gospel if our family seems unaware of the Spirit, if friends avoid church or see no need for God, if the name of Jesus spills from colleagues' lips as an expletive rather than as praise?

We get some clues from the friends of the blind man – but some serious questions are raised for each of us as well.

They *knew* what Jesus was like – what does my personal experience of Jesus, of God, tell me?

They *believed* that Jesus could transform their friend's life – do I really believe that Jesus can radically change for good the lives of those I love?

When the time was right, they *put their faith into action* – am I listening for the Holy Spirit's prompting?

They *confidently asked* Jesus to address the man's needs – to what extent am I confident that Jesus *will* act?

They *entrusted* their friend to the care of Jesus, who *draws* all people to himself and does not need to cajole, entrap, drive or scare people into the kingdom – how ready am I to relinquish control and let God be God for my loved ones?

Almighty God,
you search us and know us:
may we rely on you in strength
and rest on you in weakness,
now and in all our days;
through Jesus Christ our Lord.

COLLECT

Wednesday 21 September

Psalms 49, 117
I Kings 19.15-end
2 Timothy 3.14-end

Matthew, Apostle and Evangelist

2 Timothy 3.14-end

'All scripture is inspired by God ...' (v.16)

Two aspects of faith formation are visible here: nurture within family life and interaction with the Word of God.

Paul commends the spiritual foundation given to Timothy by his mother and grandmother, especially his exposure to 'sacred writings'. Paul, true to his Pharisaic background, emphasizes Scripture's God-given capacity to guide, correct and 'train in righteousness'. His experience clearly lies more with studying Scripture than praying with it. Yet *praying* with Scripture helps *us* move from knowing *about* God to *knowing* God – a transition Paul made when he was rendered powerless on the Damascus road as the Word broke into his life, reminding him that God seeks *relationship*, not simply obedience to a set of principles.

Today, the ancient prayer practice of *lectio divina* (sacred reading) is being reclaimed in Christian circles. The daily discipline of unhurried reading of a small portion of Scripture, discovering connections with our own context, making our response and gently resting in the love of God opens the gateway to contemplation, that state of graced availability to God accessible to all Christians.

Whether or not *our* upbringing encouraged our fledgling faith, we can choose both to study *and* to pray with Scripture, giving space for our God to love us, inspire us and equip us for service.

COLLECT

O Almighty God,
whose blessed Son called Matthew the tax collector
to be an apostle and evangelist:
give us grace to forsake the selfish pursuit of gain
    and the possessive love of riches
that we may follow in the way of your Son Jesus Christ,
who is alive and reigns with you,
in the unity of the Holy Spirit,
one God, now and for ever.

Thursday 22 September

Mark 9.2-13

'This is my Son, the Beloved; listen to him!' (v.7)

What did the chosen disciples expect as they tramped up the mountainside, pausing to catch their breath, looking out over the wide plains to Galilee? Surely not the sight of two foundational figures evoking the law and the prophets standing alongside Jesus, the fulfilment of both? Nor Christ, lit as if from within, his purity and holiness shimmering out in uncommon brilliance around them? Nor the sudden cloud cover and the voice from nowhere echoing around their startled ears, the words of God affirming his Son?

This profound religious experience comes without warning, revealing Jesus as the Light, as the Beloved, and leaving the observers stunned. We can understand Peter's impulsive attempt to capture the moment, to hold it still long enough to make some sense of what was happening before their astonished eyes.

But soon they have to come down from the mountain – and Jesus, knowing that this event will only make real sense *after* the resurrection, warns the disciples not to dissipate the intensity and wonder of their experience by conjecture, nor to incite envy among the other disciples, but to keep it to themselves.

This will not be the end of their – or our – encounters with the fullness of Christ.

All they, and we, need to do for now is listen. Listen to Jesus.

Almighty God,
who called your Church to bear witness
that you were in Christ reconciling the world to yourself:
help us to proclaim the good news of your love,
that all who hear it may be drawn to you;
through him who was lifted up on the cross,
and reigns with you in the unity of the Holy Spirit,
one God, now and for ever.

COLLECT

257

Friday 23 September

Mark 9.14-29

'All things can be done for the one who believes' (v.23)

Themes of despair and hope, uncertainty and confidence, belief and unbelief, weave through this narrative, drawing us into the powerful human drama of a father's last-ditch plea to Jesus, whose disciples have failed to heal his ailing son.

This passage confronts us with the reality that much of Jesus' ministry is described in terms of exorcism, freeing people from forces that prevent them from living a full life. Whether, as postmodern Christians, we prefer to use reason and science to 'explain' miraculous healings, or whether we gladly accept the reality of divine power, we come to realize that, whatever the *cause* of the boy's illness, it is the *outcome* of Jesus' intervention that is paramount. After all, what is more amazing? That Jesus could command an 'unclean' spirit to leave its host and depart, screaming in protest, or that he could speak words of authority to completely heal the boy of what might today be named epilepsy?

Whatever *we* believe, we cannot deny that, in Jesus' action, resourced by the deep wells of intense, God-focused prayer, there is something uniquely powerful and beautifully restorative at work.

Jesus still liberates us from our 'demons' today, when we choose to say: 'Lord I believe; help my unbelief!' (v.24).

COLLECT

Almighty God,
who called your Church to bear witness
that you were in Christ reconciling the world to yourself:
help us to proclaim the good news of your love,
that all who hear it may be drawn to you;
through him who was lifted up on the cross,
and reigns with you in the unity of the Holy Spirit,
one God, now and for ever.

Mark 9.30-37

*'Whoever welcomes one such child in my name
welcomes me …' (v.37)*

The tension is mounting for both Jesus and the disciples as he anticipates the events that will culminate in his death and resurrection. Poignantly, Jesus speaks about 'the Son of Man', as if holding the frightening reality at arm's length as he grapples with the fast-approaching end to his life.

His words and wariness alarm his disciples, but, instead of risking a direct question, they take refuge in jostling among themselves for status, more intent on establishing some sort of 'pecking order' than on acknowledging Jesus' impending suffering and their own responsibility to further the kingdom of God.

Once in the safety and privacy of Capernaum, settled in the house near the lake's edge, Jesus reminds his disciples of the virtue of humility, and wearily confronts them with their power-seeking. Reversing the cultural norms of rank, he elevates to centre stage the lowest of all: a child. Embarrassed, the disciples watch as Jesus takes this little one in his arms and speaks of the grace of welcome, painting a clear picture: the arms and hearts which welcome, in Christ-like love, the least important, are welcoming Jesus and his Father.

May we have the humility to set aside our ego's need of recognition, and live a welcoming life.

Almighty God,
you search us and know us:
may we rely on you in strength
and rest on you in weakness,
now and in all our days;
through Jesus Christ our Lord.

COLLECT

Mark 9.38-end

'Do not stop him …' (v.39)

Jesus' inclusiveness extends to 'outsiders' who are doing 'deeds of power' in his name, but John seems anxious to control, to 'manage' the spread of the good news. Jesus reminds him, and us, that anyone who values Jesus' teachings and reaches out to heal others in his name will inevitably be drawn closer and closer to Jesus, drawn by the Truth to the Truth.

Conversely, those who are plotting against Jesus and putting 'stumbling blocks' in the way of those who, in child-like trust, seek Jesus are heading for destruction as they increasingly distance themselves from the reality of Jesus' identity and purpose. Emphasizing the gravity of the situation for such people, Jesus uses a reference to Jerusalem's smouldering, worm-ravaged rubbish dump, formerly a place of child sacrifice, to symbolize the consequences of that distancing from God.

His main point is made using not literal language but graphic hyperbole: *nothing* must get in the way of living our lives in accordance with the will of God. Recognizing, and letting the Spirit excise, our unholy habits may be as painful as an amputation, but ruthless honesty about our contrariness, wilful resistance and diluting of the standards God sets is needed, if we are to 'keep our saltiness' and serve God with joy.

COLLECT

Almighty God,
whose only Son has opened for us
a new and living way into your presence:
give us pure hearts and steadfast wills
to worship you in spirit and in truth;
through Jesus Christ your Son our Lord,
who is alive and reigns with you,
in the unity of the Holy Spirit,
one God, now and for ever.

Psalms **5**, 6 (8)
Zechariah 6.9-end
Mark 10.1-16

Tuesday 27 September

Mark 10.1-16

'… and the two shall become one flesh' (v.8)

The Pharisees are still trying to catch Jesus out, but he answers their question with a question of his own, pointing them to the law of Moses who, conscious of human frailty, had made provision for divorce.

To his disciples, however, Jesus reinforces God's ideal: monogamy. In this exclusive commitment to each other, a man and a woman become one flesh joined by God, thus providing mutual support, social stability, a nurturing environment for their children and, importantly, mirroring the faithful covenantal relationship between God and his people. *THEOLOGICAL SIGNIFICANCE*

God always wants the best for us, the optimum in relationships, vocation, service and the joy of a life lived fully in the will of God. But if that ideal falters or fails under the weight of grief, violence, deceit or apathy, a way out of the pain into the light of a fresh start is offered.

That journey, from sad endings to new freedom within the kingdom of God, requires not hardness of heart but courageous inner searching, aided by the Holy Spirit. Jesus will never turn anyone away who comes to him in child-like trust and with confidence that God, as loving parent, will meet us at our point of need and set us once more on the path towards wholeness.

Merciful God,
your Son came to save us
and bore our sins on the cross:
may we trust in your mercy
and know your love,
rejoicing in the righteousness
that is ours through Jesus Christ our Lord.

COLLECT

Wednesday 28 September

Mark 10.17-31

'Jesus, looking at him, loved him' (v.21)

Kneeling before Jesus is an earnest man. He calls Jesus 'Good teacher' but draws a surprising reproof. Only after affirming that goodness is found in God alone does Jesus remind the man of the conventional Hebraic wisdom – the commandments. The man's hopeful response indicates his diligence in attending to his duty under the law, but still does not attract the approval he is seeking.

Instead Jesus *looks, really looks* at the man, aware of his outward compliance with religious codes of behaviour, but seeing within to the state of the man's heart, where conflicting priorities jostle for primacy: the distractions, worries and preoccupations of wealth, and the unnamed longing to live the sort of life the man sees radiating from Jesus, a life that vividly reveals the fruits of the spirit (Galatians 5.22).

Jesus looks *lovingly* – he is not scathing of the man's attachment to wealth but compassionate, understanding humanity's struggle to exchange the spurious security of worldly wealth for the eternal reward he offers. For this reward may well include persecution, self-sacrifice and a counter-cultural ordering of priorities as well as the wonder of deep relationships based on shared faith, and the indescribable mystery of living in Christ for all time.

What would Jesus see if he *lovingly* looked at you, at me, today?

COLLECT

Almighty God,
whose only Son has opened for us
a new and living way into your presence:
give us pure hearts and steadfast wills
to worship you in spirit and in truth;
through Jesus Christ your Son our Lord,
who is alive and reigns with you,
in the unity of the Holy Spirit,
one God, now and for ever.

Psalms 34, 150
Tobit 12.6-end *or* Daniel 12.1-4
Acts 12.1-11

Daniel 12.1-4

'Many of those who sleep in the dust of the earth shall awake' (v.2)

In this apocalyptic vision, a central role is given to the archangel Michael, who is described as 'the great prince', 'the protector' of Israel. Rather than gloriously being the bearer of good news from God, as we see later in the annunciation to Mary (Luke 1.26-38), Michael will come as a warrior angel, powerful beyond imagining, taking authority over forces opposed to God.

Some might question the language of 'angels and demons', or the supernatural emphasis on the coming together of all things in a cathartic encounter reminiscent of battle scenes from *Lord of the Rings*. Others might unhesitatingly embrace the extraordinary attributes of such beings and their roles in the story of God. Whatever our viewpoint, this passage interestingly contains the first biblical reference to the emergence of *resurrected* beings, and several important Scriptural themes:

- the labouring of the creation as it comes to the fullness God intended
- all things coming to their proper conclusion in Christ, at a time to be determined by God
- accountability to God for our actions
- the virtues of wisdom and servanthood.

No matter what we may have to face in the uncertain future, may we hold fast to Christ, our still centre, who overcomes confusion, panic and evil.

Everlasting God,
you have ordained and constituted
the ministries of angels and mortals in a wonderful order:
grant that as your holy angels always serve you in heaven,
so, at your command,
they may help and defend us on earth;
through Jesus Christ your Son our Lord,
who is alive and reigns with you,
in the unity of the Holy Spirit,
one God, now and for ever.

COLLECT

Mark 10.35-45

'... whoever wishes to be great among you must be your servant' (v.43)

Whether or not the audacious appeal from James and John is consistent with their nickname, 'sons of thunder', it reveals the universal, human dynamic of wanting to be first, 'a cut above' everyone else.

Jesus responds to their request for places of honour by questioning their understanding. Their eyes still shuttered by ego-driven needs, the wider wonder of the nature of the kingdom of God eludes them. Nor can they grasp the cost of discipleship when, without hesitation, they answer 'yes' to Jesus' question: 'Can you drink …?' They are oblivious to the solemnity of his reply – they *will* 'drink his cup' and experience the same 'baptism', but not in the way they expect. Their request naturally angers their fellow disciples and draws a clear reminder from Jesus that he came to *serve* and that that is what he expects of his disciples – then and now.

The miracle is that, in the early days of Christianity, both James and John lived and died *in the service* of others. Their attitude of 'me first' was transformed by the Holy Spirit into 'others first', expressed in James' martyrdom and in John's foundation of a vibrant community and, authenticated by recent scholarship, the gift of the Gospel which bears his name.

Are we living a 'me first' or an 'others first' life?

COLLECT

Almighty God,
whose only Son has opened for us
a new and living way into your presence:
give us pure hearts and steadfast wills
to worship you in spirit and in truth;
through Jesus Christ your Son our Lord,
who is alive and reigns with you,
in the unity of the Holy Spirit,
one God, now and for ever.

Psalms 20, 21, **23**
Zechariah 9.1-12
Mark 10.46-end

Mark 10.46-end

'What do you want me to do for you?' (v.51)

Bartimaeus is living a restricted, precarious life until, like a sweet fragrance, the name of Jesus touches his senses. Rough words do not stop his shouts for mercy, and soon he hears the voice of Jesus inviting him closer. The crowd's annoyance changes to encouragement as Bartimaeus throws off the minimal security of his sheltering cloak and is guided forward by suddenly helpful hands.

Jesus reaches out to touch the man, holds him steady in front of him, looks lovingly into the sightless eyes and the stunted soul within. Jesus can heal him at once, of course, but instead he asks a seemingly redundant question: 'What do you want me to do for you?'

The watchers may well have muttered: 'Can't you see he's blind?' Jesus, however, knows how difficult it can be for someone who has lived a life of dependence, who has imagined the marvellous moment of regained sight time and again in his mind, to be faced with imminent, life-changing healing. So, Jesus provides time for the man to feel the gentle warmth of Jesus' presence and gain the confidence to name his need and claim his freedom.

Jesus asks us this same question. Will we 'take heart' and name our need to Jesus so we may have life in all its fullness?

Merciful God,
your Son came to save us
and bore our sins on the cross:
may we trust in your mercy
and know your love,
rejoicing in the righteousness
that is ours through Jesus Christ our Lord.

COLLECT

Monday 3 October

Psalms 27, **30**
Zechariah 10
Mark 11.1-11

Mark 11.1-11

'Blessed is the one who comes in the name of the Lord!' (v.9)

In his Palm Sunday procession, Jesus is deliberately exerting the imperial claims of God's redeeming love. What happened that day was, as this passage shows, intended and planned down to the last detail. Publicly, boldly, knowing exactly what he is doing, whom he is challenging and what he is risking, Jesus here makes at last a public and open assertion of his right to reign as God's appointed king. He accepts the Hosannas of the multitudes, not because of their depth or their sincerity, but because they are his due and they are true. He *does* indeed come in the name of the Lord, and he does indeed come to save God's people from the oppressive religious imperialism of the organized religion of the temple and the military imperialism of rampant Rome. How is this passage anti-terra?

In the estimation of his enemies, he looks weak and vulnerable, but – make no mistake about it – his is a love so strong that it will not yield to anybody or anything, that will go to all lengths and all depths to have its way with humanity. This king does not oppress; he liberates, his love takes him to the cross, but from that cross he reigns!

How do you know this from the passage?

COLLECT

God, who in generous mercy sent the Holy Spirit
    upon your Church in the burning fire of your love:
grant that your people may be fervent
in the fellowship of the gospel
that, always abiding in you,
they may be found steadfast in faith and active in service;
through Jesus Christ your Son our Lord,
who is alive and reigns with you,
in the unity of the Holy Spirit,
one God, now and for ever.

Psalms 32, **36**
Zechariah 11.4-end
Mark 11.12-26

THE TEMPLE, LIKE **Mark 11.12-26**

THE TREE, *'... you have made it a den of robbers' (v.17)*
BEARS NO FRUIT...

The cursing of the fig tree is the symbolic framework for the cleansing of the temple. Both must go because both have become unfit for purpose. In its worship, the temple still proclaims itself a place committed to God and the service of his people – 'a house of prayer for all the nations' – but what it is really about is raising money and institutional maintenance – 'you have made it a den of robbers' (v.17).

Of this same temple, the Jesus of St John's Gospel said: 'Destroy this temple, and in three days I will raise it up' (John 2.19). His ultimate purpose is its remaking, the reorientation of the worship and life of God's people to the purposes to which he has called them. But, before

JUDGEMENT the new can come, the old that impedes and denies it must go;
BEFORE destabilizing judgement has to be heeded before restoring grace can
GRACE rebuild. When Jesus comes, the promise of a new beginning requires the rejection of the corrupt *status quo.* The tragedy is that the people in charge of the temple will not bow to the judgement, and so they exclude themselves from the promise.

If Jesus came now with his reproving whip in his hand, where do you think he would start?

Lord God,
defend your Church from all false teaching
and give to your people knowledge of your truth,
that we may enjoy eternal life
in Jesus Christ our Lord.

COLLECT

Wednesday 5 October

Psalm **34**
Zechariah 12.1-10
Mark 11.27-end

Mark 11.27-end

'By what authority are you doing these things?' (v.27)

Sometimes we ask the right questions but cannot hear the answers that Jesus could give to them. The Palm Sunday messianic procession and the disruptive attack on the temple do indeed raise very loudly the question of the nature and authority of Jesus, and the Pharisees are fully justified in asking it.

The trouble is that the authorities that matter *to them* prevent them from recognizing the authority that motivates *him*. They know about the institutional authority of hereditary kings and priests in the succession of Aaron, but by that measure this man is neither royal nor priestly.

They say that they listen to God – but, as Jesus' counter-question demonstrates, they actually defer to public opinion; they are so in awe of what other people are saying about John the Baptist that they have nothing of their own to say about him.

The Church in our day is tempted either to take refuge in the institutional authority we have inherited from the past or to conform ourselves to the dominant culture of the present. In fact, our life and our salvation depend on seeing in Jesus the living incarnation of the intrinsic authority of the living God.

COLLECT

God, who in generous mercy sent the Holy Spirit
  upon your Church in the burning fire of your love:
grant that your people may be fervent
in the fellowship of the gospel
that, always abiding in you,
they may be found steadfast in faith and active in service;
through Jesus Christ your Son our Lord,
who is alive and reigns with you,
in the unity of the Holy Spirit,
one God, now and for ever.

Psalm **37***
Zechariah 13
Mark 12.1-12

Mark 12.1-12

'This is the heir; come, let us kill him' (v.7)

The nearer we get to Jesus, the more we see how far away from him we still are. To know what sin is, you must first know who God is. When you see the self-giving love in which he comes close to you, everything in you that resists and rejects that love is laid bare; when you see how he good he is, all the disguises are stripped away, and you see how bad you are.

The story of Old Testament Israel presented in this parable is a sorry story of judgement and rejection. When God spoke to them by his prophets, they rejected the message and persecuted the messengers; now that he has gone further in love by coming among them in his Son, they are about to go further in hate by nailing him to the cross.

This happens not because Israel is specially wicked but because Israel is specially chosen. When God comes closer to them than to any others, the sin that is latent in everybody is exposed in them. When Christ comes close, we see the same sin in ourselves and we cry to the Jesus whose love judges us: 'Have mercy on me!'

Lord God,
defend your Church from all false teaching
and give to your people knowledge of your truth,
that we may enjoy eternal life
in Jesus Christ our Lord.

COLLECT

Friday 7 October

Mark 12.13-17

'Is it lawful to pay taxes to the emperor, or not?' (v.14) — IS π ?

Jesus' answer to the question put to him is a clear 'Yes'. If the state provides services, it is entitled to collect taxes to pay for them. But his answer is subtle and careful. The secondary claims of Caesar are a subset of the primary claims of God. CAESAR CLAIMS TO BE GOD !

Jesus avoids both the traps set for him. Caesar's claims are real but far from absolute and final. There is a time to be loyal to Caesar, to preserve the civil order that he guarantees, and there is a time to defy and resist Caesar out of a prior loyalty to God. As Peter put it later, 'We must obey God rather than men'.

Different Christian traditions give different degrees of priority to these potentially competing claims. Established churches are under constant temptation to kow-tow to the governments on which they depend, and too easily bless their bombs and their banners. Churches that have had to contend with state persecution can easily forget that even hostile Caesar performs services ordained by God. ➤ IMPORTANT TO REMEMBER

In an increasingly secular society, contemporary Christians need to be fully responsible citizens but must also know when to say 'No' to demands that come between them and their God.

HOW DOES THIS WORK W. FREE WILL ?

COLLECT

God, who in generous mercy sent the Holy Spirit
    upon your Church in the burning fire of your love:
grant that your people may be fervent
in the fellowship of the gospel
that, always abiding in you,
they may be found steadfast in faith and active in service;
through Jesus Christ your Son our Lord,
who is alive and reigns with you,
in the unity of the Holy Spirit,
one God, now and for ever.

Psalms 41, **42**, 43
Zechariah 14.12-end
Mark 12.18-27

Mark 12.18-27

'In the resurrection whose wife will she be?' (v.23)

The Sadducees depicted here are too earthly minded to be of any heavenly use! The question they pose to Jesus is frivolous and irrelevant; they ridicule the possibility of a resurrection life by assuming that it will be a continuation of the conditions and concerns of life as we know it now, where seven former husbands contend for the one wife. No wonder Jesus tells them that they know neither the Scriptures nor the power of God.

In response, he makes two statements, one negative and disconcerting, the other positive and reassuring. Many married couples have been upset by the statement that marriage no longer counts for anything in the fulfilled kingdom of God.

The answer to that is the positive promise that God is the God not of the dead but of the living, and that, in the life to come, we shall therefore be sharers in his love, with all the commitment, passion and joy that brings. That must mean that the love we have tasted in marriage, far from being abolished, will rather be fulfilled in ways beyond our present comprehension or imagining. May we all die and live to see the day.

Lord God,
defend your Church from all false teaching
and give to your people knowledge of your truth,
that we may enjoy eternal life
in Jesus Christ our Lord.

COLLECT

Monday 10 October

Psalm **44**
Ecclesiasticus 1.1-10
or Ezekiel 1.1-14
Mark 12.28-34

Mark 12.28-34

'There is no other commandment greater than these' (v.31)

TRUE! [Nowadays, in our secular society, many people reverse the order of the two great commandments on which Jesus and this young lawyer are both agreed.] A good relationship with other people is recognized as the overriding public imperative for everyone, but a good relationship with God is often written off as an optional extra, the private choice of a religious minority of no importance to anybody else.

But the wisdom of ancient Israel knows that how you understand the second commandment is defined by whether or not you acknowledge the priority of the first. Whom I recognize as my neighbours and what I think is involved in loving them depends on what I believe about what ultimately makes the world tick the way it does. If it is a Darwinian world ruled by the survival of the fittest, there will not be many neighbours and not much love. But if it is the world created, claimed and redeemed by the triune God of the gospel, then his love as shown in Christ will be the model that challenges and inspires all my relationships with other people. As John put it, 'We love because he first loved us' (1 John 4.19).

COLLECT

O Lord, we beseech you mercifully to hear the prayers
    of your people who call upon you;
and grant that they may both perceive and know
    what things they ought to do,
and also may have grace and power faithfully to fulfil them;
through Jesus Christ your Son our Lord,
who is alive and reigns with you,
in the unity of the Holy Spirit,
one God, now and for ever.

Psalms **48**, 52
Ecclesiasticus 1.11-end
or Ezekiel 1.15 – 2.2
Mark 12.35-end

Mark 12.35-end

'David himself calls him Lord; so how can he be his son?' (v.37)

Orthodox iconography uses reverse perspective; the further into the picture you look, the more the vista expands, widens and deepens into the mysterious background beyond.

In this cryptic passage, Jesus uses the quote from Psalm 110 to give that sort of perspective to his own messianic calling. As the son of David, he will faithfully fulfil God's promises to Israel, but he will do it against a background that is immeasurably deeper and greater than anything that Jewish expectations contemplated. He will indeed be David's son, but he will also be David's Lord.

He will be Messiah in a way that redeems not just Israel but the whole world; not by the exercise of armed violence but by the suffering and self-giving of the cross. In his person, he will not just be the ultimate Jewish king, but will embody and display an identity with Israel's God at which this claim to be David's Lord hints and points.

Jesus is the Messiah of Israel or he is nothing at all, but the more you enter into him, the more you become aware of his mysterious greatness, so that with Thomas you ultimately own him 'my Lord and my God'.

Lord of creation,
whose glory is around and within us:
open our eyes to your wonders,
that we may serve you with reverence
and know your peace at our lives' end,
through Jesus Christ our Lord.

COLLECT

Wednesday 12 October	Psalm 119.57-80 Ecclesiasticus 2 *or* Ezekiel 2.3 – 3.11 Mark 13.1-13

Mark 13.1-13

'Not one stone will be left here upon another;
all will be thrown down' (v.2)

A former dean of Salisbury used to stand every morning at his deanery door, look over to the magnificent pile facing him and say: 'O great Cathedral, the day will come when the Lord has no more use for you.'

Great buildings and the ancient traditions they incorporate can reach a point where they impede or resist the very purposes they were set up to serve, and then, like the Jerusalem temple, they become idolatrous sources of temptation that must be removed.

Universally, whenever and wherever Christ comes, the more powerful his presence, the more tumultuous is the resistance to it. The true Messiah will be challenged by false prophets, there will be outbreaks of murderous strife on an international scale; even the forces of nature will, in earthquake and famine, be stirred into a rebellion that frustrates the life-giving will of their Creator.

The Church where in word and sacrament Christ is most explicitly present will feel the full brunt of persecuting opposition and internal division, and will be driven to pray for that quality of endurance that will bring it to its goal of salvation in the fully unveiled majesty of its crucified and risen Lord.

COLLECT

O Lord, we beseech you mercifully to hear the prayers
    of your people who call upon you;
and grant that they may both perceive and know
    what things they ought to do,
and also may have grace and power faithfully to fulfil them;
through Jesus Christ your Son our Lord,
who is alive and reigns with you,
in the unity of the Holy Spirit,
one God, now and for ever.

Psalms 56, **57** (63*)
Ecclesiasticus 3.17-29
or Ezekiel 3.12-end
Mark 13.14-23

Mark 13.14-23

'But be alert; I have already told you everything' (v.23)

The gospel is a bit like contemporary climate change: the more it advances, the more frequently and severely extreme conditions prevail. It is right to pray with the *Book of Common Prayer* that 'we should pass our time in rest and quietness', because without conditions of outward tranquillity, the gospel would find it hard to take root and grow, as indeed it first grew in the relative peace that Rome gave to the ancient world. Besides, as this passage acknowledges, constant crisis is beyond human enduring.

Nevertheless, a faith untried by crisis can become soft and flabby. We only know how secure our stance is when somebody tries to push us off our perch. As the gospel advances, the Church that is founded on it will be increasingly challenged by adverse natural and cultural environments, by persecuting opponents and heretical false Messiahs – and the pain, suffering and confusion will be sore and real.

But when everything is being shaken, the things that cannot be shaken will emerge more and more clearly, and chief among them will be the words of Jesus. On these words, and specifically on his warnings to be ready for a crisis, the Church and its members will survive the storms and stand.

Lord of creation,
whose glory is around and within us:
open our eyes to your wonders,
that we may serve you with reverence
and know your peace at our lives' end,
through Jesus Christ our Lord.

COLLECT

Friday 14 October

Mark 13.24-31

*'Then they will see "the Son of Man coming in clouds"
with great power and glory' (v.26)*

There is an ongoing scholarly debate about what is meant by the coming of the Son of Man in verse 26. Where does he come from and where is he going to? The traditional answer is that he is coming for the second time from heaven to earth, from his reign at the right hand of the Father to fulfil and complete work of judgement and salvation that he inaugurated in his first coming.

The challenging view points back from this text to Daniel 7.13, on which it is clearly based. There the journey is in the opposite direction; the Son of Man comes to the Ancient of Days, is presented to him and is given 'dominion and glory and kingship'.

So, is Jesus speaking here of his coming to God in his ascension or his return to earth in his *second coming*? Does it refer to the beginning of the last days or to their culmination? Leaving the scholars to argue their corner, we can be content to see that, between ascension and *parousia*, we are living in these last days where Jesus already reigns hiddenly from heaven, looking to the time when at last he will reign openly on earth.

COLLECT

O Lord, we beseech you mercifully to hear the prayers
    of your people who call upon you;
and grant that they may both perceive and know
    what things they ought to do,
and also may have grace and power faithfully to fulfil them;
through Jesus Christ your Son our Lord,
who is alive and reigns with you,
in the unity of the Holy Spirit,
one God, now and for ever.

Psalm **68**
Ecclesiasticus 4.29 – 6.1
or Ezekiel 9
Mark 13.32-end

Mark 13.32-end

*'Beware, keep alert; for you do not know
when the time will come' (v.33)*

The first line of an old hymn runs: 'My times are in thy hands' – and
that summarizes this passage well. It speaks first of the timing of
Christ's second coming, and categorically forbids us to speculate on its
date. The time of Christ's final appearing is hidden so deep in the heart
of God the Father that not even Jesus, the Son of the Father, has
access to it.

'You do not know when the time will come' (v.33). That applies not
only to the time of the second coming but to many other times as
well. It was in a time of his own choosing that God sent his Son to be
incarnate among us; it is in a time of his own choosing that God calls
each of us into committed Christian discipleship. We do not know the
day or the hour when a great life-transforming decision will be
required of us; we do not know how long God will take to answer our
prayers; we do not know when and how we shall suffer or even die.
Therefore, so as not to miss God's hand in all these times, we are
commanded to alertness and bidden to stay awake.

Lord of creation,
whose glory is around and within us:
open our eyes to your wonders,
that we may serve you with reverence
and know your peace at our lives' end,
through Jesus Christ our Lord.

Monday 17 October

Psalm 71
Ecclesiasticus 6.14-end
or Ezekiel 10.1-19
Mark 14.1-11

Mark 14.1-11

'... she broke open the jar and poured the ointment on his head' (v.3)

We are near the end of Mark's Gospel, and the plot to kill Jesus is now in an advanced state of preparation. It is not a question of if, but when. And today's reading offers us an anointing flanked by two forms of betrayal. Judas, one of the Twelve, and so an insider, is paired with the religious leaders who are portrayed as the jealous and threatened outsiders. Yet it is the anointing that steals the show.

Here, Mark has Jesus at the house of Simon, and an unknown woman comes in to anoint Jesus with some expensive perfumed oil. The act is redolent with symbolism. This is both the anointing of a king and the anointing of death – with the added grist that Judas wilfully 'reads' the act as an expensive waste of resources.

But the act is also symbolic in other ways. For the woman is a kind of mirror to Jesus in these last days – a kind of 'theophany', if you will (a sign or revelation of God, like the burning bush). Like God, she takes the initiative, and boldly so. Like the Spirit, the oil is poured out in consecration. Like Christ, she seeks the lost – in this case, Jesus himself, who is about to be betrayed and given up.

Mark knows that in setting the anointing at Bethany in the midst of two betrayals – those of the religious leaders and Judas – he is placing Jesus' kingship and death in a new context. This king, and the glorious new kingdom, will come about through death of the king. The woman may know this too, and Jesus commends her: 'what she has done will be told in remembrance of her'. Just as bread will soon be broken 'in remembrance of me'.

COLLECT

Almighty God,
you have made us for yourself,
and our hearts are restless till they find their rest in you:
pour your love into our hearts and draw us to yourself,
and so bring us at last to your heavenly city
where we shall see you face to face;
through Jesus Christ your Son our Lord,
who is alive and reigns with you,
in the unity of the Holy Spirit,
one God, now and for ever.

Psalms 145, 146
Isaiah 55
Luke 1.1-4

Tuesday 18 October

Luke the Evangelist

Isaiah 55

'I will make with you an everlasting covenant' (v.3)

'I came that they may have life, and have it abundantly' (John 10.10). John's Gospel is pregnant with the possibility of abundant life, and, almost from the outset of his Gospel, new disciples are inducted into the *CAREFUL* secrets of the kingdom that will bring a life of abundance that can barely *SOUNDS* be dreamed of. It is implied in the miracle at Cana, revealed to the *GNOSTIC* woman at the well, and preached to Nicodemus.

Yet this is no new gospel. It is, rather, one that reaches back to the iconic and halcyon imagery to be found in the Old Testament, such as we find in Isaiah today. The abundance of nature will testify to the glory of God; a created and redeemed world will speak of the glory of God revealed in the world around us.

For an arable people who constantly lived between the extremes of fertility and famine, and between the wilderness of the desert and the abundance of the Promised Land, such imagery would speak powerfully. Yet here Isaiah goes one step further. The cypress will replace the thorn, and myrtle the brier (v.13).

This is why the covenant with God is so vital to Isaiah's audience – and to us today. Obedience and faithfulness will always yield a reward of plenty. The word of God will accomplish its task; it will never return to God empty. Our task, therefore, is to forsake our ways for his – to seek the Lord while he may be found, and call upon him while he is near. This is our vocation. And, through being both called and found, we are then able to be sent out in joy and led back in peace.

Calling

Almighty God,
you called Luke the physician,
whose praise is in the gospel,
to be an evangelist and physician of the soul:
by the grace of the Spirit
and through the wholesome medicine of the gospel,
give your Church the same love and power to heal;
through Jesus Christ your Son our Lord,
who is alive and reigns with you,
in the unity of the Holy Spirit,
one God, now and for ever.

COLLECT

279

Wednesday 19 October

Psalm **77**
Ecclesiasticus 10.6-8, 12-24
or Ezekiel 12.1-16
Mark 14.26-42

Mark 14.26-42

'You will all become deserters ...' (v.27)

There are many different kinds of betrayals taking place in these last few days of Jesus' ministry. Those of Judas and the religious leaders – plotting in the shadows, as it were – are perhaps the most obvious. The failure of the authorities to carry out a fair trial is another kind of betrayal. And the fickle crowds – so moved and impressed by the carpenter from Galilee earlier on – offer another kind of insight into the betrayals that Jesus suffers.

Peter's betrayal is, however, perhaps more predictable. Indeed, Jesus goes to the trouble of telling Peter that he will deny him three times. Peter, of course, denies this will happen. And Mark is careful to remind his readers that all of the disciples join with Peter in affirming their loyalty to Jesus. They will not run or hide, they say; even if they have to die, they will stay with Jesus.

The stage is now set, therefore. We move to Gethsemane, and to a time of intense prayer and anguish for Jesus. Yet the disciples drift off to sleep. In the chaos of the brewing storm – just as Jesus slept on the boat when the winds and waves threatened to overcome them all – so now the disciples sleep. INTERESTING PARALLEL...

But this is the difference. The disciples, when roused, cannot calm the storm that is now to overcome them all. Instead, they will save themselves and abandon Jesus to his fate. The stage is now set for the last few acts of Mark's epic drama.

COLLECT

Almighty God,
you have made us for yourself,
and our hearts are restless till they find their rest in you:
pour your love into our hearts and draw us to yourself,
and so bring us at last to your heavenly city
where we shall see you face to face;
through Jesus Christ your Son our Lord,
who is alive and reigns with you,
in the unity of the Holy Spirit,
one God, now and for ever.

Psalm **78**.1-39*
Ecclesiasticus 11.7-28
or Ezekiel 12.17-end
Mark 14.43-52

Mark 14.43-52

'All of them deserted him and fled' (v.50)

Out of the shadows of the night comes Judas. Escorted by others, with clubs and swords, the ultimate signal of betrayal will actually be a gesture of intimacy – a kiss. This is one of the darkest acts in the Gospels – where the bonds of trust and love between Jesus and a disciple are ultimately shattered through a gesture that now signals betrayal. Can any kiss in history have ever been so false?

But Mark does not dwell on this. Remember, this is a Gospel where the pace never slackens and almost every verse is a headline. The action quickly moves from false intimacy to violence, and a slave loses an ear in the brief armed struggle, causing Jesus to surrender immediately. He is happy to be taken – 'let the Scriptures be fulfilled'. The disciples then flee, just as Jesus had predicted, escaping with their lives into the night.

Mark then concludes this narrative in Gethsemane with a short story unique to him. A man wearing a linen cloth is caught and presumably mistaken for a disciple – indeed, perhaps he is one. But the captors cannot stop him, and he wriggles free, fleeing naked. The emphasis is not surprising. Mark is telling us that, just as everyone once ran to Jesus, now they cannot get away fast enough. Even if it means leaving with nothing, Jesus is no longer the person to be seen with. The sense of foreboding closes in as the night gets darker. Risk hanging out with Jesus, and you risk losing your life. Which is ironic, as you can't say that Jesus never promised anything less than this: 'he who loses his life for my sake ...'.

PARALLEL TO GEN 3!

Friday 21 October

Psalm **55**
Ecclesiasticus 14.20 – 15.10
or Ezekiel 13.1-16
Mark 14.53-65

Mark 14.53-65

'But even on this point their testimony did not agree' (v.59)

And so we turn to the show trial. The verdict was never in doubt, and the sentence was decided long before the jury had met. Jesus now finds himself reduced to the role of an actor in a shameful charade. The testimonies of others are noted by Mark, but not their detail. We must presume that some of the witnesses offered careful, balanced and measured statements. Others were perhaps more vitriolic and impassioned in their outright condemnation. Some bent the truth; some just lied; and some merely got their facts wrong.

But it hardly matters, does it? The defence, we already know, is pointless. Mark places particular emphasis on the silence of Jesus. Indeed, the only lines Mark gives to Jesus are construable as heresy, which is why the high priest tears his cloak. One can sense that Jesus' silence, and then a few carefully chosen words, merely intensify the fury of his accusers.

The lights go out at this point. Jesus is condemned to death. It is the darkest hour of the night. Yet he is blindfolded at this point – so he cannot see who strikes him and spits at him. This is one of the ugliest scenes in the Gospel, for Jesus is utterly defenceless, and his attackers are at liberty to strike at any time, in any place and in any manner. Mark spares his audience the details once again, but we must assume that this is now a form of torture to rival anything we would know in modern times. A vicious, vindictive assault on a blindfolded man means that the attackers can hide their crimes. Only obeying orders, this is arguably the ultimate act of betrayal on this final night.

COLLECT

Almighty God,
you have made us for yourself,
and our hearts are restless till they find their rest in you:
pour your love into our hearts and draw us to yourself,
and so bring us at last to your heavenly city
where we shall see you face to face;
through Jesus Christ your Son our Lord,
who is alive and reigns with you,
in the unity of the Holy Spirit,
one God, now and for ever.

Psalms **76**, 79
Ecclesiasticus 15.11-end
or Ezekiel 14.1-11
Mark 14.66-end

Saturday 22 October

Mark 14.66-end

'Certainly you are one of them; for you are a Galilean' (v.70)

In all this darkness of this darkest night lurks Peter, who has followed 'at a distance'. He is sufficiently hidden by the shadows and near the flickering flames of the courtyard fire – presumably still able to see but not be seen. Jesus has already been handed over to the darkness, and the stage is now set for Peter. Will he risk the light, and perhaps be identified as a disciple of Jesus, or seek the cover of darkness? Perhaps he cannot make up his mind, which is why he lurks in the half-light.

But he does not have to wait for long to discover that even the half-light of the courtyard fire will expose him. It is ironic that it falls to a slave girl of the high priest to point the accusing finger, just as her master has done to Jesus. But whereas Jesus' response to his accusers was silence and then Scripture, Peter cannot speak fast enough. Three times he denies knowing Jesus. Three times. And culminating in an oath confirming his denial – the very antithesis of Jesus' answer to the high priest.

Mark doubtless intends the subtle interplays between darkness and light, and between Jesus' response to his accusers and those of Peter. We now have an epic drama, in which humanity and divinity now seem to be dividing, at least for tonight. Yet these are not perhaps the divisions one might expect. Jesus is led off into the coldness of his cell – to darkness and yet truth. This leaves Peter with some light and consoling warmth – yet also betrayal and denial. The contrast could hardly be more vivid.

Gracious God,
you call us to fullness of life:
deliver us from unbelief
and banish our anxieties
with the liberating love of Jesus Christ our Lord.

COLLECT

283

Monday 24 October

Mark 15.1-15

'... and after flogging Jesus, he handed him over to be crucified' (v.15)

The trials and tribulations are, however, not yet finished. In what now remains of Mark's breathless narrative, Jesus must come before Pilate, be betrayed again by the crowds, face the perverse ignominy of Barabbas' life being preferred to his, and then be led to death. But no one wants blood on their hands. No one wants to be ultimately responsible for this death. So, first Pilate will wash his hands. And then the crowds will wash theirs, by handing Jesus over to their hated oppressors, the Romans, who will simply be an instrument of death in the name of justice.

But this is no justice. This is all about the pacification and vindication of a crowd that is wound up and angry. Justice is a search for the truth, and often at considerable cost. Pacification and vindication, at least in Mark's narrative, are all about the sating of desires, self-justification and the pursuit of something that is not true but simply convenient. The crowd go home happy, and the peace is kept for another day. But justice and truth are not served.

We do not witness mock trials and crucifixions today. But our daytime television schedules are hardly lacking for programmes that pitch families, partners and friends against one another, and whip the studio audience into a frenzy of anger. The subject is unlikely to be blasphemy. Invariably, such programmes focus on betrayal and infidelity.

Yet the dynamics are the same today as they were 2,000 years ago. People are hungry for justice and truth, but settle instead for pacification and vindication – and leave the studio feeling self-justified and self-righteous. Barabbas, then, is an unsurprising choice for the crowd.

Blessed Lord,
who caused all holy Scriptures to be written for our learning:
help us so to hear them,
to read, mark, learn and inwardly digest them
that, through patience, and the comfort of your holy word,
we may embrace and for ever hold fast
    the hope of everlasting life,
which you have given us in our Saviour Jesus Christ,
who is alive and reigns with you,
in the unity of the Holy Spirit,
one God, now and for ever.

Psalms 87, **89.1-18**
Ecclesiasticus 17.1-24
or Ezekiel 18.1-20
Mark 15.16-32

Tuesday 25 October

Mark 15.16-32

*'After mocking him, they stripped him of the purple cloak
and put his own clothes on him' (v.20)*

In C. S. Lewis' *The Lion, the Witch and Wardrobe*, the mocking of Aslan is perhaps the most distressing and moving scene in the whole book. It is here, perhaps, rather than at the actual point of death, that we really begin to encounter the weakness of Aslan. He has surrendered his life and his strength, and is now too weak and passive to resist the taunts of the creatures that Lewis has circling round our beloved lion.

Mark's Gospel is nearly at its climax. But, before we can see the death of Jesus and the powerful and disturbing reality of his resurrection, all his remaining strength and dignity is stripped away. It is heartbreaking.

First, already stripped, Jesus is mocked and reclothed as a king. One can imagine the taunts and the gestures. Second, there is the laughter of the soldiers that will summon up the necessary bravado for the next stage of this execution. Third, there is yet more spitting and insulting, just as there was in the high priest's palace. Fourth, with no strength and dignity left, he must carry the instrument of his own death to the place of that death. It is too much, however, and one Simon of Cyrene is recruited to help. Fifth, he is crucified – and even here, the taunts continue.

Mark wants us to see that the Jesus who started out with many friends and followers is now deserted. Alone, he hangs there, with just his accusers, some criminals and casual bystanders for company. He saved others, but he cannot save himself.

Merciful God,
teach us to be faithful in change and uncertainty,
that trusting in your word
and obeying your will
we may enter the unfailing joy of Jesus Christ our Lord.

COLLECT

285

Wednesday 26 October

Psalm 119.105-128
Ecclesiasticus 18.1-14
or Ezekiel 18.21-32
Mark 15.33-41

Mark 15.33-41

*'When it was noon, darkness came over the whole land
until three in the afternoon' (v.33)*

Themes of darkness and light once again return to throw Mark's narrative into heightened relief. The shadows and flames of the previous night, in which Peter lurked, are now dominated by a darkness that came over the whole land (v.33). It is the afternoon, however, so this darkness, both literally and metaphorically, seems to be Mark's way of acknowledging the whole of creation's bereavement at this point.

We are, of course, at the point of abandonment. Jesus is not being saved. He is dying. He is not saved. He is dead. The loud cry and the last breath are a cue for the temple curtain to be torn in two, as though in this death, paradoxically, all division between humanity and divinity is now finally ripped apart.

This is why one witness – the centurion – is given the ultimate words of testimony at this point in the narrative: 'Truly this man was God's Son' (v.39). Yet, just as our focus comes to a single point on a single hill in Palestine, Mark skilfully directs our gaze to some unremarkable figures in the background. Mary, Mary Magdalene, Salome and others – a few who have followed Jesus – turn out to be companions to the end. We cannot know what risks they took to be there, but their witnessing of these events will have important consequences for what happens next. It is to these women that the task of recognizing Jesus in the light of Easter will fall. Those who saw him die will be the first to see him alive.

COLLECT

Blessed Lord,
who caused all holy Scriptures to be written for our learning:
help us so to hear them,
to read, mark, learn and inwardly digest them
that, through patience, and the comfort of your holy word,
we may embrace and for ever hold fast
    the hope of everlasting life,
which you have given us in our Saviour Jesus Christ,
who is alive and reigns with you,
in the unity of the Holy Spirit,
one God, now and for ever.

Psalms 90, **92**
Ecclesiasticus 19.4-17
or Ezekiel 20.1-20
Mark 15.42-end

Mark 15.42-end

'Mary Magdalene and Mary the mother of Joses saw where the body was laid' (v.47)

Although Jesus is now dead, Mark is careful to note that Pilate is surprised at this. There is almost an implication of nonchalance on the part of Pilate as Joseph of Arimathea petitions him for the body of Jesus. One can imagine Pilate distancing himself from the events of the day with casual small talk: 'Is he dead already? Really? Someone go and check, will they? Ah, it seems he is – well, I never. They usually last a bit longer on the cross … Ah well, yes, I suppose you can have the body. I mean, why not?'

So, after the drama and desolation of the death of Jesus, Mark brings us some unexpected consolation and coolness to the narrative. There is Pilate's rather disturbing diffidence in it all. And then the burial of Jesus itself is quite carefully detailed in five short verses, in sharp contrast to the speed with which his death is breathlessly narrated. We learn about who owns the tomb, the linen cloth in which Jesus is to be wrapped, and the arrangements for burial and sealing of the grave. Mark goes to some trouble to point out that the burying of Jesus has been handled with a meticulous care and attention to detail.

We are, in other words, now with the undertakers. Jesus' life is over, and Mark is giving us the details any reader would normally expect: how and where he was buried, and presumably how you can now remember him. Pay a visit to the shrine, perhaps? Except this is not how any of the Gospels close; death is not the end after all, but only a beginning.

Merciful God,
teach us to be faithful in change and uncertainty,
that trusting in your word
and obeying your will
we may enter the unfailing joy of Jesus Christ our Lord.

COLLECT

Friday 28 October
Simon and Jude, Apostles

Luke 6.12-16

*'And when day came, he called his disciples
and chose twelve of them ...' (v.13)*

Our readings today remind us that we are all called to be saints. Each and every one of us is called to a life of commitment and dedication, and together we make up the Communion of Saints, with Jude, Simon and all the others … Myrtle, Tamsin, Joey, Darrell – you and I; all of us.

Our task as the Church is to be like any saint. Not clinging to our lives but to God, and being imbued by the light and fire of the spirit. Living like this, we are all saints. As one Eastern Orthodox prayer puts it: 'Set our hearts on fire with love for thee O Christ, that in that flame we may love thee and our neighbours as ourselves.'

This allows us to say four brief things about all saints. First, saints are not perfect: they can sin, and all sinners can be saints. Second, saints are loaned to life, and they live their lives in this knowledge and in this light. They expend their energy with passion and enthusiasm, not counting the cost. They are a gift. Third, they sit lightly to life. They are already close to God, and their union and absorption with the true light act as a conduit for grace in this life. To know a saint is to know something of the presence of God. Fourth, all saints have a spark about them. It glows with the breath of the Spirit, and it illuminates the darkness, setting the world alight. The Spirit is always the flame, but the saint – God's fuel – is truly aflame.

COLLECT

Almighty God,
who built your Church upon the foundation
    of the apostles and prophets,
with Jesus Christ himself as the chief cornerstone:
so join us together in unity of spirit by their doctrine,
that we may be made a holy temple acceptable to you;
through Jesus Christ your Son our Lord,
who is alive and reigns with you,
in the unity of the Holy Spirit,
one God, now and for ever.

Psalms 96, **97**, 100
Ecclesiasticus 21.1-17
or Ezekiel 24.15-end
Mark 16.9-end

Mark 16.9-end

*'... when they heard that he was alive and had been seen by her,
they would not believe it' (v.11)*

Just as Mark's Gospel began abruptly, so it ends in the same way. He
ends his narrative with these words – *ephobounto gar* in Greek – 'for
they were afraid' (v.8). What kind of conclusion is that? The resurrection
has apparently just happened, and the salvation of the world set in
motion – but 'they were afraid' does not inspire confidence.

Yet, as Eugene Peterson points out (*Under the Unpredictable Plant*,
1992), this word *gar* is transitional; no Greek writer would end a
sentence with *gar*. It is a word that gets you ready for the next part of
the sentence – except there isn't one. So Chapter 16, verse 8 is an end,
but not a very good one, which is why other later revisions of the text
soon began to supply their own, including the disciples running off into
the sunset, happily believing and rejoicing.

But I much prefer the original director's cut. Mark finishes mid-sentence,
I think, deliberately. *Gar* leaves us off-balance, mid-stride; where will the
next step be? This is artful reticence; a conclusion is withheld from the
disciples and the reader. It is up to you to say what happens next. In
other words, the Christian faith cannot be wrapped up as a finished
product. The frame is open; the picture not completed. As Peterson says:
'write a resurrection conclusion with your own life'. Quite so. That is the
invitation Mark poses to us. What will your next step be?

Blessed Lord,
who caused all holy Scriptures to be written for our learning:
help us so to hear them,
to read, mark, learn and inwardly digest them
that, through patience, and the comfort of your holy word,
we may embrace and for ever hold fast
the hope of everlasting life,
which you have given us in our Saviour Jesus Christ,
who is alive and reigns with you,
in the unity of the Holy Spirit,
one God, now and for ever.

COLLECT

Monday 31 October

Isaiah 1.1-20

'Come now, let us argue it out' (v.18)

Isaiah is read up to Christmas and prepares us for the celebration of the incarnation, with the powerful twin themes of God's wrath and mercy, divine threat and promise. God is referred to as the 'Holy One of Israel', showing both the holy transcendence of God and his immanence (immediate presence) to his chosen people. This recalls how God comes to the manger as both judge and saviour, intimate physical human but also hidden God.

The opening setting is a law court, with the heavens and earth as witnesses, and the Holy One is not to be placated by acts of worship. The case is argued out, and a reorientation of life is required: 'cease to do evil, learn to do good' (vv.16-17). → REPENT

Isaiah is addressing Israel, but the reading can be applied to us. The
WHY? action of God in our lives brings a courtroom-style conviction – we fall
WERE WE short of the glory of God. However, we are not left to be condemned.
INTENDED The gospel we proclaim is one of freedom: we can accept forgiveness
TO MEASURE and are set free from the consequences of our actions – 'though your
UP TO sins are like scarlet, they shall be like snow' (v.18). In the Christian
GOD'S Scriptures, Isaiah is the most quoted Hebrew prophet; like John the
GLORY? Baptist, he prepares the way of the Lord.

COLLECT

Almighty and eternal God,
you have kindled the flame of love
    in the hearts of the saints:
grant to us the same faith and power of love,
that, as we rejoice in their triumphs,
we may be sustained by their example and fellowship;
through Jesus Christ your Son our Lord,
who is alive and reigns with you,
in the unity of the Holy Spirit,
one God, now and for ever.

Tuesday 1 November

All Saints' Day

Isaiah 35

'... streams in the desert' (v.6)

The collect for today, All Saints' Day, begins: 'Almighty God, you have knit together your elect in one communion and fellowship.' The Isaiah reading reflects the life of this elect. This passage was probably written towards the end of Israel's captivity in Babylon, and the imagery evokes the Exodus, a journey into freedom.

The language of 'highway' and 'Holy Way' (v.8) recalls the path through the wilderness taken by Moses and the people. However, there is one consistent change showing that this new blessing is for all and not just for Israel. In the Exodus, references to water at the Red Sea or the Jordan are to its parting for a few. In Isaiah, the theme is abundance of water on 'burning sand' or 'thirsty ground' (v.7). There will be gladness and rejoicing for all creation. Salvation is not for a chosen group of people but for all.

Creation still waits with longing for salvation – particularly human salvation from the idolatry of greed and status. The environment is becoming sterile while we, in the West, amass ever more possessions. Water courses, such as Lake Victoria, are being drained to feed production. As God's people, we are called to 'one communion and fellowship' – but that is not just with fellow Christians, it is with the whole of creation.

Almighty God,
you have knit together your elect
in one communion and fellowship
in the mystical body of your Son Christ our Lord:
grant us grace so to follow your blessed saints
in all virtuous and godly living
that we may come to those inexpressible joys
that you have prepared for those who truly love you;
through Jesus Christ your Son our Lord,
who is alive and reigns with you,
in the unity of the Holy Spirit,
one God, now and for ever.

COLLECT

Wednesday 2 November

Isaiah 2.1-11

'... swords into ploughshares ... spears into pruning-hooks' (v.4)

The people fail in their calling to live as God's people. They have succumbed to fortune-tellers, opulence and idolatry. If Israel lived as God's people, the nations would stream to the temple, and the peaceful kingdom of God would be established. Armaments would be unnecessary, and the conversion of weapons into agricultural tools may recall the fertility of Eden. Unfortunately, because of their behaviour, the people of Israel fail to make God widely known.

The nations should have streamed to Jerusalem and now they should stream to Christ, who is called 'the way'. Luther said: 'People flow to [Christ] just as water flows by its own effort and needs no one to push it.' Sometimes this doesn't happen, maybe because the Church, like Israel before it, fails to live its calling adequately. If the Church were a foretaste of the kingdom, then, according to the feminist theologian Elisabeth Schüssler Fiorenza, it would always practise 'justice and well-being for all'. Instead, faith is lived as a kyriarchy (the rule or domination of a lord or master). The Church is sometimes structured as a hierarchical pyramid.

If the church turns to idolatry of power and status, the danger is that this stifles human flourishing and conflicts with the message of Jesus, whom we proclaim.

COLLECT

Almighty and eternal God,
you have kindled the flame of love in the hearts of the saints:
grant to us the same faith and power of love,
that, as we rejoice in their triumphs,
we may be sustained by their example and fellowship;
through Jesus Christ your Son our Lord,
who is alive and reigns with you,
in the unity of the Holy Spirit,
one God, now and for ever.

Isaiah 2.12-end

'The Lord of hosts has a day' (v.12)

'It is the time for the Lord to act', calls the deacon at the start of the celebration of the Orthodox Eucharist. When we gather for worship, God's time breaks into our time.

There are two Greek words for time in the Bible. One is *chronos*, the linear passing of time; the other is *kairos*, which has an urgency – it is the right or opportune time. Thus Jesus begins his ministry with: 'The time (*kairos*) is fulfilled, and the kingdom of God has come near' (Mark 1.15). Isaiah is making a similar proclamation saying that God has a day.

God's day has arrived because of a crisis; all that is 'proud and lofty ... lifted up and high' (v.12) has come between God and his people. Crisis is often an important precursor to *kairos*, and a theme of liberation theology is discerning how God's time often breaks into the bleakest human time.

A crisis of 2010 was the huge oil spill in the Gulf of Mexico. Was this a *kairos* moment? We have an opportunity to see that we have been 'proud and lofty' regarding our use of scarce and polluting resources. A *kairos* moment would mean that everything has changed – or have we failed to discern God's opportunity in this crisis?

As the kingdom continues to invade, what isn't "a kairos moment"?

God of glory,
touch our lips with the fire of your Spirit,
that we with all creation
may rejoice to sing your praise;
through Jesus Christ our Lord.

COLLECT

293

Friday 4 November

Psalms **16**, 149 *or* **139**
Isaiah 3.1-15
Matthew 4.1-11

Isaiah 3.1-15

'... the Sovereign, the Lord of hosts' (v.1)

'Anarchy in Jerusalem' is my Bible's heading for today's verses. Anarchy reigns, scarcity follows, because the sovereignty of the Lord of hosts is ignored. But what does this name for God mean?

The 'Lord of hosts' is a full military title. When applied to God, it may have indicated that God was the Lord of all the celestial hosts or powers. This heavenly meaning is used in the contemporary Message Bible translation, 'God-of-the-Angel-Armies'. The heavenly emphasis developed further, through a reflection upon the Exodus experience, to include God's earthly power. As nations were driven out to make way for God's chosen people, God seemed to have power over earthly sovereigns, armies and peoples.

The military 'hosts' of the Lord may be seen as all who do God's work, just as Paul later saw Christians as soldiers (Ephesians 6.10-20). In our reading, Israel is scrabbling around for a leader – and those called, with minimal discernment, are shirking responsibility. An understanding of God, as the Lord of hosts, leaves the Lord centre stage in our lives, and our lifetime's work is one of discernment.

How does the Lord call me so that God may be Lord of my life, and how do I share the Lord God with others?

"*Lord of Hosts*" ⟶ *military title...*

COLLECT

Almighty and eternal God,
you have kindled the flame of love in the hearts of the saints:
grant to us the same faith and power of love,
that, as we rejoice in their triumphs,
we may be sustained by their example and fellowship;
through Jesus Christ your Son our Lord,
who is alive and reigns with you,
in the unity of the Holy Spirit,
one God, now and for ever.

Saturday 5 November

Isaiah 4.2 – 5.7

'My beloved had a vineyard' (5.1)

The singer Sinead O'Connor sings today's text. She introduces the song by saying that, for her, Jerusalem refers to the Israelis and Judah refers to the Palestinians. She takes an ancient reading and places it in a contemporary context.

The vineyard of the Lord has always been a provocative parable; the story refers to God's people 'planted' in the promised land. They are to bear fruit; the hewed-out wine vat and best vines indicate the expectation of a good harvest. However, fruit is not borne, and Jerusalem and Judah are now invited to pass judgement on themselves.

God is present as the vineyard is established. In the introduction, cloud, smoke and fire are all Exodus symbols of God's presence. He gives the protection of shade and shelter but the Lord's people still turn to oppression and bloodshed. This is a parable of both unfruitfulness and unfaithfulness.

This parable challenges because it is easy to take God's blessings for granted and to forget that we, in turn, are to bless others. Both the Israelis and Palestinians, in Sinead's song, are blessed by having Abraham as their father and their home in the promised land. This blessing has led to violence, walls and blockades, she says. Today, let us consciously live as people blessed by God.

God of glory,
touch our lips with the fire of your Spirit,
that we with all creation
may rejoice to sing your praise;
through Jesus Christ our Lord.

COLLECT

295

Monday 7 November

Psalms 19, **20** *or* 123, 124, 125, **126**
Isaiah 5.8-24
Matthew 4.23 – 5.12

Isaiah 5.8-24

'... you who call evil good and good evil' (v.20)

The people aren't living free. They are held captive by social injustice, drunkenness and confusion. Death has become an animated force of oppression: 'Sheol has enlarged its appetite and opened its mouth beyond measure' (v.14).

The sin of the people has distorted values. Words are corrupted, and false propaganda is peddled by those in power. Heroism is found in binge drinking, rather than honour, as Israel descends into self-inflicted pain. The instructions and words of God are rejected.

For Isaiah, a right relationship with God implies a right relationship with your fellow human. As St John later points out (1 John 4.20), if we don't love those around us, whom we can see, how can we love God, whom we cannot see?

How did we get here?

The Eucharist often concludes: 'Go in peace to love and serve the Lord.' We are sent out to honour God by serving other people; when the worship is over, the service begins. How can we share bread and not care for those who hunger? How can we celebrate with wine and not care for those in misery? In her autobiographical *Take This Bread*, Sara Miles shows how provisions for those in need at St Gregory's of Nyssa, San Francisco, are distributed from the altar table. Worship and service are intentionally intertwined.

COLLECT

Almighty Father,
whose will is to restore all things
in your beloved Son, the King of all:
govern the hearts and minds of those in authority,
and bring the families of the nations,
divided and torn apart by the ravages of sin,
to be subject to his just and gentle rule;
who is alive and reigns with you,
in the unity of the Holy Spirit,
one God, now and for ever.

Psalms **21**, **24** *or* **132**, **133**
Isaiah 5.25-end
Matthew 5.13-20

Tuesday 8 November

Isaiah 5.25-end

'... the anger of the Lord was kindled' (v.25)

How do we read a text where God inflicts violence? The God who is love bringing pain; the creator bringing corpses to the streets.

One way is to read this passage as a reflection upon the writer's contemporary situation. Israel has already suffered a catastrophic defeat by the Assyrian army, yet Isaiah wishes to record this as an event directed by God. To me, it seems easier to accept God's part in violence when it is presented in a symbolic way. Earlier in this chapter, the vineyard, Israel, had its hedge and watchtower removed, and was then overrun with briers and thorns. *[handwritten: SOFTEN THE BLOW]*

To assume that this is a reflection upon God's involvement in violence leaves us with a theological problem. This violence is recorded in sacred Scripture; thus God is traditionally accepted as an agent of violence. *[handwritten: PROB!]* Sometimes God's aggression is interpreted as something ethical or spiritual, rather than physical. Therefore, a past violent situation, involving God, is now reinterpreted as the purging of vices: the greed, oppression and idolatry seen by Isaiah. Reading this as the purging of vices may help with interpretation today, but it seems a long way from Isaiah's original intention. So, we will read with a (hopefully fruitful) tension between our modern sensibilities and the original context.

[handwritten: THIS IS UNHELPFUL...]

God, our refuge and strength,
bring near the day when wars shall cease
and poverty and pain shall end,
that earth may know the peace of heaven
through Jesus Christ our Lord.

COLLECT

Wednesday 9 November   Psalms **23**, 25 *or* **119.153-end**
Isaiah 6
Matthew 5.21-37

[handwritten:] ISAIAH 6.3 IS REPEATED ALL OVER THE PLACE.

Isaiah 6

'Holy, holy, holy is the Lord of hosts' (v.3)

This verse is repeated in the Book of Revelation and in our Eucharistic prayer – but what does it mean?

Holiness is to be set apart, and, as God is uniquely set apart in his uncreatedness and transcendence, holiness is a quality belonging to God. Joining in this holiness is God's gift to us, and our worship allows us to grow personally into God's holy nature.

Our calling to holiness is shown in our Eucharistic prayers. We sing 'Holy, holy, holy, Lord God of hosts' just before we ask God to enact change, thus making holy. Following this chant, we invoke the Holy Spirit over the bread and the wine, and over the people. We also repeat the transforming words of Jesus: 'this is my body ... this is my blood'. We call upon God's promise of transformational holiness.

The early African bishop Augustine reminds us that this is not primarily about transforming bread and wine, but about our own calling to change. We are to become holy by being the body of Christ. Augustine shows this in his reflection on receiving communion: 'What you hear ... is "The body of Christ", and you answer, "Amen". So be a member of the body of Christ, in order to make that Amen true.'

[handwritten:] EUCHARIST IS A CALL TO HOLINESS → A CALL TO BE THE BODY. I LIKE THIS...

COLLECT

Almighty Father,
whose will is to restore all things
in your beloved Son, the King of all:
govern the hearts and minds of those in authority,
and bring the families of the nations,
divided and torn apart by the ravages of sin,
to be subject to his just and gentle rule;
who is alive and reigns with you,
in the unity of the Holy Spirit,
one God, now and for ever.

Psalms **26**, 27 *or* 143, 146
Isaiah 7.1-17
Matthew 5.38-end

Thursday 10 November

Isaiah 7.1-17

'… shall bear a son, and shall name him Immanuel' (v.14)

The book of the prophet Isaiah is sometimes called the fifth Gospel, as it points forward to the life and person of Jesus – but is this a fair way of reading Isaiah?

Verse 14 is used by the evangelist Matthew as a sign of Jesus' coming as Immanuel, 'God with us'. Matthew develops Isaiah's prophecy to imply the motherhood of Mary by using the term 'virgin' rather than 'young woman'. Isaiah *may* have originally meant virgin, to emphasize God's action in this prophecy, but this would need to be implied, as it is not actually stated.

Isaiah was originally trying to rally the courage of King Ahaz as he faces enemy invasion. Isaiah is promising a sign from God that Ahaz's enemies will be destroyed before a child reaches maturity or knows 'how to refuse the evil and choose the good'. The king, or house of David, struggles to respond to prophesied deliverance.

Christians have held that the house of David, in the person of Joseph, fully responded 2,000 years ago. The sign was accepted, and Joseph played his role in the gospel of salvation. When writing the passage, this could not have been Isaiah's intention, but God's inspiration left it open to this later prophetic interpretation.

CAN WE, IN GOOD CONSCIENCE, READ IT LIKE THIS?

God, our refuge and strength,
bring near the day when wars shall cease
and poverty and pain shall end,
that earth may know the peace of heaven
through Jesus Christ our Lord.

COLLECT

299

Friday 11 November

Psalms 28, **32** *or* 142, **144**
Isaiah 8.1-15
Matthew 6.1-18

Isaiah 8.1-15

'*... this people has refused the waters of Shiloah that flow gently*' *(v.5)*

Assyria is dominating the entire region, and these are confusing times for God's people – both Israel and Judah. Isaiah indicates imminent invasion by naming his son 'Swift-Plunder, Hastening-Booty' (the translation of 'Maher-shalal-hash-baz', vv.1,3). However, this sign is not accepted by Israel or Aram, and 'this people' rebel, refusing the gentle waters of Assyrian control. Judah is addressed by Isaiah and is encouraged not to join this doomed and mistaken campaign.

Misguidedly, the people assume that, because God is with them, Immanuel (v.8), they are invulnerable. They have forgotten that the name Immanuel implies both deliverance and reckoning, and not unconditional protection. Salvation and judgement are part of Immanuel's character, so making our forthcoming Advent season one of both anticipation and penitence.

Israel fights against Assyrian domination, and Judah is swept up in the ensuing flood. However, the hand of the Lord remains upon those who are open to guidance, and God can lead them away from the will of the crowd. In this sense, God is a rock who is both a sanctuary and a stumbling block. God is both the gospel of his gift of presence, later experienced in Christ Jesus, and also the law, which can motivate us to live differently but may trip up those who behave wrongly.

COLLECT

Almighty Father,
whose will is to restore all things
in your beloved Son, the King of all:
govern the hearts and minds of those in authority,
and bring the families of the nations,
divided and torn apart by the ravages of sin,
to be subject to his just and gentle rule;
who is alive and reigns with you,
in the unity of the Holy Spirit,
one God, now and for ever.

Psalm **33** *or* **147**
Isaiah 8.16 – 9.7
Matthew 6.19-end

Isaiah 8.16 – 9.7

'The people who walked in darkness have seen a great light' (9.2)

Verses 9.2-7 are well known from carol services. They are read as a promise, looking forward to the coming of Christ and God's kingdom. However, their original intention was not prophetic.

The passage contains no references to the prophet or God's inspiration. It also contradicts the previous oracles, predicting disaster, and is written so as to avoid a timeframe. These verses are here not to prophesy but to encourage hope from the resources of faith.

Existential despair has fallen upon Judah, and, in the darkness of despair, reliance upon God grows. Jerusalem is not going to save itself; it needs miraculous deliverance or 'the zeal of the Lord of hosts' as when Gideon overthrew Midian. The people have a messianic hope of God's personal deliverance when all traces of bloody conflict are burnt. This is similar to the alcoholic who, in the pit of addiction, calls upon a higher power to deliver. Freedom comes from God, but it often takes a crisis before we turn to God and no longer rely upon ourselves. The names proclaimed before God are throne names: 'Wonderful Counsellor, Mighty God, Everlasting Father, Prince of Peace' (9.6). The hope proclaimed is that we enthrone God, not *despite* our despair, but *because* of it.

God, our refuge and strength,
bring near the day when wars shall cease
and poverty and pain shall end,
that earth may know the peace of heaven
through Jesus Christ our Lord.

COLLECT

301

Monday 14 November

Psalms **46, 47** *or* **1, 2, 3**
Isaiah 9.8 – 10.4
Matthew 7.1-12

Isaiah 9.8 – 10.4

'For wickedness burned like a fire' (9.18)

You will either be a prisoner or a corpse. You will have no one to call for help and nowhere to go to escape. The passage for today gives this terrifying prediction and seems to suggest that God allows these traumatic military invasions. This wrath of God consumes wickedness like a fire, consuming briers and thorns. This seems very vindictive and even has some of the characteristics of genocide. How can this be the work of a God of love?

In the Old Testament, we are given revelations of God's arm, whereas in the New Testament, we are given revelations of God's face: Jesus the Christ. So, the Old Testament, in this prophecy of Isaiah, discerns the consequences of God's action in the sweeping away of injustice and wickedness. For a Christian reader, the focus is on the justice of God consuming oppressive statutes, which turn the needy away from the justice they seek, and where people in poverty are robbed of their right, where widows and orphans are devoured by cruel authorities and heartlessness in high places.

In Christ, we know that God's judgement is centred in God's mercy, and we now read what happens to us in terms of grace and truth. This is why we were given a new covenant, a new kingdom and a new king.

COLLECT

Heavenly Father,
whose blessed Son was revealed
    to destroy the works of the devil
and to make us the children of God and heirs of eternal life:
grant that we, having this hope,
may purify ourselves even as he is pure;
that when he shall appear in power and great glory
we may be made like him in his eternal and glorious kingdom;
where he is alive and reigns with you,
in the unity of the Holy Spirit,
one God, now and for ever.

Psalms 48, **52** *or* **5**, 6 (8)
Isaiah 10.5-19
Matthew 7.13-end

Tuesday 15 November

Isaiah 10.5-19

'By the strength of my hand I have done it, and by my wisdom' (v.13)

Everything that happens and unfolds, including conflict, uncertainty and the unexpected, comes about through the interaction of divine and human wills. In a way, events can be seen as 100 per cent human will and 100 per cent divine will, because God does not take away our freedom and, therefore, the power of our own will. Yet God reigns even when we choose evil or destruction. God can ride a lame horse, God can carve rotten wood. Our text today assumes that God chose Assyria to deal with Israel; however, the arrogant will of the king of Assyria took over, and so the divine will responds. The king of Assyria did not respect God's justice reigning in Jerusalem, and so God intervenes.

The good use of power with justice can carry out God's will, but absolute power, without respect for God's law, will corrupt. For us personally, this can mean becoming a control freak, with the consequent damage to our relationships or work style. There must be room for humility, contemplative calm and perspective, self-examination and the wisdom that comes from consultation and good advice. The real heroes are neither the individual military invaders nor the lone-ranger tough leaders. If you want to go fast, go alone. If you want to go far, go together: walk with God.

Heavenly Lord,
you long for the world's salvation:
stir us from apathy,
restrain us from excess
and revive in us new hope
that all creation will one day be healed
in Jesus Christ our Lord.

COLLECT

Wednesday 16 November

Psalms **56, 57** *or* **119.1-32**
Isaiah 10.20-32
Matthew 8.1-13

Isaiah 10.20-32

'A remnant will return' (v.21)

If you have ever narrowly escaped death or, even worse, been among a few who have survived a major catastrophe, you will know that those who remain feel changed for ever. Some report a new lease of life, and some give the rest of their lives as a thanksgiving for the fact that they are still alive.

This sense of 'remaining', or remnant, is crucial for the people as they come out of exile following the destruction of their nation and their deportation. They will carry the tremendous responsibility and opportunity of starting again. Nothing will then be taken for granted; the slender thread by which life hangs each day concentrates the mind and focuses the spirit. Every day is to be a sacred gift.

Our reading announces that only a few people will remain to carry the promise, but that these remnants are to be the beginnings of a new community of faith. This is a message of liberation and freedom from oppression. Burdens come off shoulders, and yokes are destroyed from off the neck. There is a huge responsibility here, though, to give the rest of the life that remains to the cause of liberation and freedom.

As the Rabbi Hillel, a teacher from the time of Jesus, said: 'If I am not for myself, then who will be? But if I am for myself alone, then what am I?'

COLLECT

Heavenly Father,
whose blessed Son was revealed
    to destroy the works of the devil
and to make us the children of God and heirs of eternal life:
grant that we, having this hope,
may purify ourselves even as he is pure;
that when he shall appear in power and great glory
we may be made like him in his eternal and glorious kingdom;
where he is alive and reigns with you,
in the unity of the Holy Spirit,
one God, now and for ever.

Psalms 61, **62** or 14, **15**, 16
Isaiah 10.33 – 11.9
Matthew 8.14-22

Isaiah 10.33 – 11.9

'A shoot shall come out from the stock of Jesse' (11.1)

The hope that is proclaimed here is breathtaking, life-changing and a transforming vision for the whole earth. The words describe a relationship between justice, mercy and peace, interwoven with a new and deep harmony in nature. It is good to recall that this text is often used at Christmas time when, in church, within the view of the hearer, there is a crib scene. This scene depicts the same interweaving of justice, mercy and peace arriving in the form of a baby with the stillness and beauty of a natural and cosmic harmony: a small nuclear family who will become the beginning of a new creation, together with people of different socio-economic backgrounds and races, together with tended animals and stars.

How to make this vision real? Our reading today is the message of a prophet who promises that God will move through nitty-gritty social and political challenges, like poverty and corruption, so that God's peace and justice may come through more and more. The world is, therefore, heading for the peace and harmony that will one day be real when the kingdom of God reaches its fullness for people, for domestic animals and for races and nations. The Bible ultimately reveals that this kingdom comes through a pregnant mother and a faithful father, in the humblest circumstances, in the person of a once and future king who reigns from the heart of all who have faith.

Heavenly Lord,
you long for the world's salvation:
stir us from apathy,
restrain us from excess
and revive in us new hope
that all creation will one day be healed
in Jesus Christ our Lord.

COLLECT

Friday 18 November

Isaiah 11.10 – 12.end

'Shout aloud and sing for joy' (12.6)

To draw water with joy from the wells of salvation and to give thanks to God, singing praises and shouting aloud of the greatness of the holiness of God, is indeed the highest form of human worship. 'God listens to me when I pray, but God loves me when I sing.' This is to be the calling and destiny of the people. This will come from a deep appreciation of God's saving grace and liberating comfort. This is to name the worth-ship of God: to celebrate the great value that God is to us and within us, because we have been ransomed, healed, restored and forgiven. As the Jesuit theologian Teilhard de Chardin once said: 'Worship is ... to lose oneself in the unfathomable, to plunge into the inexhaustible, to find peace in the incorruptible ... to give of one's deepest to that whose depth has no end.'

The message of hope in the act of worship described is not for a special clique or a single city. It is a proclamation of God's name in all the earth. Those who sing do so for the whole world, and so we are reminded that worship in a particular congregation is actually centred in God's concern for everyone and every nation. This worth-ship of God finally enriches our own worth as part of the great worth of all that lives and breathes.

COLLECT

Heavenly Father,
whose blessed Son was revealed
    to destroy the works of the devil
and to make us the children of God and heirs of eternal life:
grant that we, having this hope,
may purify ourselves even as he is pure;
that when he shall appear in power and great glory
we may be made like him in his eternal and glorious kingdom;
where he is alive and reigns with you,
in the unity of the Holy Spirit,
one God, now and for ever.

Psalms **78.1-39** *or* 20, 21, **23**
Isaiah 13.1-13
Matthew 9.1-17

Saturday 19 November

Isaiah 13.1-13
'... the day of the Lord is near' (v.6)

Are we meant to celebrate the suffering and death of our enemies, as this text seems to suggest? No. But we are called, in this text, to get a sense of what it feels like to have been so utterly crushed and devastated by oppression that a cry for justice will, for ordinary human beings, have a cry for retribution within it. Hate needs to be named so that it can be exorcized and confessed, so that it can be forgiven.

When deep xenophobia and military jingoism have been expressed, named and cleansed, then the possibility of a higher form of thinking arrives. The thoughts of God may come through more clearly in our own thinking – and, of course, these thoughts are always higher than our own thoughts, so they lift our gaze and expand our vision. Then we think no longer in terms of the destruction of our enemies, but in terms of the overcoming of evil, arrogance and tyranny themselves. And this overcoming will begin within our own hearts and minds, the removal of a plank of wood from our own eye before we look for specks elsewhere. We come to see that an eye for an eye may actually mean, in the end, that the whole world goes blind. Darkness cannot drive out darkness, only light. Hate cannot drive out hate, only love.

Heavenly Lord,
you long for the world's salvation:
stir us from apathy,
restrain us from excess
and revive in us new hope
that all creation will one day be healed
in Jesus Christ our Lord.

COLLECT

Monday 21 November

Psalms **92**, **96** *or* 27, **30**
Isaiah 14.3-20
Matthew 9.18-34

Isaiah 14.3-20

'How the oppressor has ceased!' (v.4)

This text seems to rejoice in the death of a Babylonian king. There is, nevertheless, the underlying principle of justice and righteousness being vindicated in the end, no matter how pompous, powerful or wicked the oppressor is. Everything that looks important from a political or military point of view, in an oppressive regime, will ultimately disintegrate because, in the end, it isn't of God. Even the natural environment celebrates the death of a tyrant who would cut it down. There is a challenge here to the spread of city technologies and industries if they use and deplete natural resources to the point where deserts are all that are left. The trees were 'needed' to make cities and weapons.

And so, from a text which could have been written off as an ancient piece of prejudice and primitive jingoism, we find a salutary challenge to our way of life today. Babylon was not a sacred city, and the splendour and glory of urbanization and empire led to arrogance and all-consuming pride. This proved to be the way to perdition. Shall we follow? Christ considered the lilies of the field and said that Solomon in all his glory was not arrayed like one of these. He called us to centre ourselves in a new creation of the heart and not of the material. This is the way of humility, literally meaning living down to earth.

COLLECT

Eternal Father,
whose Son Jesus Christ ascended to the throne of heaven
    that he might rule over all things as Lord and King:
keep the Church in the unity of the Spirit
and in the bond of peace,
and bring the whole created order to worship at his feet;
who is alive and reigns with you,
in the unity of the Holy Spirit,
one God, now and for ever.

Psalms **97**, 98, 100 *or* 32, **36**
Isaiah 17
Matthew 9.35 – 10.15

Isaiah 17

'For you ... have not remembered the Rock of your refuge' (v.10)

This passage challenges the worship of idols, for example, in the growing of ritual gardens for fertility, considered then to be a form of magic. The basic point here is that Isaiah is challenging the belief that, by performing magic rituals in the name of false gods, you will shape the future. This superstition held that you could cause certain things to happen by performing ritualistic acts. This is a selfish and mechanistic view of the divine.

We can preoccupy ourselves with the promises of false gods such as wealth, television, cyberspace, the mirror, alcohol or personal security, believing that bowing to them will bring future happiness or comfort.

Or, in fact, we can trust that the Creator of all is the author of our future as a whole, with whom we are called to co-operate. We can say: 'Draw us O God to the wellspring of grace, lead us O God in the way of justice, guide us O God on the pathways of peace.' What we are called to do is to 'love kindness, practise justice and walk humbly with our God', as Micah the prophet said (Micah 6.8). There is no manipulation of God and no ultimate control on our part, but a willingness to trust that God's ways lead to freedom of the spirit and the realities of divine love. This is better than an attempt at thinking that the future is all about us.

God the Father,
help us to hear the call of Christ the King
and to follow in his service,
whose kingdom has no end;
for he reigns with you and the Holy Spirit,
one God, one glory.

COLLECT

Wednesday 23 November

Isaiah 19

'The Lord will make himself known to the Egyptians' (v.21)

At the beginning of chapter 19, we could be forgiven for thinking that here is an example of the Hebrew peoples' believing that God was their personal property – or at least that they were his only people. This can lead people to think that God will bless them especially, because there is special favour, and that God is not equally interested in people who are racially different or culturally strange. Chapter 19, having talked about idols in Egypt trembling at the presence of God (v.1), and the princes of Zoan and Memphis lost in foolishness and confusion (vv.13-14), ends with a 'United Nations under God'. Egypt and Assyria are offered healing, intimacy in worship and the vocation to be a blessing in the midst of the earth. God actually says: 'Blessed be Egypt my people, and Assyria the work of my hands, and Israel my heritage' (v.25).

God is the God of all the earth in this prophecy. This has to mean both that God does love us specifically and especially that God loves everybody else in the same way. This has to mean a radical challenge in the way that we think of others. To see others as God sees them means not only to see God's image in them but also to look at them as God does – as special, as people of blessing, called to be blessed and to become a blessing to others.

COLLECT

Eternal Father,
whose Son Jesus Christ ascended to the throne of heaven
    that he might rule over all things as Lord and King:
keep the Church in the unity of the Spirit
and in the bond of peace,
and bring the whole created order to worship at his feet;
who is alive and reigns with you,
in the unity of the Holy Spirit,
one God, now and for ever.

Psalms **125**, 126, 127, 128 *or* **37***
Isaiah 21.1-12
Matthew 10.34 – 11.1

Isaiah 21.1-12

'Fallen, fallen is Babylon' (v.9)

This text is describing the fall of Babylon, imaging the world in chaos. The fall of Babylon is cast in the form of a vision. The main message of the vision is that the Lord of hosts is God over all the nations of peoples, sees all things and oversees all things. This means that the destruction of the Babylonian images (her false gods) is a sign of the authority of the one and only true God.

The false gods cannot endure because they are ultimately made up of nothing and have the seeds of their own destruction within them; that is their own unreality. Oppressive evil is ultimately made up of shadows of illusion and of attempts to assert power. But this power turns out to be hollow in the end, and only the power of God creates abundant and eternal life.

We need visions of this sort from time to time to remind us that, in the end, every emperor has no clothes and that God looks on the emperor as a human being of flesh and blood, not someone pretending to be a god or to rule like a god. In this kind of vision, we are called to let the love of God, which is perfect, cast out our fear in the face of the principalities and powers around us.

God the Father,
help us to hear the call of Christ the King
and to follow in his service,
whose kingdom has no end;
for he reigns with you and the Holy Spirit,
one God, one glory.

COLLECT

Psalm **139** *or* **31**
Isaiah 22.1-14
Matthew 11.2-19

Isaiah 22.1-14

'Let us eat and drink, for tomorrow we die' (v.13)

This verse of chapter 22 has become part of common parlance for many centuries. It has rightly been understood that, from this context, it is like an ostrich putting its head in the sand. The inhabitants of Jerusalem, faced with death from a dangerous military siege from the Assyrians, thought that eating and drinking was the only best response.

Isaiah strongly challenges this myopia and indicates that, if all you live for is the moment, either to resign yourselves or to celebrate, then that is all indeed that you will get. Isaiah calls us instead to be serious in the face of trouble, to repent and trust God. Leave your future open; not even the very wise can see all ends, as Tolkien once said. Never give up hope. In the presence of God, even in the face of apparent defeat, when there seems no way out, it is still possible, as William Temple, former Archbishop of Canterbury, used to say, 'to quicken the conscience by God's holiness, to nourish the mind with God's truth, to purify the imagination with God's beauty, to open the heart to God's love, and above all, to surrender the will to God's purpose'. We can affirm the life and time we have been given (which is the way to peace) rather than fly to immediate pleasure or hedonism.

COLLECT

Eternal Father,
whose Son Jesus Christ ascended to the throne of heaven
    that he might rule over all things as Lord and King:
keep the Church in the unity of the Spirit
and in the bond of peace,
and bring the whole created order to worship at his feet;
who is alive and reigns with you,
in the unity of the Holy Spirit,
one God, now and for ever.

Psalms **145** *or* 41, **42**, 43
Isaiah 24
Matthew 11.20-end

Saturday 26 November

Isaiah 24

'The earth lies polluted under its inhabitants' (v.5)

Nothing could be more relevant than the message of these words today, that it is people who are capable of polluting the earth. This text talks about religious and moral pollution; about what is clean and unclean. Today, the sustainability of the earth and the state of the environment mean that what is 'clean' and 'unclean' has a life-and-death meaning.

Many scientists think that the earth may well choke or cook in the future, unless people change their ways, unless there is a carbon-neutral planet, unless the greenhouse gas problem is decisively addressed, unless we recycle conscientiously. Our home is God's earth, and what we do to the environment we live in, we do to God, because God gave it to us. God makes the earth from nothing (Genesis 1.1; John 1), God declares it good (Genesis 1.4-31; Psalm 148), God sustains it in love (Psalm 104; Job 38).

For Christians, Christ is the centre of the earth where creation is set free and all things are reconciled to God, where all things are made new. We are called to discipleship, in and with Christ, to heal and redeem the whole earth. This is dominion, not domination, to serve and preserve, refreshed by a sabbath of rest for the land and the people. We seek a kingdom come on earth, this earth on which we live and breathe.

God the Father,
help us to hear the call of Christ the King
and to follow in his service,
whose kingdom has no end;
for he reigns with you and the Holy Spirit,
one God, one glory.

COLLECT